Regulating the Press

Tom O'Malley and Clive Soley

Regulating the Press

Pluto **Press**
LONDON • STERLING, VIRGINIA

First published 2000 by
PLUTO PRESS
345 Archway Road, London N6 5AA
and 22883 Quicksilver Drive,
Sterling, VA 20166–2012, USA

www.plutobooks.com

British Library Cataloguing in Publication Data
A catalogue record for this book is available from
the British Library

Library of Congress Cataloging in Publication Data
O'Malley, Tom, 1955–
    Regulating the press / Tom O'Malley and Clive Soley.
        p. cm.
Includes bibliographical references and index.
    ISBN 0–7453–1198–9 — ISBN 0–7453–1197–0 (pbk.)
    1. Freedom of the press—Great Britain. 2. Journalistic ethics—Great
Britain. 3. Press Council. 4. Press law—Great Britain. I. Soley,
Clive. II. Title.
    PN4748.G7 O47 2000
    323.44'5'0941—dc21
                                                        00–009391

ISBN 0 7453 1198 9 hardback
ISBN 0 7453 1197 0 paperback

09   08   07   06   05   04   03   02   01   00
10   9   8   7   6   5   4   3   2   1

Designed and produced for Pluto Press by Chase Production Services
Typeset from disk by Stanford DTP Services, Northampton
Printed in the European Union by TJ International, Padstow, England

Contents

Introduction   1

Part I   The History of Self-Regulation
     Tom O'Malley

1   Putting the Press into Perspective   7
2   The Meanings of the Press   19
3   Working on the Law: Employers,
     Journalists and the Legal Framework   36
4   A Sense of Doubt: The Origins and
     History of Self-Regulation up to 1972   51
5   Nothing Resolved:
     Self-Regulation, 1972–98   71
6   Organising and Defining Self-Regulation   97
7   Self-Regulation at Work – An Overview   120

Part II   Cases and Issues
     Clive Soley

8   The Problem of Accuracy in the UK Press in the 1980s
     and 1990s   145
9   The Distorting Mirror. The Problem of Misrepresentation
     in the Press in the 1980s and 1990s   154
10   Privacy and Self-Regulation   165

Part III   Reforming Regulation
     Tom O'Malley and Clive Soley

11   Rights and Responsibilities: The Need for Reform   177

Appendix   Freedom and Responsibility of the Press Bill   191
Notes   199
Bibliography   221
Index   233

Introduction

Newspapers have been a central part of social experience of people in the UK for a long time. They play an important part in cultural and political life by informing, entertaining, exasperating, delighting and infuriating their readers. Within the press there has always been a range of content, from the simple, popular style of papers like the *Sun* to the more considered tones of papers like the *Guardian*.

The modern daily press emerged over a period of around 300 years, from the early 1600s to the early 1900s. During that time the state moved from trying to control all of the outpourings of the press through the use of various forms of direct and indirect controls, to a position where, formally at least, it claimed no power to interfere significantly in the content of the press. This idea that the state should not control the press was the product of a long historical development and became a central part of the way people, within and without the industry, have understood the relationship between the press and the people.

When broadcasting emerged in the early part of the twentieth century successive governments claimed the right to exercise controls over the content of materials broadcast for a variety of reasons. Some of these were to do with a desire to exercise political and cultural control over a powerful new medium; others were to ensure that standards remained high. Governments have continued to exercise these controls and there are many who would argue that under the new regime since the 1990s explosion of TV channels in the UK there needs to be more government intervention to prevent monopoly ownership and to promote higher standards for all.

The press has, however, remained immune from the kinds of requirements that have governed broadcasters in the UK. This would be fine, were it not for the fact that the press has, as we outline in this book, had a long record of printing inaccurate and misleading information as well as breaching the privacy of ordinary citizens. The damage and upset this causes has led, especially since 1945, to calls for a system that regulates standards in the industry without infringing on the freedom of expression so rightly prized by all.

The industry's answer to these calls was to decry any attempt to set standards by law as a threat to press freedom, and to establish, under pressure, its own self-regulatory bodies, the Press Council (1953–90) and the Press Complaints Commission (1991). These bodies have had some success, but they have failed, as we demonstrate, to stop either abuses by the press or to stem demands for statutory reform. In the UK at the beginning of the twenty-first century it was still possible for the press to print inaccurate and misleading information about people and be subject, with the exception of a limited number of expensive libel actions, to very little rebuke or penalty.

Whether the press should be subject to statutory regulation or whether it should be allowed to continue to have its own self-regulatory system has been the subject of fierce, sometimes bitter, political debate in the twentieth century. It is this debate and the issues it raises that are the subject of this study.

This book therefore combines historical survey with political argument. It aims to provide much needed historical perspective on the debates in the UK over the self-regulation of the press since the 1940s. It also argues a particular case. This is that there are no sound reasons, in principle, or in practice, why self-regulation of the press should not be replaced by laws that guarantee the right to correction of factual inaccuracies in the press and promote press freedom. We hope the amount of detail presented here will be informative and, for many interested in the subject, fresh. We also hope our arguments will persuade. We have surveyed an area that has not, as yet, had the benefit of being extensively examined by contemporary historians; there are, therefore, many other areas that need much more detailed examination if we are to understand the historical processes surrounding the evolution of ideas and practices about the regulation of the press. In particular there needs to be a detailed study of aspects of the decisions taken by the Press Council so as to link the institution more closely to the changing political and cultural framework of which the press was a part; something which, for reasons of time and space, we could not do here. In addition Press Council rulings have not been satisfactorily analysed to illuminate the continuities and discontinuities in decision-making and the implications of often complex cases for regulatory practice. Also, the history of criticisms of the press since the seventeenth century is only sketched here. Our account is meant to provide a context for understanding debates in the twentieth century. Readers who seek a richer, more informed account of the nature, sources, variety and wider significance of this long-running body of public discourse can begin to explore these issues through our references. Nonetheless we hope we have made a useful start in recovering the history of debates about self-regulation as well as contributing to them ourselves. In an age when the power of media conglomerates is growing, the issues here will be of interest to those in other countries who are seeking to deal with the thorny issue of press regulation.

We come to this work as two people who have been closely involved in the subject matter of the book since the 1980s, and have both campaigned for a statutory right of reply. We have therefore argued a case for reform, but at the same time tried to do justice to the range of materials and arguments that we have surveyed regardless of whether they support the overall view that we take.

Self-regulation of the press is defined, for our purposes, as the right of the newspaper industry to regulate itself on matters of standards, and as exemplified in the actions of the Press Council and its successor the Press Complaints Commission. The press is hemmed around with all sorts of laws, and although these play an important part in our discussion they are not the focus of the book. Chapters 1, 2 and 3 of the book are designed to place the whole question of the relationship between the state and the press, and the questions of press standards, in a long-term perspective. We want to show that whilst orthodoxies about the relationship between the press and the state exist, they do not reflect the variety of views or practices that have held sway over time about the proper relationship between the press and the state. This provides a context for the detailed account of the range of debates on these issues that occurred in UK politics from the 1940s onwards and which are the subject of Chapters 4 and 5. Here we try to show that self-regulation of the industry never won the wholehearted consent of significant bodies of political, pressure group and journalistic opinion, and survived, in the last analysis, because of the reluctance of Labour and Conservative politicians to challenge the influence of proprietors. We recover a long tradition of people, of all hues of opinion, who have wanted some form of enforceable mechanism to bring redress to those people who are the victims of press malpractice.

In Chapters 6 and 7 we provide an analysis of the Press Council and aspects of its successor body the Press Complaints Commission. Whilst recognising that these bodies performed some useful functions, our overall assessment, based on the evidence we present, is that they were designed to stave off assaults on the interests of the proprietors as well as to, in effect, act as a mechanism for rejecting the vast majority of complaints they received. In Chapters 8, 9 and 10 we take a closer look at the way the Press Council and the Press Complaints Commission have acted in particular cases. This illustrates points made earlier in the book, that the self-regulatory process has lacked both teeth and conviction when it came to promoting high standards in the press. Finally, in Chapter 11, we review some of the key themes in the book and propose that some form of statutory reform of the framework of press regulation is needed. We reproduce a copy of Clive Soley's Press Freedom and Responsibility Bill in the Appendix, as we hope it will be an aid to further study, discussion and debate of these issues.

We hope that this book will help students and interested people grasp the fundamental fact that what is at stake in this debate is an argument about power – the power of those who own and run the media versus the power of those who consume it. As in other areas of life, such as local government, education, and health, it has long been recognised that providers of services, be they private or public, need to be accountable, often through law, for their practice. We consider that this should apply in the media, and in the press in particular. There has been no shortage of proposals for reform of the system of self-regulation over the years. What has been absent has been the power to implement them in the face of opposition from proprietors. We do not consider that the interests of the community are served by allowing the way that the press is run to be defined by owners, or for that matter editors. It is far too important a social institution for this to be so. We would like to see the balance of power in the press, and the media at large, shift away from proprietors and towards journalists and citizens. That would be a major advance, albeit only a small one, in the ongoing campaigns to make the media in general more accountable to the people they are meant to serve.

In writing this book we have accumulated a large number of debts. We would like to thank the following. Professor Eric Barendt, Anne Beech of Pluto Press, Michael Bromley, Professor James Curran, Peter Goodwin, Nick Hallet, Mark Turner, Barry White, Tim White and Granville Williams read the manuscript. We very much appreciated their comments and suggestions. We would also like to thank Mike Jempson and Jo Treharne who assisted Clive Soley in the early stages of the project and Nora McCleod who played an important role in Clive Soley's office throughout all stages. We have been greatly assisted by the courtesy and efficiency of the staff at the House of Commons Library, the Public Record Office, Kew, and the Learning Resource Centre of the University of Glamorgan. Tom O'Malley would like to thank the University of Glamorgan's School of Humanities and Social Sciences Research Committee for a grant towards the costs of researching this book, and to its Social Policy Research Committee for funding teaching relief to free time for writing. We would like to thank the many people involved in the Campaign for Press and Broadcasting Freedom whose work and ideas have been central to the development of the ideas expressed in this book. Any errors of fact or interpretation are the responsibility of the authors.

PART I

The History of Self-Regulation

Tom O'Malley

1

Putting the Press into Perspective

The central theme of this chapter, and of the next two, is that the relationships between the state and the press have shifted over time as has the understanding of those relationships by individuals, journalists, employers, politicians and commentators. The origins and significance of the debates about self-regulation after 1945 have to be seen in the context of this longer development in order to be understood.

Ways of thinking about the press

By the mid-1950s the idea that the struggle over the centuries for freedom of the press from state control was central to the development of democracy in the United Kingdom was common in academic discussions of the industry. For instance, H.C. Strick argued that:

> journalists and their employers, possibly more than any other members of society, made modern democracy possible in the first place ... They, at least equally with any other power in the state, can determine whether democracy is to be given the inspiration and the information without which it must inevitably die.[1]

The work of the socialist, literary critic and cultural theorist Raymond Williams on the popular press, first published in 1961, sketched a more complex model of press history. In this account commercial forces and changes in literacy and economics interacted with the legislative framework to form the mass popular, daily press that had emerged in the UK by the 1940s.[2] Williams's work was part of a tendency amongst historians writing from the 1960s onwards to criticise the reductionism of views that defined the history of the press largely in terms of the struggle for relief from selective state controls. Yet he also retained an appreciation of the value of the freedoms won by the press during the industry's protracted development.

Writing in 1978 Williams argued:

> Every necessary campaign against the capitalist press, every attempt to move beyond its specifically restricting forms, must begin from an unequivocal acknowledgement of what a capitalist and bourgeois press has historically achieved. There are freedoms that by its nature it can not attain, but this is no warrant for underplaying the freedoms it has and the attainable freedoms it still needs.

This appreciation led him to be cautious about advocating state intervention in the press. He warned against the 'radical confusion between popular interest and the state' that could lead to forms of public intervention by people who 'for their own reasons, want a more visibly controlled and "protected" society'.[3] So whilst Williams helped widen the focus of study away from simply the question of how state controls were shed, he retained a perspective coloured by a suspicion of state intervention in the press.

In the late 1970s George Boyce attacked the 'myth' of the press as the Fourth Estate of the realm. This is the idea that the press is, after the three Estates of the Lords Spiritual, Lords Temporal and House of Commons, the Fourth, quasi-constitutional Estate of the realm. In this model the press acts as a constitutional watchdog, enhancing the freedoms of the citizen by acting as an independent monitor of government actions. Boyce argued that, whatever the kernel of truth in this idea, it was always a highly selective and misleading characterisation of reality, designed to help the legitimate press 'take its place in society' by creating a myth about its constitutional role.[4]

In a similar vein, James Curran drew attention to the question of whether those people who had campaigned in the 1830s and 1840s for the lifting of financial controls on the press did so to free the industry from state-imposed restraints or, by tying it more closely to the operations of the market, to make it a more efficient form of social control.[5] Curran's interpretation was challenged by Brian Harrison. Harrison argued that the changes in the press laws needed to be viewed through the prism of a particular conflict that was 'central to nineteenth-century politics':

> that [was] between aristocracy on the one hand, and a radical alliance between members of the middle and working classes on the other. Given the aristocratic predominance within the nineteenth-century political system, the mid-Victorian victory for a free press seemed a major radical triumph at the time.[6]

Other work after 1970 has highlighted both the range of factors shaping the history of regulation and the variety of interpretations that co-existed in the nineteenth century about the nature and significance of the press. One study of the historical development of the libel laws has argued that 'generally speaking there is a very close relationship between the developments of the capitalist system and of the libel laws. This relationship is expressed in many different socio-economic contexts: the political, technological, economic and moral-evaluation.'[7] Another important consideration includes attending, as Aled Jones has, to the multitude of ways in which people in the nineteenth century understood, interpreted and responded to the rapid expansion of the newspaper industry. Jones has demonstrated that the press was the subject of a 'long argument' in nineteenth-century culture, an argument that included conflicting views about its worth and status.[8]

Circulation

If we define a newspaper as something that is printed, published at regular and frequent intervals and concentrates on current events, then, as a form, it was slow to emerge. Printing came to England in the 1470s, but news periodicals do not appear until the 1620s, and then only as accounts of European politics printed at Amsterdam and imported into England. These publications were known as 'corantos'.[9] The exigencies of politics in seventeenth-century England led to periods of repression followed by periods, such as the English Civil War, 1642–49, when controls broke down and a flood of newsbooks, as they were then known, appeared.

During times like the Civil War, or the constitutional turmoil associated with attempts to prevent James Duke of York succeeding his brother, King Charles II (the Exclusion Crisis, 1679–81), 'the potential scale of the demand for news and the ability of printers to respond to that demand emerges very clearly'. Once pre-publication censorship lapsed in 1694 the way was open for a steady exploitation by printers of the market for news.[10]

Newsbooks in this period, up at least until the 1660s, had short lives relative to their successors in the nineteenth century. They were produced in London although their readership extended throughout England, Scotland and Wales. Determining their circulation is difficult. Frank has argued that the circulation of one coranto in the 1620s might have been between 250 and 500 per issue, with an average of 500 for the 1640s, sometimes rising to 750 or 1000.[11] One estimate for 1666 puts the print-run of the official government newspaper, the *London Gazette*, between 12,960 and 15,552.[12] Although demand for news periodicals was growing in the seventeenth century these publications were small fry by the standards of contemporary print culture. When in 1664 the London wholesaler Charles Tias died, his stock 'included 90,000 chapbooks, that is, one for every fifteen families in England and Wales. He also held over 37,000 ballad sheets.'[13] News periodicals were therefore a small part of people's experience of print and news. They had other sources of information, including social networks, rumour, gossip, letters, proclamations, contact with the church and, occasionally, with the courts of justice.[14] It is no accident that control of print in general, rather than news periodicals in particular, exercised the minds of the authorities in the seventeenth century.

The eighteenth century, after the lapse of the Licensing Act in 1694, witnessed growth in the number of titles and total circulation of news periodicals in England and Scotland. The first daily paper, the *Daily Courant*, appeared in 1702 and the first evening paper, the *Evening Post*, in 1706, whilst this period also saw the emergence of a provincial press.[15] Estimates, although based on sparse evidence,[16] show a steady increase in circulations. The growth was uneven, stronger in periods of war and political turmoil than at other times. It was based not on the development of titles with massive circulations, but on the fact that 'the number of titles published multiplied as the century progressed and, with it, the overall circulation of newspapers'. Estimates of circulation are based on returns from the payment of stamp duty, a tax placed on newspapers in 1712. Using these figures it has been suggested that in 1713 the annual sale of newspapers was around 2.5 million copies. In 1750, 7.3 million stamps were purchased by the press, 9.4 million in 1760 and 12.6 million in 1775. In 1801, 7 million stamps were issued for London and 9 million for provincial papers. Impressive as these figures may seem, they were small when compared to developments in the nineteenth century. Many more newspapers failed than succeeded in the eighteenth century and the pattern of growth of the provincial press was uneven. The development of a larger market was limited by constraints imposed by the 'technology, content, and, to a lesser degree, illiteracy and poor communications'.[17] Nonetheless, compared to the preceding century, there can be no doubt that regular news periodicals became an established part of print culture.

It was during the period after 1800, especially after the 1850s, and, again, after the 1890s, that newspaper circulations rose dramatically.[18] The most enduring feature of this expansion was the gradual emergence by the first decades of the twentieth century of a mass popular daily newspaper press.[19] The Sunday press was the immediate forebear of this development. In 1812 there were at least 18 Sunday papers published in London. Because stamp duties made daily papers expensive, it was cheaper to buy just one on Sunday. These papers concentrated mainly on crime and sport although they were 'nearly all outspokenly radical'. Once the stamp duty was lowered in the 1840s the circulation of the

Sundays grew. *Lloyd's Weekly News* was selling between 60,000 and 70,000 in 1852 and, in 1854, over 100,000. *The News of the World* was selling over 100,000 per week in the 1850s and *Reynolds' Weekly News* nearly 50,000 per week by 1854.[20]

Newspapers were part of the expansion in the production of cheap printed material in the nineteenth century.[21] There was also an expansion in trade papers and specialist weeklies.[22] Table 1.1 illustrates the rapid growth in the circulations and numbers of newspapers in the United Kingdom.

Table 1.1   Newspapers in the UK: 1800–1914

Percentage increases in circulations[1]	
1816–1836	36%
1836–1856	70%
1856–1881	600%
Numbers of newspapers established in the United Kingdom[2]	
1800–1830	136
1830–1855	415
1855–1861	492
Numbers of daily and evening London and provincial papers in England[3]	
1856	30
1900	203
1914	153

Notes
1. R. Williams, *The Long Revolution* (London: Pelican, 1973), p. 216.
2. A. Jones, *Powers of the Press. Newspapers, Power and the Public in Nineteenth-century England* (Aldershot: Scolar Press, 1996), p. 23.
3. A. Lee, 'The structure, ownership and control of the press, 1855–1914', in G. Boyce, J. Curran and P. Wingate (eds), *Newspaper History: from the seventeenth century to the present day* (London: Constable, 1978), p. 121, Table 6.1.

By the 1890s a new phase of expansion was about to get under way based initially on Alfred Harmsworth's innovation of the halfpenny *Daily Mail* in 1896. Building on the techniques of the established Sunday and weekly popular papers, Harmsworth's *Daily Mail* helped trigger an expansion in the circulation of the press that eventually spread the readership of cheap daily newspapers to the working classes. It is possible to get some sense of the pace and expansion involved in this process. In 1880 the sales of the daily press were around 700,000, compared with a figure of about 1,725,000 for the Sunday papers in 1890. By 1900 the number of daily papers sold had grown to

1,500,000 and by 1910 to 2,000,000. In 1920 the dailies reached 5 million and the Sundays 13 million. By 1947 the figures were 15 million and 29 million respectively.[23]

The period from the 1850s onwards witnessed the emergence of a process that extended over almost a century. This process included the proliferation of different types of newspaper and periodical publications on an unprecedented scale. It also included the gradual, absolute and relative expansion in the total circulation of newspapers, a process that finally brought the working classes into the orbit of daily press readership. By 1947 both the daily and the Sunday press had become central to the social experience of the majority of the population in the United Kingdom.

Content

The names used to describe news serials over the centuries reflect the indeterminate nature of their content: coranto, newsbooks, periodicals, newspaper and tabloids. As a form they have often been closely linked to other types of print: advertisements, ballads, accounts of executions, newsletters, etc. They have always been unstable forms and as such have provoked a variety of responses.

The corantos of the 1620s resembled the manuscript newsletters that circulated amongst social elites in the sixteenth and seventeenth centuries. Their content, largely foreign affairs, and style situated them firmly within elite cultural circles. Once pre-publication censorship broke down after 1642 the range of news-orientated print forms exploded. Ballads, newsbooks and pamphlets flooded onto the market. These varied in content, some separating, some mixing up the serious and the scato-logical, the secular and the providential. The reassertion of central control in the 1660s saw the *London Gazette*, the official newspaper of the government, address its audiences with content that mixed political with foreign news, religious propaganda, shipping news and advertisements for books, events, thieves and stolen goods.[24]

Diversity was the chief characteristic of the eighteenth-century papers. Cheap or unstamped papers of the first half of the century were aimed at a popular audience with accounts of trials and murders. The legitimate, normally priced papers, appealed to readers 'who followed domestic and international events closely, who could recognise leading political and social personalities through allusions and innuendoes, and who boasted at least some familiarity with classical literature and history'. Adver-tisements were a key part of the press in this period and covered everything from runaway servants and stolen goods to notices of sporting events.[25]

In the early nineteenth century the high political content of the legitimate press, such as *The Times*, could be read alongside the radical working-class press and the Sunday papers whose 'main emphasis was not political, but a miscellany of material basically similar in type to the older forms of popular literature: ballads, chapbooks, almanacs, stories of murders and executions'.[26] These contrasts persisted after the repeal of the duties, with the popular Sundays continuing their interest in sensation, whilst the dailies, at least until about the 1880s, retained a more sustained focus on the serious.

The major development after 1880 was the spread and development of popular styles from the Sundays to the dailies. Under pressure from competition and, to some extent, influenced by developments in the press in the US, a less turgid, more popular style gradually asserted itself in the daily press. This development was called, at the time, the 'new journalism' and consisted of a mix of journalistic and typographical devices designed to make newspapers easier and more attractive to read. Shorter paragraphs, simpler, longer headlines, more illustrations and the use of the interview gradually spread across the press. Newspapers that had previously filled columns with verbatim accounts of speeches by politicians cut back and made space for other material. Even the quality dailies like *The Times* were willing to devote extensive space to scandals, such as the trial of Oscar Wilde.[27]

The growth of cheap daily papers like the *Daily Mail* (1896) and the *Daily Mirror* (1903) in the first half of the century led to the institution-alisation within the daily press of divisions that had previously separated the daily from the Sunday press in the nineteenth century. Whilst populist techniques of writing and presentation developed in all papers, it was in the mass-market dailies that the drive towards entertainment rather than serious news was most pronounced. This was the context within which divisions between 'quality' daily papers, such as *The Times*, the *Manchester Guardian* and the *Daily Telegraph*, and the 'popular' press, the *Daily Mail*, the *Express* and the *Daily Mirror*, emerged.

Readers

Literacy is commonly measured in periods before the twentieth century by the ability to sign one's name. This is because reading was generally taught before writing. Thus before 1500 only 10 per cent of English adults could read and write. This had risen to about 50 per cent of the population by 1750. These figures say nothing about the level of sophis-tication of readers. But they remind us that a mass market existed for other forms of popular print in the seventeenth and eighteenth centuries, and it was the cost of eighteenth-century news serials that restricted their availability to this wider market.[28] By 1840 about 66 per cent of men and 50 per cent of women could sign their names.[29] In 1850 about 61 per cent of the population were literate, in 1868 about 75 per cent and by 1900 it was over 95 per cent.[30] The acceleration in the growth of literacy in the nineteenth century was due to a number of factors, including the spread of schooling and of economic- and leisure-orientated incentives for working people to acquire literacy. For example, 'the demand of the labor market for literate workers was increasing' and newspapers provided access to information on jobs. The growth of working-class interest in football interacted with the spread of sports coverage in papers. The development of cheap publications in the nineteenth century exploited the existence of a sizeable market of working people who previously had limited their purchases of print because of cost. The expansion of literacy in these years added to this growth.[31]

Although literacy was not universal in the eighteenth and early nineteenth centuries we know that people of all classes, literate or not, were keen to read or hear news. This was achieved by communal purchase, reading in pubs, coffee houses and specialist reading rooms where a range of papers were kept, by hiring copies of papers and reading out loud to illiterates. These practices had existed, in one form or another, from at least the seventeenth century and meant that even though access to news was restricted by cost and literacy, it was possible for publications to have a readership, and listenership, well beyond the limits set by the size of their print-run.[32] Thus, throughout our period the growth of literacy was creating ever-increasing opportunities for the printing industry.

Controls

Printing arrived in England in the 1470s. From then until 1695 various governments used a range of devices to regulate the printing presses. F.S. Siebert has described the situation under the Tudor monarchs (1485–1601), the Stuarts (1601–49, 1660–89) and the Common-wealth and Protectorate (1649–60) thus:

> The authority to control and regulate the printing press in England was claimed for two centuries by the Crown as one of the prerogative rights. Beginning with Henry VIII, this authority was consistently and persistently exercised by the king himself, by the Council, or by officers appointed by the king. Through royal proclamations, licences, patents of monopoly, Orders in Council and Star Chamber decrees, the press of England was effectively held in check throughout the Tudor period. The succeeding Stuart kings were less successful in operating the elaborate machinery that they inherited from their predecessors, and with the Revolution of 1688 the system of control through the royal prerogative finally collapsed.[33]

Note the variety of devices used to control the press at a time, in the sixteenth century, when the printing industry was small and news serials did not exist. One device was to encourage the industry to collaborate in implementing controls in return for economic privileges. In 1484 an Act to encourage printers was passed, and in 1534 another one was passed to protect English printers from foreign competition. In 1557 the leading figures in the book trade were given a Royal Charter and became the Stationers Company. In return for granting them monopoly rights in printing, the Crown expected members of the Company to police the industry. Over the years the Crown supplemented these measures by instituting a system of pre-publication censorship that was embodied in various Acts of Parliament and other initiatives dating from 1538, through to the Licensing Act of 1662 until the last licensing Act expired and was not renewed in 1694.

The illegal printing of unlicensed material recurred over and over again after 1500 and the breakdown in official controls during the English Civil War revealed that a substantial market existed for news publications. During the reign of Charles II (1660–85), press censorship was reimposed, but there were plenty of individuals and groups who flouted the law with relative impunity, like the early Quaker movement. The emergence of over 40 short-lived news periodicals in London alone during the period 1679–82, when a constitutional crisis weakened royal controls over the press, illustrated the existence of an infrastructure and market ready to exploit weaknesses in the system.[34] This capacity to print news serials co-existed with an eager market thereby making the task of pre-publication censorship and policing the system commercially undesirable from the printing industry's viewpoint and increasingly impracticable from the government's.

The lapse of the Licensing Act in 1694 has to be viewed in this context, but it did not end attempts by governments to control print, or to punish the producers of particular newspapers. Governments developed an approach that substituted for pre-publication censorship a range of devices suited more to establishing the boundaries within which the press should work than to controlling the detail of its content. In this task successive governments in the eighteenth century were assisted by the content of the newspaper press. During this period most newspapers were not seditious. Though many did challenge the government, and by the early 1800s working-class publications were challenging the political system as a whole, newspapers were a conservative influence on eighteenth-century political developments and at times 'enabled the state and parliamentary classes, at crucial moments, to reinforce their hold over society'.[35]

Again, the devices used varied. A tax on newspapers, the stamp duties, plus a duty on advertisements and on paper, were introduced in 1712 and increased in 1757, 1776, 1780, 1789, 1797 and 1815, pushing up the price of newspapers each time, thereby restricting their potential market by making them too dear for the majority of the population.

These taxes became known in the nineteenth century as the taxes on knowledge. The sheer inconvenience and risk involved in being prosecuted was an incentive to conformity and the use of secret service money to pay journalists and to support friendly papers was common.

During times of heightened tension, such as the period between the French Revolution and the end of the Napoleonic Wars (1789–1815), and the working-class agitation that extended into the early decades of the nineteenth century, controls were intensified. Nonetheless this marked the last phase in the use of openly, wide-ranging repressive measures. These were the steps of governments seeking to contain an external military threat from France and pressure for social and political reform from a labouring population whose working conditions were undergoing rapid change as a result of industrialisation. In 1789 a law was passed forbidding the hiring of papers from hawkers. In 1798 and 1799 steps were taken to force printers and publishers to put their names on their material and to register their presses.[36] The Publications Act of 1819 raised the price of popular papers in order, according to its preamble, to keep 'pamphlets and printed papers containing observations upon public events and occurrences' out of the hands of the working class. The Act had the effect of limiting the emerging working-class press, whilst leaving 'respectable' newspapers untouched.[37]

From the 1830s onwards a series of largely middle-class led campaigns developed that pressurised successive governments to lower and repeal the stamp, advertisement and paper duties. This was a long, drawn-out process. These campaigns were part of wider movements for both an extension of the electoral franchise to include more middle-class voters, and for the establishment of free trade in a range of industries. In addition, there was a variety of opinions amongst reformers about the likely social effects of reform, some of which stressed the benefits of encouraging a commercial, politically safe press, which would counter the influence of cheap, scurrilous and more politically orientated working-class publications.[38]

In 1833 advertisement duty was reduced. A reduction in stamp and paper duties in 1836 was accompanied by an increase in the amount of security required by the government from publishers thus making transgression more costly. This also had the effect of bringing previously unstamped publications into the system. Agitation by reformers in the 1840s and 1850s led to the abolition of advertisement and stamp duties in 1853 and 1855 respectively. In 1861 paper duties were abolished, followed in 1869 by the abolition of the security system.[39] This slow process of reform is indicative of the divisions of opinion within the ranks of government and reformers, which took time to crystallise into a modified set of attitudes towards the press.

These reforms were the culmination of tendencies evident in the seventeenth and eighteenth centuries: the growth of a market for print in all forms from the 1600s onwards; the pressures from those in the industry to repeal unnecessary constraints; and the difficulty of effectively policing both pre-publication censorship and financial controls, especially in times of crisis. These difficulties were countered by governments developing a range of relationships with the press, including the use of official publications like the *London Gazette* in the late seventeenth century, and the use of secret service monies to subsidise publications, bribes and advertisements. All of these factors contributed by the mid-nineteenth century to a climate in which social elites conceived of print and serial publication as a form that could not be stifled, but could be contained or managed.

After the 1860s the state continued to intervene in the workings of the press and, as the industry became more capital intensive and market driven, the inherently conservative inclination of proprietors and journalists, a factor evident from the earliest days of serial production, asserted itself to inject what turned out to be a major element of stability into the system. Indeed the commercial forces, which by the twentieth century shaped the economic environment of the press, also dictated its content. James Curran has argued that the dependence on advertising income by the national press, combined with the drive to build circulation, helped both squeeze out left-of-centre newspapers from the national newspaper market in the 1950s and 1960s and contributed to the depoliticisation of the press. This process was an increasingly important part of the system. Stephen Koss has detailed, exhaustively, the close links between political parties, editors, proprietors and journalists up to the 1940s in England and Wales. He has shown how the press as an industry was integrated into the political system. The rise of a mass circulation daily press in the first four decades of the twentieth century disrupted the direct political ties of papers to political parties; the old direct forms of subsidy and party-based partisanship were modified by the financial independence achieved by owners of commercially successful papers. This process was uneven, with some papers like the Labour movement's *Daily Herald* retaining its direct party links. Where changes occurred, however, this meant that politicians and proprietors evolved new kinds of relationship predicated on a mutual regard for the established political structures of the state, even if there were occasional fierce differences of view on particular issues. Thus the range of links between politicians and the press helped to stabilise the post-1869 relationship.[40]

From the 1860s onwards the state gradually developed a variety of responses to managing new forms of communication and to setting the boundaries of permissible expression. Thus in 1868 it nationalised the telegraph system. In 1889 the first Official Secrets Act was passed and was followed by the 1911 Official Secrets Act, its more long-lasting successor. The press co-operated with the aims, if not always agreeing with the methods, of the state during World War I (1914–18), not because there was coercion, but because the majority of proprietors, editors and journalists accepted the premises on which the war was fought.[41]

The new communication industries of the twentieth century were subjected to varying degrees of control. As the film industry emerged the state encouraged, with industry support, a system of pre-publication censorship and by the 1930s was liaising with newsreel production companies to influence the coverage of the sensitive question of rearmament in the content of weekly newsreels.[42] When broadcasting was set up in 1922 the state established a system in which firm pre-publication censorship was exercised by the BBC, at times with direct intervention from the government.[43] Wartime controls of the press (1939–45) were followed by a heated debate about the future of the press and broadcasting. The Labour government's decision to reopen the questions of the role and responsibilities of the press by setting up the 1947–49 Royal Commission on the Press can be seen as part of a wider process in which successive governments of all parties in the first decades of the twentieth century assessed and adjusted their relationships to the new forms of mass communication, the mass press, film and broadcasting, that emerged after the 1890s.[44]

Changes in the relationship between the state and the press between 1600 and 1947 were therefore bound up with a range of factors such as the nature of the industry, changes in content, the attitudes of elites, the growth of a market for print, and the changing social composition of the readership of newspapers. The forms of regulation have been various: from blunt measures like licensing, to the use of collaboration, such as when the Stationers' Company censored the industry on behalf of the state or when after the 1860s the state and proprietors maintained close, if varying kinds of relationships.

If we therefore view pre-publication censorship and the taxes on knowledge in context, they become two, amongst many, manifestations of the relationship between the state and the press. They were imposed and removed because of shifting pressures on the state occasioned by the problem of controlling a form of print media that over time became increasingly difficult to regulate. Other kinds of relationship that involved devices for controlling and manipulating press content remained after the 1860s and formed part of a wider set of tools which successive governments used to influence the development and content of other forms of mass communications like radio and film. Viewed in this way, press history is not dominated by a simple, heroic battle for freedom, but by the development of different kinds of relationship with the market, readers and the state that have always been subject to change. In the next chapter we examine some of the ways in which people have understood and responded to the press and state relationship up to 1947.

2

The Meanings of the Press

In 1947 the Labour Prime Minister, Clement Attlee, announced the establishment of the first Royal Commission on the press. No similar government-sponsored inquiry had occurred since the repeal of the stamp and advertisement duties in the mid-nineteenth century. It came about after the National Union of Journalists, reflecting a much wider discontent over questions of ownership and standards within the industry, put pressure on the government to initiate an inquiry. The Royal Commission was the first of a host of other official and unofficial inquiries into the industry after 1945. Its findings were to influence official pronouncements about the relationship between the press and the state for the next 50 years.[1]

Chapter 1 suggested that one way of understanding the meanings people attributed to the press is to use the idea, developed by Aled Jones, of a 'long argument'.[2] This idea is helpful and can be extended backwards to the seventeenth and forward to the twentieth century. It has the merit of focusing on the conflicts and debates through which people came to understand the press. It also allows us to appreciate that in any historical period views exist that both endorse and challenge the economic, legal and political status quo within which the press operates.

A free press, the state and the law

> [T]he superiority of England in the great family of nations is, in a vast measure, owing to her free, untrammelled, outspoken and patriotic press.
>
> (W.G. Robinson, 1858)[3]

By the middle of the nineteenth century there existed a view that the press in the UK was independent of state control. This independence had been won in a long battle, extending from before the lapse of the licensing laws in 1694 to the repeal of the taxes on knowledge. This battle had, in turn, been part of a wider social struggle for the extension of the franchise and the development of democratic institutions. The freedom enjoyed by citizens in the UK was, in part, a result of the success of this struggle for press freedom. Indeed the maintenance of democracy was regarded as being linked with the continuation of a press free from pre-publication censorship and government interference. This view remained profoundly influential in public discussion about the media throughout the twentieth century. For instance, as late as 1986 a government-sponsored inquiry into the finances of the BBC, known, after its chairman, as the Peacock inquiry, repeated a version of this history:

> Pre-publication censorship came to an end when Parliament refused to renew the Licensing Act in 1694, in part because of the corrupt practices of the Stationers' Company. The abolition of pre-publication censorship was described by Macaulay as a greater contribution to liberty and civilisation than either the Magna Carta or the Bill of Rights.[4]

This version of history obscures more than it reveals.[5] It also draws attention away from the variety of ways in which people thought about the relationship between the press and the state.

In the mid-seventeenth century John Milton viewed the issue through a religious perspective. In *Areopagitica* (1644) he attacked pre-publication licensing because it was inefficient, unworkable and denied humans the right to exercise their God-given powers of reason. An individual's virtue, he thought, needs to be tested against error. Suppressing wrong opinions in the end weakens virtue by leaving it untested. There were limits, however, to his tolerance. As a Protestant convinced of the moral dangers of Catholicism he was not prepared to extend tolerance to Roman Catholic writers.[6]

During the eighteenth century, after the lapse of the licensing laws, and in spite of the existence of the stamp and advertisement duties, Henry Fielding in his novel *Jonathan Wild* (1743) wrote so as to assume that the press had a good deal of latitude to criticise politicians. The problem was not so much the financial controls on the press about which reformers in the nineteenth century were to agitate, but the ambitions of politicians, who, discomfited by criticism, hankered after stricter controls:

> Indeed, many inconveniences arise to the said GREAT MEN from these scribblers publishing without restraint their hints or alarms to society, and many great and glorious schemes have been thus frustrated, wherefore it were to be wished that in all well-regulated governments such liberties should be by some wholesome laws restrained, and all writers inhibited from venting any other instructions to the people than what should be first approved and licensed by the said GREAT MEN,

or their proper instruments, or tools – by which means nothing would ever be published but what made for advancing their most noble projects.[7]

Others considered that, whilst the press was free, its freedom was from pre-publication restraint, not from punishment for what it printed. In 1765 William Blackstone argued that: 'The liberty of the Press is indeed essential to the nature of a free State; but this consists in laying no previous restraints on publications, and not in freedom from censure for criminal matter when published.'[8]

Even the anonymous writer of the celebrated *Letters of Junius*, a series of letters that appeared in the *Public Advertiser* between 1769 and 1771 attacking corruption in government, accepted the need for some restraints. Like Milton and Blackstone, the writer was making an argument for liberty, but liberty within boundaries determined by the general need to restrain malice and slander:

> A considerable latitude must be allowed in the discussion of public affairs, or the liberty of the press will be of no benefit to society. As the indulgence of private malice and personal slander should be checked and resisted by every legal means, so a constant examination into the characters and conduct of ministers and magistrates should be equally promoted and encouraged ... In the state of abandoned servility and prostitution, to which the undue influence of the crown has reduced the other branches of the legislature, our minister and magistrates have in reality little punishment to fear, and few difficulties to contend with, beyond the censure of the press and the spirit of resistance which it excites among the people.[9]

Indeed it was the question of post-publication penalties rather than the pre-publication restraints of duties and subsidies that concerned James Mill in 1811. Mill felt, contrary to Blackstone, that the liberty of the press was in a sense a myth as 'Our Law in favour of the liberty of the press consists in mere general expressions, and these not engrossed in statutes.' It was all very well for Blackstone and others to assert that there was liberty, but the law of libel, as used by the government, was so general in its application, that 'to point out any fault in the government, is a liberty not allowed to the press by the law of England'. For Mill of 'all the dangers at the present day besetting our liberties, the danger of leaving a door open for the destruction of liberty of the press, by a vague and indeterminate law of libel, is by far the greatest'.[10] Whether the press was 'free', or what the nature of that freedom was, remained, therefore, a subject of debate in the eighteenth and early nineteenth centuries.

Writing in 1859, however, J.S. Mill argued that it was wrong to impose any restraint on freedom of expression. Suppressing even wrong opinions was to be deplored, for 'If the opinion is right, they [i.e. the public] are deprived of the opportunity of exchanging error for truth; if wrong, they lose, what is almost as great a benefit, the clearer perception and livelier impression of truth produced by its collision with error.'[11]

But this position, in its libertarianism, was certainly out of step with the views of Milton, Blackstone and Junius. In fact J.S. Mill's position, although superficially appealing, was also out of step with the realities of mid-Victorian politics. Governments were still willing to interfere with freedom of expression, as they did by passing the censorious Obscene Publications Act in 1857. In drawing attention to the logical conse-quences of an unqualified commitment to freedom of expression, Mill raised the question of how realistic such a commitment could be.

During the period after 1850 a number of histories of the press were written, usually by editors or journalists who, in articulating the idea that the press was free and had reached a pinnacle of achievement, were, in a sense, producing a self-justification both for mid-Victorian society and their own industry.[12] Viewed in a longer historical perspective, these writers appear as a few amongst many who had explored the relationship between the press, freedom and the state. They had neither the first, nor the last word, on the subject.

Truthfulness, impartiality and accuracy

Of similar importance to ideas about the freedom of the press from state control was the idea that what was printed should be truthful, impartial and accurate. In the seventeenth century there was a view that ordinary people were liable to believe almost anything. The philosopher Thomas Hobbes, writing in the first half of the century, believed that 'the Common-peoples minds, unless they be tainted ... are like clean paper, fit to receive whatsoever by Publique Authority shall be imprinted in them'. This was also a period of poor physical communications, in which rumours could spread easily. As a result claims to truth, accuracy and impartiality were important in establishing the worth of a publication and encouraging sales.[13]

During the seventeenth century: 'A profession of factual accuracy and objectivity became the facile claim of all journalists. Of the periodicals begun then, more than 40 contained the word 'perfect' in their titles, 27 more the word 'true', 17 'moderate', nine 'faithful', while others were 'exact', 'impartial', 'certain', and 'particular''.

In 1632 the Reverend Christopher Foster prayed for 'the saviour to inspire the curranto-makers with the spirit of truth' and during the English Civil War many of the newsbooks, operating within a context of wartime disruption and rumour, advertised their purpose as 'To Prevent Misinformation'. In 1680 an official proclamation asserted that 'all News

Printed and Published to the People ... should be agreeable to Truth' to avoid the spread of 'Lyes or vaine Reports, which are many times raised on purpose to Scandalize the Government'.[14]

This concern continued after the lapse of pre-publication licensing. In 1702 the editor of the *Daily Courant* stressed the truthfulness of the paper by refusing 'to give any Comments or Conjecture' of his own. He would 'Relate only Matter of Fact'. In 1782 the *Edinburgh Advertiser* offered its readers 'a very full and impartial detail of PARLIAMENTARY DEBATES', and the *Preston Review and County Advertiser* asserted in 1793 that 'A Faithful Historian is of no country; and the conductor of an impartial Newspaper is of no party.'[15]

As the nineteenth century progressed, these ideas became firmly embedded in the minds of some writers as a standard to which all newspapers should aspire and which, in turn, justified a relatively high social status for the industry. In 1832, when developing a 'Prospectus of a Morning Paper', the Utilitarian philosopher, Jeremy Bentham, asserted that in his paper 'The strictest impartiality would be observed as to the insertion of well-written communications from men of all political opinions, and the proposed newspaper would become a register of the current notions of the day on all topics of public interest.'

The equation of 'impartiality', along with the idea that the paper would in so being become a 'register', illustrates how the concepts of impartiality and truth (for a register's value resides in its truthfulness) were frequently linked. The editor of *The Times* argued in 1852 that the duty of the journalist was 'the same as that of the historian – to seek out truth, above all things, and to present to his readers not such things as statecraft would wish them to know but the truth as near as he can attain it'.[16]

These ideas were transmitted[17] to the twentieth century, and found their most famous expression in 1921 in the words of C.P. Scott, the editor of the *Manchester Guardian*:

> A newspaper is of necessity something of a monopoly, and its first duty is to shun the temptations of monopoly. Its primary office is the gathering of news. At the peril of its soul it must see that the supply is not tainted. Neither in what it gives, nor in what it does not give, nor in the mode of presentation must the unclouded face of truth suffer wrong. Comment is free, but facts are sacred.[18]

In 1938 the former editor of *The Times*, Henry Wickham Steed, extended this to arguing that the obligation to write truthfully was the very basis of the bond between writers and readers:

> The underlying principle that governs, or should govern, the Press is that the gathering and selling of news and views is essentially a public trust. It is based upon a tacit contract with the public that the news

shall be true to the best of the knowledge and belief of those who offer it for sale, and that their comment upon it shall be sincere according to their lights.[19]

The editor of the *Spectator* from 1932 to 1953, Wilson Harris, asserted in 1943 that 'news columns must by their impartiality and objectivity supply the reader with dependable data'. This data had to be truthful:

> the first function of the Press is to tell the truth ... It is a question of giving – or endeavouring honestly and persistently to give, for in this matter there can be no full attainment – an accurate, adequate and faithful picture of life as a whole, in which things intrinsically important are presented as important and things intrinsically trivial as trivial.[20]

This collection of attitudes about truthfulness, impartiality and accuracy survived throughout our period. The 1947–49 Royal Commission on the Press found evidence that they were central to the way people in the industry justified their activities. Odhams Press Ltd, publishers of the *Daily Herald* and *John Bull*, argued that 'A newspaper has a responsibility to the public to report facts as accurately and as fully as the circumstances of the publication allow and to be honest in the expression of opinion.' London Express Newspapers Ltd, publishers of the *Daily Express* and the *Sunday Express*, asserted that a newspaper should give 'a correct and balanced account of what is happening'. The Co-operative Press, publishers of *Reynolds' News*, argued that a newspaper should 'strive constantly to report fairly and objectively what is significant'.

Whilst accuracy in this context often referred to factual accuracy, the Communist-controlled People's Printing Society Ltd, which published the *Daily Worker*, pointed out that 'Accuracy in a newspaper is not only a matter of the correctness of the news that it carries, but of the accuracy with which the newspaper as a whole reflects the significant news of the day.'[21] The People's Printing Society was illustrating a basic problem with the terminology. Words like 'accuracy', 'truth' and 'impartiality' were open to different interpretations. But their power had resided, and continued to reside, in their ability to conjure up a standard to which the press should aspire, and which some papers felt they achieved. It also, implicitly, underpinned Fourth Estate theory, as no newspaper press could aspire to a quasi-constitutional position in a democracy unless it could claim that, in some sense, it was printing the news truthfully, accurately and, if needs be, impartially.

The Royal Commission backed these ideas. For the Commissioners one of the 'essential requirements which in our view newspapers individually and the Press collectively ought to fulfil' was truthfulness: 'if a newspaper purports to record and discuss public affairs, it should at least record them truthfully. It may express what opinions it pleases ... but opinions should be advocated without suppressing or distorting the relevant facts.' Elsewhere they made the link between this essential requirement and the political function of the press. Echoing the mid-nineteenth century view that the press was central to the political process, the Commissioners implied that this held good only in so far as the press aspired to truth: 'Democratic society, therefore, needs a clear and truthful account of events, of their background and their causes; a forum for discussion and informed criticism; and a means whereby individuals and groups can express a point of view or advocate a cause.'[22]

So, over the centuries the idea that the newspaper press should be truthful, accurate and impartial had at least two uses. From being a selling point in those times, such as the seventeenth and eighteenth centuries, when rumour or gossip, ignorance and misinformation were common, during the nineteenth and twentieth centuries they became central to claims about the social usefulness of the press and, by implication, the status of journalism. Assertions of the sort surveyed here were made, not only to sell papers and to set up a standard for aspiring practitioners, but also to insist upon the value of journalism when many people, especially from the mid-nineteenth century onwards, were sceptical of, and sometimes downright hostile to, the claims made by the industry for its usefulness and value.

Attitudes and abuses[23]

1600–1840

Some criticisms of the press are timeless. In 1644 the anonymous author of the Gentle Lash, a publication attacking a newsbook called The Continuation, argued that it was the 'nature and property' of diurnals 'to Lye ... I feare it goes against your conscience to print a truth'.[24] As well as lies, superficiality was attacked. In the eighteenth century Dr Johnson argued that the press 'affords sufficient information to elevate vanity, and stiffen obstinacy, but too little to enlarge the mind into complete skill for compensation'.[25] In 1788 the Morning Post delivered a similar verdict on the superficiality of the press, whilst at the same time heaping blame on the buying public: 'Newspapers have long enough estranged themselves in a manner totally from the elegancies of literature, and dealt only in malice, or at least in the prattle of the day. On this head, however, newspapers are not much more to blame than their patrons, the public.'[26]

The Morning Post was guilty of publishing 'prattle' for, in the same year, it revealed intimate details of the Prince of Wales's private life. Other papers were more than willing to accept financial support from the government. From the late 1780s until 1802 The Times received 'contradiction and suppression fees' plus a sum 'to support Measures of the government'.[27]

In the early nineteenth century Sunday papers were accused of distracting men and women from worship and attracting them to public houses where the papers were read. They were attacked in Parliament for encouraging atheism. From a radical perspective William Cobbett argued, in 1807, that 'The English Press, instead of enlightening, does, as far as it has Power, keep the People in Ignorance. Instead of cherishing Notions of Liberty, it tends to making of the People Slaves; instead of being their Guardian, it is the most efficient Instrument in the Hands of all those who oppress or who wish to suppress them.'[28]

The commercialism of the press was seen as a problem in the 1820s yet, at the same time, there were those who argued that a freer press would promote political stability. As one commentator put it in 1824, giving more freedom to the press would lead to 'the suppression of intense and angry political feelings among the labouring population' and to a reduction in 'party zeal'.

Uncertainty about the nature of newspaper influence was part of a wider concern about the likely social effects of the growth of a mass readership for print. Writing in 1821 the Tory essayist and MP John William Croker speculated on 'Whether the mass of men is made better by learning *such* learning as the mass can obtain, or whether ... the *good* effects can counteract the *bad* effects of a free press.'[29] Croker was satirised in Benjamin Disraeli's *Coningsby* (1844), where the character of Rigby (modelled on Croker) was attacked for allowing himself to be bought by Party bosses and for writing 'slashing articles' which 'whispered as the productions of one behind the scenes, and ... were passed off as genuine coin, and took in great numbers of the lieges, especially in the country'.[30]

1840–1900

In 1840 the Reverend Jenkins of Dowlais in South Wales warned his congregation against reading Chartist publications which were 'as full of poison to the mind and soul, as the Bible is full of grace and mercy'.[31] In the late 1840s there were criticisms of press intrusions into the private lives of the Royal Family, but neither this kind of activity, nor the condemnation of the likes of the Reverend Jenkins, prevented the former Chartist Henry Vincent pointing out that the printing press was 'the great friend of everything liberal and progressive' and that it had ' refused to be the vassal of Government or of priestcraft'.[32]

But, as Aled Jones has pointed out, there was no consensus on the benefits of a press free from the taxes on knowledge and driven by commercial motives. In 1863 the Manchester Literary Society debated the question 'Is not our Newspaper Press as at present existing more mischievous than beneficial?' The Society voted in favour of the press. In 1866 the Reverend Brook Herford considered that the press acted as a unifying force, a 'helpful, softening, humanising, christianising influence'. This was not the view held by reformers in Newcastle upon Tyne who, in 1859, had been so angered by the refusal of the *Northern Daily Express* to print letters from Liberals that they publicly burnt copies of the paper. The question of just how a potentially mischievous press could be dealt with was raised in 1867 when Louis Blanc, a French journalist living in London, suggested there should be a legal 'Right of Reply' to attacks on individuals in newspapers.

Another response was to establish your own paper. On 12 September 1869 the members of the Sunday Evening Debating Society at the Hope and Anchor Inn, Navigation Street, Birmingham, were 'almost unanimously in favour' of the question 'Would the establishment of a working man's newspaper in the midland counties be beneficial, and was the proposed plan to start "the Radical" commercially sound?'[33] This reflected a wider movement that, in the 1870s, tried to set up a national system of radical working-class newspapers. By the mid-1870s papers had sprung up in Staffordshire, Shropshire, Gloucestershire and South Wales, but a combination of low circulation, a narrow appeal, amateurish production techniques and a weak financial base meant that by the end of the decade the initiative had ended. Nonetheless the voices of Labour and of socialists were to figure prominently in public criticisms of the press, from the 1870s and 1880s onwards.[34]

This, in turn, was part of a wider critical response to the Victorian press. For, as Brian Harrison has argued, 'in the long run, the free press disappointed the hopes of the early Victorian radical'. John Morley was one of these. In 1874 he complained that the removal of newspaper taxes had 'done much to make vulgar ways of looking at things and vulgar ways of speaking of them stronger and stronger'.[35] As the forces of an expanded, post-reform press were felt, so there developed a strain of piercing criticisms of its shortcomings. John Ruskin believed the employees of newspaper companies were 'the worst form of serfs that ever human souls sank into – partly conscious of their lying, partly, by dint of daily repetition, believing in their own babble'.[36] George Gissing attacked journalists in his *Thyra: A Tale* (1880). The press's influence had meant that 'every gross-minded scribbler who gets a square inch of space in the morning journal has a more respectful hearing than Shakespeare'.[37] For the socialist Belfort Bax, commenting in 1884, the failure of journalism lay in the way the journalist wrote to order acting as the 'paid hack of the dominant class'.[38] The unease was shared by the Birmingham Ladies Debating Society who in 1890 carried a motion calling for 'the liberty of the press' to be 'curtailed'. Their fellow citizens in the Birmingham and Edgbaston debating society debated whether newspapers were a curse in 1889 and whether 'the influence of the Press at times of national crisis has a tendency to evil rather than to good'.[39]

As the century drew to a close the emergence of 'new journalism' and the prodigious expansion of the market exemplified by the success of the *Daily Mail* (1896) helped intensify debates about the press. These debates included socialists and social conservatives, alarmed by the repressive or negative social effects of the press, as well as those with more confidence in the beneficial impact of the industry.

In 1884 the socialist paper *Justice*, echoing the frustrations that led to the failed attempts to establish a network of Labour papers in the 1870s, declared, 'capitalists own almost the whole Press ... they are masters of the ordinary means of distribution. We must consequently organise a distribution of our own.' A more sanguine view was taken in 1887 by Henry Richard Fox Bourne when he published his *English Newspapers: Chapters in the History of Journalism*. Bourne was a working journalist and felt confident to assert that 'Newspapers are now thrones and pulpits, and journalism assumes to itself the right and power to control and reform the world.' Nonetheless, he was concerned about the effects of commercialism on the press, arguing that one remedy was for all those associated with the industry to regard themselves as professionals and to adopt an appropriate professional ethos.[40]

A similar note of confidence, tempered by doubt, was struck by a pioneer of the 'new journalism', W.T. Stead, in 1886: 'A man without a newspaper is half-clad, and imperfectly furnished for the battle of life. From being persecuted and then contemptuously tolerated, it has become the rival of organized governments.' Yet he was still concerned that 'the journalistic assumption of uttering the opinion of the public is in most cases a hollow fraud'.[41] J.A. Spender's experience as a journalist on the *Eastern Morning News* in the late 1880s illustrated one part of the problem: the willingness of journalists, under pressure, to put words into people's mouths. 'In despair I have written and put into Mr Gladstone's mouth eloquent sentences which he ought to have spoken and which at any rate seemed necessary to make his peroration suit his exordium.'[42]

For Matthew Arnold, writing in 1887, the 'new journalism', in spite of its 'novelty, variety, sensation, sympathy, generous instincts' tended to throw 'out assertions at a venture, because it wishes them to be true' and 'does not correct either them or itself, if they are false'. Delegates at the 1896 conference of the Institute of Journalists complained that falsity was encouraged by advertisements as an 'advertisement given to a paper influenced the editorial columns, and often men could not write what they thought because of this fact'.[43] In addition there were concerns about the effect of journalism on public morals. In 1895 an East Grinstead debating club focused on the extent to which the stress on crime, sensational trials, racing and betting, and the influence of advertising, militated against the elevation of public morals. At the same time there was a concern about the sporting press, which was increasingly popular at the end of the century. These papers allegedly encouraged 'the social evil of gambling and the corruption of sport that, it was thought, inevitably accompanied it'.[44]

1900–47

The early years of the twentieth century saw the continuation of the trends established in the nineteenth, only this time in the context of a rapid, systematic expansion of the mass circulation press. W.T. Stead attacked the jingoism, sensationalism and inaccuracy of the London press in 1904, over the way it covered an incident at Dogger Bank when a Russian warship fired on some British trawlers, mistaking them for the ships of its then enemy, Japan. He was also critical of the way the British press was 'afflicted' by 'a pestilential school of German phobists'.[45] Another concern, echoing the delegates at the 1896 Institute of Journalists' conference, was about the influence of advertising on standards. The planting of promotional editorial copy, or 'puffs', in return for the placing of advertisements was such a problem that it provoked *The Times* on 31 December 1907 to assert:

> It is certain now that in a great number, the majority in fact, of London morning newspapers of reputation, the criticisms and reports printed about cars and things connected with them are not, as in the public interest they most unquestionably ought to be, wholly and absolutely, independent of advertisements 'given' or 'refused'.[46]

In the following year members of the NUJ protested against 'the practice of employing convicted murders and criminals as journalists'. G.K. Chesterton raised questions about the ethics of the employers when, in a telegram to the NUJ in 1911, he praised the profession, whilst echoing widespread fears about how the industry was being run in the interests of a few rich owners: 'Journalism was meant to be a voice from below (democracy). The peril is that it has become the voice from above (plutocracy). I see no remedy but democratic organisation of journalists, and therefore I drink your health.' At the annual conference of the Institute of Journalists in 1913, its president noted that in the previous 20 years there had been 'a check in the increase of newspapers' and 'a concentration of ownership' in fewer hands.[47]

After World War I (1914–18) the Labour Party emerged as a party of government. The Labour Party and Trade Union movement subsequently voiced major criticisms of the press, criticisms that raised questions of ethics and of the ways in which private ownership of the mass commercial press, distorted political news and promoted triviality and sensationalism. The party was therefore developing ideas that had been in circulation during the nineteenth century, but in the context of a changed political situation; in particular the emergence of organised Labour as a major political force with the potential to respond, collectively, to the problems posed by the press.

One Labour leader, Philip Snowden, asserted in 1919 that:

> A Labour Newspaper is at a disadvantage from the point of view of establishing a circulation by feeling under an obligation to maintain a higher moral standard than that observed by ordinary newspapers ... The ordinary newspaper ... is primarily a commercial venture. It has no scruples which are allowed to interfere with the success of its appeal for popular support.

In the same year, the Trade Union leader Ernest Bevin argued that the Labour press had to be 'a real educational factor' not 'full of the caprices of princes, the lubricities of courts and the sensationalism produced by display of the sordid'.[48]

The Labour and trade union movement's critique of the press called into question the political independence of the industry and attacked notions that the press, as constituted, was a socially and politically desirable institution. In 1922 the Labour Research Department published a pamphlet, *The Press*, in which it argued that the ownership of 'the great majority of the London Press ... is in the hands of capitalist groups who are interested either in making direct profits ... or in using it as a means of maintaining the system with which profit-making is possible'. Owners were careful not to offend the interests of advertisers. Whilst recognising the merits of quality papers like the *Sunday Times* and the *Observer*, Labour Research argued that in most papers 'Details of divorce proceedings, of suits for nullity of marriage, and of murder trials, accounts of robbery with violent and indecent assault ... take up the main part of their columns.'

The propagandistic role of these papers was rooted in this kind of content. The *Daily Mail*'s 'concern was the systematic diversion of the minds of the workers from their growing realisation of economic and industrial conditions'. In this context the 'attitude of the journalist and printer [who] ... by ceasing work [or insisting] ... upon the standard of news being of a certain quality, becomes increasingly important'. It praised the attempts of compositors at the *Daily Express* who in 1919 insisted on the paper giving a fair hearing to striking railway workers.[49]

In the same year H.G. Wells stressed the importance of journalists as the defenders of high standards: 'The activities of rich adventurers in buying, and directing, the policy of groups of newspapers is a grave public danger. A free-spirited, well paid, and well organised profession of journalism is our only protection against the danger.'[50]

For the South Wales Labour movement a more direct response to the failings of the press was deemed appropriate. During the General Strike of 1926 the Maerdy miners banned the *Western Mail* and the *South Wales Daily News* from the Maerdy Institute because they had been printed by strike breakers and in May 1926 Aneurin Bevan and others publicly burned copies of the *Western Mail* on a hillside. In 1928 Kingsley Martin, writing an article in *The Encyclopaedia of the Labour Movement*, asserted that 'Labour has long ceased to look for a fair statement of its case in the Capitalist Press.' Labour movement leaders continued to attack the press for similar reasons in the 1930s, and the party put a great deal of faith in seeking to counter the effect of the capitalist press through its own publications.[51]

The Labour movement's complaints about the press in the inter-war years were shared by others who were concerned about the nature and impact of the mass circulation press and the intense competition in the industry. These concerns were, in part, a continuation of the disdain felt by some intellectuals for mass culture: D.H. Lawrence, T.S. Eliot and F.R. Leavis, all of whom attacked the mass press. Evelyn Waugh in *Scoop* (1938) and Graham Greene in *Brighton Rock* (1938) took a highly critical view of the morality and competitiveness of the industry.[52] But these views were, as has been indicated, more widely held than a focus on intellectuals and literary figures might suggest.

By the 1930s even the owners of newspapers were becoming aware that the activities of the press were causing problems. One proprietor, addressing the Newspaper Society in 1936, argued: 'The struggle for sensation, to go one better than one's competitors, the intrusion into private grief, the utter lack of good taste which are the principal characteristics of a large and widely read section of the press are a cause of much lack of sympathy in the very real difficulties we face today.' These 'difficulties' were the tendencies of juries in libel cases to award, as the owners saw it, increasingly larger sums of money to plaintiffs. The problem was so acute that the owners supported a Private Member's Bill in 1936 that, had it been passed, would have taken the right to determine the amount of damages away from juries and handed it to judges.[53]

Earlier, in March 1931, the leader of the Conservative Party, Stanley Baldwin, although specifically exercised by his own conflicts with the owners, showed he shared the kinds of insights and concerns we have been outlining in his now celebrated attack on proprietors:

Their methods are direct falsehood, misrepresentation, half truths, the alteration of the speaker's meaning by putting sentences apart from the context, suppression, and editorial criticism of speeches which are not reported in the paper ... What the proprietorship of these papers is aiming at is power, but power without responsibility – the prerogative of the harlot through the ages.[54]

Complaints abounded. Invasions of privacy provoked concern as did the intrusive behaviour of photographers at funerals. The Chief Constable of Blackburn believed that a recent 'suicide mania' was fed by gruesome stories in the press and suggested that there might be a danger of the curtailment of reporters' rights to report inquests.

As the 1930s progressed, the question of the British government's relationship with fascist regimes in Italy and Germany became a subject of controversy; sections of the Labour movement and the Conservative party pushed for a more aggressive anti-fascist stance in opposition to the government's policy of appeasement. Journalists were concerned about the apparent failure of some newspapers to take a more robust line. In 1938 the ex-editor of *The Times*, Henry Wickham Steed, asked, with reference to Italy and Germany: 'Why have we seen prominent British public men, including owners of influential newspapers, bow before the Leaders of those systems and, overlooking the foul crimes for which those Leaders have been responsible, hearken to their words and extol their deeds?'[55]

Steed's book, along with the publication by Political and Economic Planning – a non-partisan collection of businessmen, academics and public officials – of its report on the British press (1938), were fairly sustained articulations of concerns that had mounted through the decade, but which had been increasingly evident since the turn of the century. Steed noted the reluctance of newspapers to criticise public companies who advertised their annual reports in their pages and how advertisers in 'a dozen ways ... seek to influence the Press to their own advantage'. One remedy for this was to encourage advertisers to set aside 10 per cent of their outlay on press advertising to fund 'periodical and other publications that seek to instruct and to educate rather to [sic] amuse their readers'. He also felt that advertising free broadcasting provided a model for the future:

> public men are no longer quite at the mercy of the newspaper Press. They can speak to millions direct through the broadcasting microphones. They can help to build standards of taste and judgement to which the pressure of public feelings would compel the controllers of newspapers to conform. No care can be too great and no safeguard too stringent to preserve the independence of broadcasting. In so far as the press prostitutes to the business of money-making its mission of instructing and educating the people, that mission should be carried on by other means.[56]

These concerns, and particularly the search for a remedy, remained acute during World War II (1939–45).

In 1943 the NUJ's official historian attacked:

> the low-down kind of journalism which exploits the bawdy and the horrific and cares not how it gets its stories of frailty, folly, crime and

the abnormal. There is plenty of healthy thrill in life without raking the sewers. Many styles of journalism, both the plain and the coloured varieties, are practised without provoking decent, good-mannered people. It is the sensationalism which goes beyond that which must be banned.[57]

In the same year two journalists published pamphlets on the press. Ivor Thomas, an MP and former journalist on *The Times*, conceded that 'misleading reports, misleading headings, and even downright errors are commoner to-day than good journalists would wish'.[58] The editor of the *Spectator*, Wilson Harris, reflected on whether there was a chance that the future would lead to even more concentration of ownership, a move 'decidedly against the public interest'. Whilst not as critical of the industry as some, he considered that there were problems. His view was that the industry should police its own standards:

Study, indeed, of one or two popular journals, daily or Sunday, sometimes raises the question whether more restraints ought not to be imposed ... But it is far better that restraints should be imposed by the journalistic profession itself. It has influential organs, the Newspaper Proprietors' Association and the Newspaper Society, representing London and provincial proprietors respectively, and the Institute of Journalists and the National Union of Journalists representing working journalist of all grades. They have it in their power, the latter particularly, to set standards honourable to the profession, and to a considerable extent they are doing it.[59]

In September 1943 *The Economist*, in looking to the postwar period, argued that measures needed to be taken to provide 'professional guidance' and to maintain high standards. Similar concerns existed in the United States of America, where the Hutchins Commission was established through a private initiative, in 1944, to look into the state of the American press. When this Commission reported in 1947 it recommended, *inter alia*, that there should be an 'opportunity to reply'.[60]

When World War II ended in 1945, the Labour Party won the subsequent general election with 48 per cent of the vote and the support of papers that controlled about 35 per cent of national daily circulation, including the *Daily Mirror*, the *Daily Herald*, and *Reynolds' News*. In left and Labour circles the power of the right-wing press remained a source of real concern and underpinned demands for an inquiry. George Orwell, for instance, writing in 1946, counted 'the press lords', along with 'film magnates and bureaucrats', as 'the immediate enemies of truthfulness'. The Labour government, acting under pressure from the NUJ and Labour MPs, established a Royal Commission in 1947. In so doing it took advice from a key civil servant in the office of the Lord President, Herbert

Morrison, to the effect that if the press wanted to claim the quasi-constitutional position of a Fourth Estate it should not, therefore, be immune from occasional public inquiries similar to those undergone by broadcasters.[61]

The Royal Commission was established

> with the object of furthering the free expression of opinion through the Press and the greatest practicable accuracy in the presentation of news, to inquire into the control, management and ownership of the newspaper and periodical Press and news agencies, including the financial structure and the monopolistic tendencies in control, and make recommendations thereon.[62]

These terms of reference allowed the Commissioners to range over the content and ownership of newspapers. The Commissioners deliberated on long-standing concerns about inaccuracy, bias and sensationalism, which, as has been shown, were particularly acute in the first three decades of the century. For instance, when reflecting on the pre-war position, they attacked the

> intrusion on the privacy of individuals necessary to satisfy the appetite for intimate personal detail about the lives and affairs of people who are, perhaps, quite accidentally, in the news ... but journalists whose papers compete in publishing material of this sort are inevitably under some pressure, direct or implied, to obtain information regardless of the feelings of those concerned: and it is clear both from Questions asked in the House of Commons before the war and from correspondence in *The Times* that there was at that time considerable public resentment of the methods employed.[63]

Although the conclusions reached by the Commission have been criticised heavily for their conservatism[64] this should not obscure the fact that it provided a context within which many of the concerns about inaccuracy, intrusion and sensationalism gained a relatively systematic airing.

The concerns that led to the establishment of the 1947–49 Royal Commission on the Press were therefore of long standing. Traditional concerns had been magnified and supplemented by the expansion, after 1900, of a mass circulation daily press, dominated by a few companies. This development and the anxieties it provoked provided the context in which an inquiry into the press could be proposed. In addition, the existence of an organised Labour movement, in government from 1945, with its own critique of the press, provided the conduit through which the concerns outlined in this chapter could gain a systematic and authoritative hearing.[65]

Thus the Commission was part of a 'long argument' about the press which had not been resolved by the repeal of the taxes on knowledge. Public discussions about the relations between the press and the state developed in the seventeenth and eighteenth centuries, reflecting differences of opinion over what constituted a free press and whether a completely free press was desirable. Running parallel with these discussions were ideas about the relationship of the press to truth, accuracy, impartiality and democracy. These ideas served, initially, to help sell papers by drawing attention to their value in an age of rumour and poor communications but by the twentieth century they had developed into a justification for according a special role in society to the press and journalists. Yet they were also, by implication, a standard against which others could judge the industry and find it wanting as did working people, literary figures, politicians, and even owners.

The interventions cited in this chapter illustrate that there has never been a consensus amongst those who thought and commented on the industry about its social value nor on how, or whether, it should be held accountable to society as a whole. What is clear is that the idea that the press should be free from pre-publication censorship and levies was only one, albeit powerful and influential, idea amongst many others about how best to order the relations between the press and society.

3

Working on the Law: Employers, Journalists and the Legal Framework

The relations between the state and the press have shifted across time. So too have ideas about the role of the press in society and its relationship to the state. The people who have played a major role in influencing these relations and ideas have been employers, journalists and politicians. This chapter explores the interactions between these groups and the development of aspects of the legal framework governing the press.

Employers

On the 25 April 1836 a meeting of the proprietors of provincial newspapers was convened in London. Eighteen attended and twelve sent letters of support. The purpose was to determine what they could do to ease the burden of government-imposed restrictions on their trade, including stamp, advertisement and paper duties. They arranged a deputation to the Chancellor of the Exchequer and, in May, formed the Provincial Newspaper Society. As Strick has pointed out about the Society:

> Its time, efforts and financial resources were spent in fighting campaigns over such matters as scales of charges for newspaper parcels operated by railway companies, charges for press telegrams ... admission of the Press to meetings, censorship, the law of libel, wartime legislation, copyright and divorce court reporting.[1]

Its membership rose from 23 proprietors in 1837 to 300 in 1888, representing 750 newspapers. As the press expanded in mid-century, so the need for collective organisation became more widely accepted amongst proprietors. In 1889 the organisation changed its name to the Newspaper Society, but shortly afterwards there occurred the start of a process of organisational fragmentation which was to gather pace in the 1900s and last until the 1920s. The rapid growth of the industry increased the complexity of the tasks facing the Society, not least of all on matters relating to trade unions. The Society ruled that it could not negotiate with unions and so, in 1894, a separate organisation, the Linotype Users' Association, was set up to negotiate with the major print workers' union, the Typographical Association. This process went further in 1904 when a separate Lancashire Newspaper Society was formed and, in 1906, the Fleet Street proprietors set up a local section of the Newspaper Society, which eventually ceded in 1916. Separate owners' organisations emerged in Southern England in 1909, in Wales in 1913 and Scotland in 1915.

The growth of trade unionism in the industry and the need to reverse the fragmentation of employers' organisations led to an amalgamation in 1921 of the major federations under the auspices of the Newspaper Society, which from then onwards had the authority to conduct national negotiations with the trade unions. By 1936 the Newspaper Society had 400 members, publishing 1000 daily and weekly papers of the total of 1600 printed in England and Wales. Many of the remaining 600 were small circulation papers.[2]

By the time the Royal Commission on the Press was set up in 1947, proprietors had been organised for over 130 years. The Commission felt that 'proprietors and directors' whilst 'keenly concerned for the good name both of their own papers and of the Press as a whole' had 'taken little effective action' on questions of standards. Whilst true, this judgement underestimates the effectiveness of the actions taken in defence of their interests by employers' organisations (see the section on the legal framework below) and, in a sense, misunderstands the purpose of these bodies. For to appear to be concerned about standards whilst taking no effective action and getting away with it could, from an employers' perspective, be deemed a success.[3] These bodies were there not to proclaim, in the spirit of Fourth Estate theory, the independence of the press from the state, but to negotiate with it in order to promote their members' interests. After 1953 the Press Council became an extension of this process.

The struggle for professional status

Since the nineteenth century journalists have been unclear about their standing in society. There have been disagreements, amongst themselves and amongst commentators outside the industry, about whether journalism is a craft or a profession. These disagreements have had consequences the most important of which is that journalists have been unable to agree on a form of organisation, which would be similar to that of doctors and lawyers, that could control entry and regulate standards. As a result, journalists have not achieved similar status nor been able to act effectively to prevent the intrusions into privacy, the sensationalism and inaccuracies that have been a recurrent source of complaint against the industry. Nonetheless, through their organisations, notably the NUJ, they have been able to intervene in the political process to influence the legal framework within which they work.

Estimates for the number of journalists show a growth that mirrors the expansion of the press outlined in Chapter 1. Numbers have been estimated as being about 2000 in 1861, rising to around 10,000 in the 1930s. As the nineteenth century developed, words appeared in the language describing different aspects of journalism, which, in illustrating the recognition of the different tasks associated with the work, also conjure up the fluidity of the idea of a journalist. In 1821 the publishers of the *Carnarvon Advertiser* 'described the role of the "journalist" as one of "reporting discoveries", linking such reporting with "the Progressive advance of Philosophical Knowledge"'. According to Lucy Brown, the first recorded reference to an 'editor' of a newspaper is in 1830; of a 'reporter', 1813; a 'sub-editor', 1834; and 'Leader-writer', 1888. Journalism was an evolving occupation in the early nineteenth century and it is no surprise, therefore, that public understanding of it was uncertain.[4]

Aled Jones has noted the 'ambivalence' that was 'ingrained in popular and political attitudes' towards journalists well into the nineteenth century. In 1846 Charles Mitchell in his *Newspaper Press Directory* observed that 'English editors, unlike those of their class in France, hold, at best, but a dubious position in Society'. In his memoirs of journalism Sir Wemsys Reid (1842–85) gave reasons why journalists were held, by some, in low esteem: 'The Press, at all events in provincial towns, was the reverse of respectable in the eyes of the world, and surely there was some reason for the low esteem in which it was held. The ordinary reporter on a country paper was generally illiterate, was too often intemperate and was invariably ill paid.'[5]

The journalist, according to Brian Harrison, occupied an 'insecure professional status' and an 'uncertain class location' and, even in the 1950s, Strick noted that the journalist 'has never been quite sure of his [*sic*] position and never quite able to reconcile his calling with the trade union approach'.[6]

Journalists worked under commercial pressures that could at anytime undercut their attempts to apply high standards and thus achieve a higher level of social esteem. They needed to satisfy advertisers, their financial backers and the assumed needs of their readers.[7] They were increasingly employees of papers, rather than self-employed like doctors and lawyers, a fact that made self-regulation harder. As Lucy Brown has pointed out they were, more often than not, 'recruited from the more insecure and impoverished section of the middle classes'. Their career often started immediately after school or university, which set them apart from politicians and literary figures, and a combination of their unsociable hours plus their tendency to socialise with each other increased their sense of separatism. A high level of job mobility, common amongst journalists in the nineteenth century, may have contributed to the perception of journalists as unsteady characters. Paradoxically, the spread of Pitman's phonetic shorthand system after the 1840s, whilst increasing the employability of journalists, may have contributed to their low status because shorthand reinforced the distinction between the craft of recording and reporting and the more creative skills of literary production.[8]

Whilst these and other factors continued to contribute to the unstable self- and public perception of journalists into the twentieth century, by the mid-nineteenth century, parallel with the changes in law and the size of the industry, there is evidence that journalism began to improve in status. As Aled Jones has argued: 'It was a measure of this new-found respectability that, having won the right to report Parliamentary proceedings, places were also reserved for reporters in law courts, local government meetings and commissions and meetings of voluntary association and trade unions.'

In London the growth of West End clubs, where aristocrats and businessmen, politicians and professionals could mix, provided a forum through which journalists could become more widely known and their craft more socially acceptable. By the 1860s and 1870s journalism was regarded as a more respectable practice than it had been in the first half of the century and for the next two decades 'professional status became ... the most highly valued and desperately sought after goal of late nineteenth-century journalists'.[9] This move can be seen as a part of a wider social process in which status was equated less with industrial and commercial wealth and more with the traditional pursuit of the ideal of gentlemanly, quasi-aristocratic, professional status. The move to become a profession reflected the socially conservative impulses of journalists. For, as Rubenstein has noted, the acquisition of professional status in the nineteenth century signalled a profound form of conservatism:

> In so far as the incorporated professionals may be assigned anywhere, it is invariably with the most conservative elements in society, to the pre-industrial urban elite or even to the aristocracy. This is obviously so with the Church and the bar, and no less true of medicine, civil engineering or accountancy – in Britain at any rate. The process of incorporation, acquisition of an expensive and palatial headquarters in central London, establishment of an apprenticeship system,

limitation on entries, and scheduling of fees, are all manifestly designed to 'gentrify' the profession and make it acceptable to society.[10]

Full professional status was never achieved by journalists, although the Institute of Journalists (IOJ) attempted it. Nonetheless, the desire to be seen as a profession, in part a reaction to the negative perceptions of the early nineteenth century, also provides further illustration of journalists' desires to be part of, not apart from, the social and political establishment. This, in turn, helps explain the willingness of most journalists during the late nineteenth and twentieth centuries to deal pragmatically with the state when it came to assessing or seeking state intervention in the industry.

The Institute of Journalists

The desire for professional status found expression in the foundation of the IOJ. Journalists, who met informally at the 1883 Royal Agricultural Show at York, discussed grievances such as the obstructions they encountered in trying to do their job, the lack of redress against charges of inaccuracy levelled at them by public figures and the problem of the welfare of sick journalists or their bereaved families. It must also be remembered that by this time journalists had before them recent evidence of the success of collective activity of employers, especially as exemplified by the reforms embedded in the Newspaper and Libel Registration Act 1881 (see below). As a result, in 1884, a National Association of Journalists (NAJ) was founded, which, in keeping with its 'professional' orientation, included employers as well as employees. Membership had reached 614 by 1887. After concerted lobbying the NAJ was granted a Royal Charter. The Charter was formerly granted in 1890 and the NAJ became the IOJ. This move established the framework for the IOJ to build a profession, but it was a framework without the all-important power to regulate entry. The IOJ set about devising examinations for entry into the profession, committed itself to promoting the status of journalists, to monitoring legislation that affected their duties or interests, to helping them find employment and to establishing a welfare fund.[11]

The Institute attempted, unsuccessfully, to devise means of restricting entry by examination, but in the process also promoted journalism courses at the Universities of Birmingham, Leeds and Glasgow. By 1892 it had grown to 3114 members, but within the ranks concerns that the inclusion of employers compromised the Institute's ability to promote the economic interests of journalists led to a split and the creation of the National Union of Journalists (NUJ) in 1907. Competition from the NUJ eventually forced the IOJ to register as a trade union in 1920, since which it has remained by far the smaller of the two organisations.[12]

An overriding theme of the IOJ was the need to sustain high standards. This led it towards advocating state intervention to solve the problems associated with lack of control over entry. As early as 1891 members were attacking the practice of reporters receiving gifts from people about whom they wrote. In 1923 one member, dissatisfied with the IOJ's effectiveness in this area, insisted that the body should take a cue from other professions:

> we must do as they did before they got the right to control the entrance to their callings ... build up the right spirit and set the right standards ... Later no doubt we shall ... insist on entrance qualifications, just as other professions have done ... we must bend our efforts towards the constitution and recognition of journalism as one of the learned professions.[13]

The problems of sensationalism, intrusions into privacy and inaccuracy led in the 1930s to an attempt by the IOJ to introduce a state register of journalists. Initiated in 1931 by the IOJ President it was picked up in 1933. A delegation from the IOJ saw the Home Secretary and a proposal, with the formal support of the organisation's Council, formed the basis of an attempt in 1935 to win Parliamentary support for the Journalists' (Registration) Bill:

> The Bill made it an offence for any unregistered person to use the title 'journalist' and contained a disciplinary clause providing for the striking off the register of any journalist held, after a disciplinary inquiry, to have been guilty of disgraceful conduct in their capacity as journalists. The register would be administered by a journalists' Registration Council consisting of members appointed by the governing bodies of the Institute, the NUJ, proprietors' organisations, unattached but duly registered journalists, and the senates of universities awarding diplomas in journalistic studies.

The NUJ opposed the idea of a state register, but this did not prevent the Institute backing two further attempts, in 1936 and 1937, to get a Private Member's Bill heard in Parliament. The onset of the crisis leading up to the second World War contributed to the demise of the proposal.[14] Nonetheless, it should be recognised as an important precedent. Firstly, it predated in time, if not in substance, the proposals made by the 1947–49 Royal Commission. Secondly, it illustrated the continuing desire for effective professional organisation, a desire not satisfied by the granting of the Royal Charter. Thirdly, it illustrates the fact that some journalists in the 1930s considered a state register of journalists as a device for raising standards rather than as a backdoor for state censorship of the press. Thus the pressure for some regulation came from within the industry. Attitudes to state intervention remained fluid and by 1935 there were plenty of examples before journalists of the successful use of state power to further the influence of employers and workers.

The National Union of Journalists

The NUJ was founded in 1907. Whilst one of its purposes was to deal with questions affecting the professional conduct of members, its main focus in the early years was on salaries and conditions rather than on achieving professional status. As its first official historian pointed out, the union 'was opposed to the ingrained prejudice of the journalist against trade unionism as applied to what he finally regarded as his profession'.[15] In its opposition to employers being part of the union it asserted both the need for industrial independence and, in a sense, the craft identity of many journalists, things which the IOJ in its search for status and incorporation into the establishment tended to marginalise. Whilst the NUJ grew and gained recognition for negotiating purposes with employers it also pursued changes to the legal framework governing journalism, thus, like the IOJ, adopting a flexible approach to the question of state intervention in the industry.

The NUJ responded to the intensification of criticisms of press practice in the 1920s and 1930s and to the IOJ's attempt to establish a register of journalists. In 1931 the union acknowledged concerns about intrusive methods used by some reporters during the collection of news, but, at the same time, recognised that these practices were often the result of pressures placed on its members by economic competition. Thus: 'An appeal was addressed to proprietors, editors and managers to endeavour to come to a common understanding as to the limits of licence which should be allowed to or imposed upon, their staffs.'

The National Executive Council (NEC) of the union proposed that reporters be forbidden from intruding into private lives, and that they should not usurp the functions of detectives. It commented that 'There seems to be a tendency on the part of some to assume that the world was made for the sole purpose of providing copy for the newspapers. There should be more restraint, more reticence and a greater sense of responsibility.'

It promised to provide moral and financial support to members who, with the support of their branch, refused to carry out instructions deemed repugnant to their sense of decency. In 1932 the Annual Delegate Meeting (ADM), in an attempt to help apply international standards on 'offenders against the principles of honesty and responsibility', agreed that all rulings of the International Court of Honour, established by the International Federation of Journalists, should apply to NUJ members.[16]

When the proposal for a state register emerged in the early 1930s, it was objected to, from within the NUJ, in part because it came from the

IOJ, a body perceived by many members as hostile to trade unionism, and in part because, as Mansfield writes, the union 'felt convinced of its ability through its own policies on education, standards of conduct and the protection of the interests of working journalists, to achieve the desired uplift'. The union's response to criticisms of journalistic standards and to the IOJ's initiative was to draft and debate, from 1934 onwards, a code of conduct. The code was passed at the 1936 ADM and became an appendix to the NUJ rule book. This 'Code of Professional Conduct' reiterated the promise of union support for those journalists who refused to do work 'incompatible with the honour and interests of the profession'. It also asserted that: 'In obtaining news or pictures, reporters and press photographers should do nothing that will cause pain or humiliation to innocent, bereaved, or otherwise distressed persons. News, pictures, and documents should be acquired by honest methods only.' Members were enjoined not to 'falsify information and private documents, or distort or misrepresent facts' and informed that 'Whether for publication or suppression, the acceptance of a bribe by a journalist is one of the gravest professional offences.'[17]

In 1937 the NEC passed a resolution to the government and proprietors offering its full co-operation in attempts to stop malpractices. In the same year the NUJ's President, F.G. Humphreys, identified the Fleet Street papers as the main culprits and, according to Mansfield, 'clung to the ideal of co-operation between proprietors and union as the most effective method of stopping intrusions on privacy'.[18] In 1940 members asked to do anything 'which offended their sense of decency' when interviewing the relatives of people lost in the conflict were advised to report to the NEC. In 1942 the union lobbied the Home Secretary over a proposal for a joint NUJ, IOJ and employers' body for 'the maintenance of a proper sense of responsibility in the Press, and control of irresponsible newspapers and journalists'. The Home Secretary, Herbert Morrison, who as Lord President in the 1945 Cabinet was to oversee the establishment of the Royal Commission, told the NUJ that he would consider sympathetically the proposal if all newspaper interests were agreed. NUJ members, concerned about wartime restraints on the press, rejected the idea on the grounds that it might become a 'most dangerous agency for the suppression of legitimate criticism, and must inevitably lead to a still further invasion of the freedom of the Press'. The NUJ was to modify its position after the war. It helped to persuade Morrison to back a Royal Commission, in the face of opposition from other sectors of the industry, and, in its evidence, supported the idea of a voluntary, industry-wide body to promote standards.[19]

Wartime conditions did not, however, mean that problems of standards could be put to one side. Writing in 1943, the union's historian, F.J. Mansfield, argued that the problems of sensationalism, whilst a perennial feature of the press, had become 'acute in recent times'.

Wartime conditions, problems of standards and the impact of concentrated ownership on working practices combined to put pressure on working journalists. As one member put it 1946: 'A newspaper man is forced to mislead the public or be sacked ... staff journalists are marionettes. They cannot be servants of both the public and their employers.' This dilemma, and concerns about the ease with which newspapers could be closed down by owners, underpinned the decision of the 1946 ADM to call for a Royal Commission to investigate monopolistic tendencies and the distortion and suppression of news. When in September 1948 a special delegate meeting met to consider the union's evidence to the Commission it argued for, amongst other things, 'the setting up of a Press Council, without representatives of the general public, but with an independent Chairman'.[20]

Politicians and the industry

Stephen Koss has described the close links that existed between politicians and journalists in the nineteenth century. The high point of these connections came after the repeal of the stamp and advertisement duties and continued into the early decades of the twentieth century.[21] The links between newspapers and particular political parties changed with the rise of the mass circulation press. Journalists and employers, however, whilst no longer seeing themselves as loyal adjuncts of a particular political party, remained intimately bound together in a range of ways.[22]

At the height of the nineteenth-century relationship between politicians and the industry, politicians gave the press 'varying amounts of encouragement; confidential information and guidelines; social inducements; professional rewards, including honours; and transfusions of capital from private and party funds'. In return newspapers, in theory at least, 'had intelligence to impart and favours to bestow; they could rally the faithful and, if necessary, harry the feckless'. This did not always happen. But the point is that the two sides stood in a mutually dependent relationship.[23]

The complexities of these links and the hypocrisy they could generate have been illustrated by Lucy Brown. In the nineteenth century successive governments held and used a list of newspapers in which it was considered politically prudent to place government advertisements.

Advertising would have consisted of such matters as government contracts: it might have been important to the finances of papers in such places as the dockyard towns ... The government list survived, in the teeth of the wind of change, and to the annoyance of civil servants, to the end of the nineteenth century: the fact that it did so suggests the partiality and self-interest of the agitation for a free press in the middle of the century. The 'taxes on knowledge' put up costs and were evil, but the government list, in a period of predominately Liberal administrations, attracted no attention.[24]

These connections were fed by what Koss has suggested was an 'appetite for newspapers' among the privileged orders which 'became an addiction'.[25] At a local level, journalists were closely involved with, or were part of, the political elites; no respectable political movement could do without its newspaper. In 1874, for example, there were 489 Liberal English provincial papers and 41 Liberal London papers, and 294 and 25 Conservative ones respectively.[26]

From the late 1860s onwards 'the journalistic presence in Parliament became more noticeable in the chambers as well as the lobbies. Newspaper proprietors and editors were elected to Parliament. J.A. Hardcastle, a Liberal MP, commented after the 1880 election that 'The entrance of so large a number of journalists to the House of Commons is striking proof of the growing influence of the press, which is one of the most important training schools of modern politicians.' He put their number at 14, which Koss considered, taking on board the number of MPs who wrote to augment their income, 'an exceedingly cautious estimate'. In 1888 there were, at a conservative estimate, at least 21 proprietors and 10 editors sitting as MPs.[27]

This tendency for the House to contain a strong presence of journalists continued into the twentieth century. Amongst the 14 NUJ members elected in 1929 there were two who occupied places in the 1929–31 Labour government: Philip Snowden and William Graham. One estimate put the number of journalists elected to the 1945 House at 40 and Strick has noted that at that election there were '20 members of the NUJ – the third largest group in the new House – of whom 19 were Labour members and the 20th an independent; and four members of the Institute, of whom two were socialist and two Conservative.'[28]

So, throughout the late nineteenth and twentieth centuries the personal, political and professional links between politicians, both local and national, and employers and journalists have remained very close. This helps explain how ideas favoured by the industry continued to gain sympathetic hearings from politicians. It also helps an understanding of why employers were adept at achieving many of the legal changes they desired and why they were also prepared to accept the continuation of state intervention in the press after the repeal of the stamp duties.

Aspects of the legal framework

The law governing the press developed in a number of areas, sometimes through the action of the courts, sometimes through initiatives by politicians and, at other times, as a result of initiatives by the industry. Whilst pre-publication censorship lapsed in 1694, the courts retained the powers to intervene in the press affairs. In 1727 the Curl case established the crime of publishing an obscene libel. Prosecutions under this law continued from time to time, and, running parallel, was the ability of the government to prosecute for criminal libel. A 'vague and indeterminate law of libel' had, by the early nineteenth century become, according to James Mill, the greatest danger to liberty. As the press grew in the early decades of the century, the libel laws came to be seen, especially by proprietors, as a major obstacle to the activities of the industry. The financial consequences to a paper stemming from the loss of a libel action could be severe. The employers' organisations began to act on this and from the 1830s the state entered into protracted negotiations with the industry over the laws of libel.[29]

In 1843, in response to a petition from Irish newspaper owners, a House of Lords Select Committee was set up to look at the libel laws. Its report led to an Act, in 1843, that benefited the industry by, amongst other things, allowing papers to avoid prosecution for libel if they could show that no malice was intended and that they would publish a full apology. It introduced a defence of justification and made it illegal to threaten to publish a libel with a view to blackmailing someone. A further Act in 1854 placed financial obstacles in the way of profiteering litigants.[30] Thus proprietors of the respectable press were able to influence the nature of state intervention to suit their interests.

Other laws continued directly, or indirectly, to affect the press. The Printers and Publishers Act 1839 required the names of printers to be published on papers alongside those of the publisher. The Limited Liability Act 1854, by allowing the creation of companies with shareholders who carried limited liability, encouraged a shift from subscription based funding for newspapers to shareholding. The old system meant subscribers could not necessarily exercise control over their publications once the money had been put up. The new system gave shareholders legal control over the publication. The state thus helped create the legal conditions for the development of more stable forms of ownership and control in the industry. In contrast, in 1857 the state, partly in response to scandalous and obscene journalism, added controls to the framework in the form of the Obscene Publications Act. In 1876 a further restraint was imposed. The Customs Consolidation Act prohibited the importation of indecent or obscene works.[31]

Between 1865 and 1867 newspaper employers backed at least three Private Member's Bills designed to provide protection to newspapers from libel actions stemming from published reports of public meetings. These attempts failed, to some extent because of fears about the damage to reputations if immunity was granted. In 1867 Louis Blanc, a French journalist living in London, joined in the debate over questions of redress by suggesting a legal 'Right of Reply' to attacks made by newspapers on individuals. Although the attempts of the 1860s to influence libel laws did not yield the desired results, proprietors benefited from the Newspapers Printers and Reading Rooms Act 1869, which by removing the requirement for all newspaper proprietors to be registered with the state, made it more difficult for a potential litigant to identify the proprietor. During the 1870s this change provided some cover for the publishers of scandalous papers, which in turn stimulated attempts, opposed at the time by the proprietors, to reintroduce registration.[32]

Employers did not focus efforts on lifting restraints on the publication and import of obscene publications in the interests of fighting state censorship. Instead, in 1878 the proprietors prepared a bill designed to achieve immunity from proceedings stemming from reports of public meetings. This led to a Select Committee on libel being set up that allowed the proprietors, some of whom were MPs, to introduce a Private Member's Bill that became the Newspaper Libel and Registration Act 1881. The Act was the product of concerted lobbying in Parliament by newspaper interests and, whilst it re-introduced the compulsory registration of the names of the proprietors of newspapers, this was a minor point when compared to the immunity it granted proprietors. It allowed magistrates to dismiss cases early on in proceedings where justification seemed likely to succeed as a defence. It also allowed them to rule on the triviality of the libel and, if they considered it proper, to then promote an early and cheap settlement. More importantly, it 'provided that a fair, accurate and unmalicious newspaper report of the proceedings of a lawfully convened public meeting should be privileged, notwithstanding that it contained defamatory reflections'.[33] The Law of Libel Amendment Act 1888 came from an initiative of the Provincial Newspaper Association and its eight parliamentary sponsors with direct affiliation to the press. It extended qualified privilege to reports of select committee hearings and to the publication of police notices and government departments.[34] So, whilst the theory of a Fourth Estate independent from the state was at its height, proprietors were simultaneously soliciting state power to bolster their legal and economic position.

Restraints on the collection and publication of information continued to be imposed while the idea that the press was independent flourished and proprietors were perfecting their powers of manipulation of the legislative process. In 1889 the Indecent Advertisements Act made it an offence to deliver obscene or indecent material on a public highway. The Prevention of Corruption Act 1889, whilst designed to restrain the use of bribery, by implication covered the selling of information by public servants to the press. In response to concerns in the government and the military about the sale and leaking of intelligence and military secrets to the press and foreign powers, the first Official Secrets Act was passed in

1889, making it an offence for a civil servant to disclose, improperly, official information.[35]

The NUJ was involved, from the early days, in seeking to win benefits from the State. George Leach, an NUJ member, was influential in securing the provision of the Local Authorities (Admission of Press to Meetings) Act 1908, which gave reporters special status at meetings of local authorities and in courts of justice. From then onwards the union continued to pursue a policy of intervening to prevent unacceptable state interference or to get the state to act, at a time when, between 1900 and 1945, the state was continually pro-active in legislating on matters relating to the press.[36]

During the early 1900s UK governments became increasingly concerned about leaks in foreign and domestic affairs. As a result, and in the wake of a diplomatic crisis sparked by Germany sending a gunboat to Morocco, legislation, based on drafts produced in 1896 and 1910, was rushed through Parliament and became the Official Secrets Act 1911. The Act made it illegal to communicate or retain official documents, and made the mere unauthorised possession of any official document an offence. This Act was designed to catch domestic as well as defence related leaks, but it was produced during a period of growing Anglo-German tension, and 'the press allowed the Act to pass without comment, as its attention was focused on fears of war with Germany'. When war did break out in 1914 the bulk of the press lost its 'independence'. Government censorship was imposed, but was regarded by the bulk of the press not as an outrageous affront to their independence but 'as an unnecessary impediment to their patriotic efforts to win the war'. Large sections of the press were, and have remained, willing to sanction government control of the flow of information to the press in the interests of definitions of patriotism and national security that are derived from the state.[37]

In 1923 the UK government signed an international convention for the suppression of obscene publications. Three years later it passed the Judicial Proceedings (Regulation of Reports) Act, which can be seen, in part, as both a form of pre-publication censorship and an attempt to counter some of the worst excesses of the mass circulation press. It made it:

> a crime to publish in relation to any judicial proceedings any indecent matter or indecent medical, surgical or physiological details which could be calculated to injure public morals ... [and] an offence to publish in relation to proceedings for divorce, or nullity any particulars other than the following; the names, addresses, and occupation of the parties, the charges, legal argument and the judge's summing up and verdict.

The Bill had been opposed, in an earlier version, by the Newspaper Society. When it reappeared the NUJ lobbied successfully to protect journalists by inserting a clause that made only the owner, editor, master printer or publisher liable to prosecution.[38]

Other examples of the state continuing to restrict freedom of expression were the suppression of Radclyffe Hall's novel about lesbianism, *The Well of Loneliness*, in 1928, and the passage of the Incitement to Disaffection Act 1934. In the latter case, according to one journalist, Ivor Thomas, writing in 1943, the Act made it possible 'to proceed against a newspaper not for an offence which it has committed but for an offence which it may commit'. Indeed, by the 1930s, in spite of the fact that the press had nominally been 'free' since the 1860s, it was hedged around by laws, some granting privileges, such as immunity from libel and rights to report, and others imposing restraints, such as the 1934 Act, or the Official Secrets Act 1911. In 1939 the newspaper proprietors attempted to gain passage of a bill to grant them immunity from actions arising out of the reports of shareholders' meetings. This led to the establishment of a Select Committee under Lord Porter which, reconvening after the war, produced recommendations that laid the basis for further relief for proprietors in the form of the Defamation Act 1952.The passage of these measures, which in a sense reduced the public's safeguards against defamatory reporting, was aided by the expectation in political circles that a Press Council, based on the recommendations of the 1947–49 Royal Commission, would be established and would provide an alternative means of redress.[39]

In fact, by the 1930s and 1940s, the legal framework that had evolved was a complex one of rights and responsibilities. In 1936 the Privy Council summarised the situation thus: 'Free speech does not mean free speech: it means speech hedged in by all the laws against defamation, blasphemy, sedition and so forth. It means freedom governed by law.'[40] The lifting of the taxes on knowledge in the 1850s and 1860s was therefore only one part of an evolving legal framework. The factors shaping that framework were many. Amongst the most significant was the interaction between the state, employers and journalists. The state continued to impose pre-publication restraints and post-publication penalties but, in response to pressures from employers and journalists, it was prepared to reduce citizens' rights over the press by making libel actions harder to mount and to grant the press rights of access to public bodies for reporters. Whilst the NUJ opposed some forms of pre-publication censorship, elements within the industry accepted state controls in wartime and, to some extent, in peacetime, including the Official Secrets Act. The IOJ were also prepared to accept some form of state registration of journalists.

Thus the legal framework within which the press has operated since the nineteenth century has evolved through negotiation between various interest groups. These negotiations have not been dominated, except in rhetorical terms, by unqualified opposition to state intervention or pre-publication censorship. The determining factors have been the power that different participants in these negotiations could exercise and the ways in which different situations have invited or thrown up different solutions to the problems faced. It is this pragmatism which has governed the development of the legal framework, a pragmatism in which the rhetoric of the Fourth Estate was not the guiding principle, merely one, albeit high profile and important, factor in the ongoing interaction between the state and the industry.

4

A Sense of Doubt: The Origins and History of Self-Regulation up to 1972

This chapter and the next outline the history of public debate about voluntary versus self-regulation of the press in the UK from the late 1930s to the 1990s. The range of perspectives on the proper relationship between the state and the press discussed in earlier chapters continued to find public expression as the political debate about the regulation of the media in general and the press in particular intensified.[1] These chapters also demonstrate the existence, in the face of sustained opposition from proprietors, editors and many politicians, of a long, postwar tradition in favour of creating a statutory framework for improving standards.

1930s–1953 – the emergence of the Press Council

Up to 1949

By the 1930s there was widespread interest in, and concern about, the press.[2] These concerns were given systematic expression in 1938, in a long and detailed report produced by a group of academics, industrialists, public servants and people from the newspaper industry known as Political and Economic Planning (PEP). PEP expressed concern about standards in the industry and noted that 'Perhaps the most acute cause of trouble is the intrusion into private lives and personal affairs which has led to considerable public indignation against sections of the press.' They ruled out statutory regulation on intrusion and the state registration of journalists, but did recommend a voluntary Press Tribunal:

It should consist of a chairman commanding unqualified general confidence, for his judicial gifts, with two assessors drawn from representative panels of proprietors and of journalists. The tribunal would need no legislative authority, and could be launched with a widely published appeal to the public from the Press that anyone feeling aggrieved by alleged journalistic intrusion should lay a complaint before it.

The sanction operated by the Tribunal would be publicity and, in time, there 'would thus be built up by a series of case decisions a working code of legitimate and illegitimate practice in newsgetting from members of the public'. Limited as this proposal was as to the question of intrusion, these ideas about a voluntary body that investigated complaints, used the power of publicity as a sanction and built up a code of conduct recurred throughout the postwar period.[3]

The idea that you could help solve the problem of press standards by producing a blueprint for a Press Tribunal was part of wider current of opinion amongst professionals in the 1930s and 1940s that stressed the importance of planning as a policy instrument. PEP was part of this current. During the war this vogue for planning gained expression in the 'professional journals' which 'were full of the cry for planning, public investment, and social development'. More specifically in September 1943, *The Economist* looked forward to a postwar regime of agencies providing 'professional guidance ... to maintain high standards, in the face of proprietorial pressures, financial considerations and the contemporary mistranslation of popularity to mean vulgarity'. By 1943 the NUJ was working on how to deal with the postwar situation.[4]

The 1945 General Election returned a Labour government that for the first time had an unassailable majority in the House of Commons. During the campaign Labour had captured 48 per cent of the popular vote and the Conservatives 40 per cent. Conservative-controlled papers accounted for 52 per cent of press circulation, with Labour just 35 per cent. This bias of the national press against Labour went back to the party's foundation in 1900 and was widely recognised in Labour circles, even though it was clearly not decisive in the election. In addition, the presence of up to 40 MPs with press connections in the 1945 intake, many of whom were Labour, provided fertile ground for discussions about the press. These factors, combined with long-standing and widespread concerns about press standards, helped create the political impetus that produced the 1947–49 Commission.[5]

Concerns about the press went, of course, beyond the question of standards. In 1946 at the Annual Delegate Meeting of the NUJ the Manchester Branch successfully moved a motion calling for a Royal Commission on the press. The Commission was meant to look at ownership and control, financing, the tendencies towards monopoly, and the influence of financial and advertising interests on the distortion and suppression of news. Speaking in favour of the motion, Preston Benson recapitulated long-standing concerns amongst journalists: 'In the last fifty years there has been a widespread exploitation of the right to print. This long development of commercial newspapers, with millions of circulation, has reduced news to the quality of entertainment and the gathering, reporting, discussing, and commenting on news has lost its social interest.'

A deputation from the NUJ met the Lord President of the Council, Herbert Morrison, in July 1946. Morrison, a key figure in the administration of Prime Minister Clement Attlee, promoted the idea of a Royal Commission within Cabinet, where he had to overcome opposition from some sceptical ministers. He saw the appointment of a Commission as justified, in part, because broadcasting had been subjected to regular public scrutiny of this sort since its beginning in 1922. So, he and his civil servants reasoned, why should the press be immune from a similar form of public scrutiny? In taking this line, Morrison was, in effect, moving on from the position held by successive governments since the 1860s, that the press should by and large be free from government initiatives which could be construed as attempts at control. In so doing he helped to create a political atmosphere in the postwar period in which government-inspired inquiries into the press could take place without being universally interpreted as attempts to curb press freedom.

With the backing of the Parliamentary Labour Party and Attlee, Morrison arranged for a government-drafted motion setting up the Commission to be debated and passed by the House of Commons on 29 October 1946. The Commission, chaired by the academic Sir David Ross, was charged in its terms of reference

> with the object of furthering the free expression of opinion through the Press and the greatest practicable accuracy in the presentation of news, to inquire into the control, management and ownership of the newspaper and periodical Press and the news agencies, including the financial structure and the monopolistic tendencies in control, and to make recommendations thereon.

The inclusion of the reference to accuracy signalled that the question of standards was on the agenda.[6]

By October 1947 the Policy Committee of the Commission was considering a raft of proposals for a body to regulate standards and promote cohesion in the industry. At a meeting of three of the Commissioners, on 17 March 1948, David Ross 'thought the proposal of a Press Council was within the Terms of Reference. The reaction of the Press has been either unenthusiastic or hostile. He thought there was a case for bringing such a Council into being, more to stimulate training than for critical purposes. He favoured a voluntary basis.'

The Commission, whilst not recommending an overhaul of ownership in the industry, eventually agreed to recommend a General Council of the Press. One of its members, Sir Geoffrey Vickers, 'was doubtful ... whether a Press Council would be a good thing' but agreed to a proposal for a voluntary Council. In the end the Commission recommended the establishment of a Council, but with reservations from two members. Sir George Waters opposed the inclusion of lay members, 'apart from an independent chairman', on the grounds that the Council would make a better start 'if the responsibility for order, decency and progress within the Press were left to the sense of honour and duty of those who own and conduct it and constitute its editorial staff'. Ensor, too, felt that 'As an old member of the journalistic profession I cannot put my name to the proposal that the General Council of the Press should have its members appointed from outside other than the chairman.'[7]

Although it rejected using legislation to establish a Council, the Commission was unclear about whether the law should be used to regulate standards. It rejected a law to curb intrusions into privacy on the grounds that it would be 'extremely difficult to devise legislation which would deal with the mischief effectively and be capable of enforcement'. This was an objection based on practicality rather than principle. In reaching this position it mirrored the verdict of its contemporary Committee on the Law and Defamation, which had reported in 1948 and asserted that 'there are great difficulties in formulating' a law to restrain invasions of privacy whilst not at the same time restraining 'the due reporting of matters which are of public interest'. On the other hand, the 1947–49 Commission objected to a proposal for a law to make papers carry a column commenting on incorrect or misleading statements because of the 'objection of principle' to compelling a newspaper to publish controversial material. When the Commission favoured a voluntary Council, it was indicating a decided preference for non-statutory measures but, as its position on privacy law implied, it did not rule out, in principle, legislation on questions of standards.[8]

The Recommendation for a General Council of the Press was as follows:

That the Press should establish a General Council of the Press consisting of at least 25 members representing proprietors, editors, and other journalists, and having lay members amounting to about 20 per cent of the total including the chairman. The lay members should be nominated jointly by the Lord Chief Justice and the Lord President of the Court of Session, who in choosing the other lay members should consult the chairman. The chairman, on whom a heavy burden of work will fall, should be paid.

The objects of the General Council should be to safeguard the freedom of the Press; to encourage the growth of a sense of public responsibility and public service amongst all engaged in the profession of journalism – that is, in the editorial production of newspapers – whether as directors, editors or other journalists; and to further the efficiency of the profession and the well being of those who practised it.

In furtherance of these objects the General Council should take such action as it sees fit :

1. to keep under review any developments likely to restrict the supply of information of public interest and importance;
2. to improve the methods of recruitment, education, and training for the profession;
3. to promote a proper functional relation among all sections of the profession;
4. by censuring undesirable types of journalistic conduct, and by all other possible means, to build up a code in accordance with the highest professional standards. In this connection it should have the right to consider any complaints which it may receive about the conduct of the Press or of any persons towards the Press, to deal with these complaints in whatever manner may seem to it practicable and appropriate, and to include in its annual report any action under this heading;
5. to examine the practicability of a comprehensive pension scheme;
6. to promote the establishment of such common services as may from time to time appear desirable;
7. to promote technical and other research;
8. to study developments in the Press which may tend towards greater concentration or monopoly;
9. to represent the Press on appropriate occasions in its relations with the Government, with the organs of the United Nations, and with similar Press organisations abroad;
10. to publish periodical reports recording its own work and reviewing from time to time the various developments in the Press and the factors affecting them.[9]

It is worth focusing on the major points in this recommendation, as they figured so much in subsequent debates. These include the fact that appointments to the Council were to be made by people not involved in the industry: the Chair was to be a lay person and paid; 20 per cent of the 25 members were to be lay people; and its remit was to be wide, to protect press freedom as well as to promote training, cohesion, a sense of public responsibility and public service. To do this it would need to monitor developments on press freedom issues, censure undesirable practice, build up a code of conduct, consider complaints from the public and act as the public face of the press in dealings with the government and international agencies. All of this implied the creation of a large, well-resourced body.

As we will see, one mark of the deep-seated unwillingness of proprietors to establish an effective body was their excessive delay in implementing even a few of these proposals. These delays, and the partial way in which the 1949 recommendation was implemented, provided the soil in which postwar demands for statutory regulation flourished.

1949–53

The Labour government agreed to back the recommendation; when the Report was debated on 28 July 1949, Morrison made this clear but also warned that 'If it should turn out – though I hope it will not be the case – that the Press should not be willing to take steps for the appointment of such a General Council the Government and Parliament would have to consider the situation which would thereby be created.' The Conservative Party spokesman, Oliver Stanley, whilst opposing the idea of a statutory measure, warned that any measure relied on the goodwill of the industry: 'Unless the Press come into the Press Council meaning to play and believing that some use can be made of it, then whether we set it up or not does not really matter because it will be just a facade.' A motion was passed welcoming 'all possible action' by the industry to implement the Commission's recommendations, but it was also clear that the option of statutory reform was not off the political agenda.[10]

Stanley's recognition of the need to gain press acquiescence proved prescient. Opposition to a Council was strong among proprietors and they proved reluctant to move swiftly.[11] The failure of the Newspaper Proprietors' Association and the Newspaper Society to agree proposals led Morrison to declare, on 16 November 1950, that 'it does not seem to me that the proprietors have acted with the full sense of urgency which Parliament was entitled to expect of them'. On 18 January 1951 the Cabinet considered the latest set of proposals from the proprietors. Morrison argued that they gave owners too much influence, that the terms of reference were narrower than those proposed by the Royal Commission and that the NUJ could not accept them. The Cabinet concluded: 'While it was not desirable that the establishment of the Press Council should be unduly delayed, some further delay would give the opportunity for opposition to develop to the undesirable features of the proprietors' scheme.' It authorised Morrison to seek modifications, and on 2 February he urged, publicly, all parties to 'reach agreement on revised proposals'.[12]

At the NUJ's Annual Delegate Meeting (ADM) in March, the President of the Union, H.J. Bradley, accused proprietors of pushing their proposals, not those of the Royal Commission. But the delays continued. In 1951 the return of a Conservative government led by Winston Churchill did little to improve matters. Churchill, when pressed by Tom Driberg MP, in November, seemed content to let the discussions proceed. But the sheer delay had, by 1952, become an embarrassment. In July 1952 two former members of the 1947–49 Commission, Violet Bonham Carter and Sir David Ross, wrote to *The Times* complaining of the delay. On 31 July, the Liberal MP Joe Grimond asked the Home Secretary whether he would 'consider some legislation to compel newspapers to publish denials ... or better still, encourage the Press to set up their own Press Council for the protection of their own journalists and the public?' The Home Secretary, in response, recognised the need for urgency in setting up a Press Council.[13]

On 20 November the Conservative Cabinet discussed its approach to a Private Member's Bill, promoted by the Labour MP C.J. Simmons, that was designed to establish a Press Council. It agreed that the Home Secretary, David Maxwell Fyfe, should consult the Newspaper Proprietors' Association, as at this point, eight days before the debate, no agreement on proposals for a Council had been reached.[14]

Simmons's Bill was intended to 'implement the one recommendation of the Royal Commission, and the will of Parliament, as expressed in the motion carried in the House without opposition on 29th July 1949' by requiring the industry to set up a General Council of the Press. Jo Grimond supported the Bill on the grounds that the press had had three and a half years 'and how long are we to wait ? ... I should have thought that if we are to have strict control of television by the Government, we can hardly object to the mild suggestion that a Council should be set up for the Press.' The Conservative W.F. Deedes accused Morrison, who backed the Bill, of wanting to 'clip the wings of the Press', an accusation he withdrew after Morrison objected. He pointed to the practical diffi- culties of deciding both who would be on a Press Council and how it would proceed. Pressed by Morrison, the Under Secretary of State at the Home Office, Hugh Lucas-Tooth, said that there was likely to be 'a satis- factory outcome' in the very near future. Morrison stressed that the delay undermined the authority of the Commission and Parliament: 'We are in danger of saying that, although a Commission has recommended this, that and the other, and although the House has approved it *nem. con.*, if the industry itself does not take action, there is nothing we are going to do about it. That seems to me to be futile and wrong.'[15]

The debate was adjourned, and was due to be resumed on 8 May 1953. Earlier that year, as a result of the public and parliamentary attacks and of pressure brought to bear on the industry by the Cabinet, agreement on a constitution had been reached. On 5 May the Home Secretary told the Cabinet that 'It would be unfortunate if this Bill ... were to receive a Second Reading when the interests concerned, under pressure from the

Government, had agreed upon the main lines of a voluntary Press Council, which it was hoped to bring into being by 1st July.'

It was decided to take action 'to ensure that the Press Council Bill should not receive a Second Reading'. The Cabinet got its wish. During the debate Simmons criticised the proposals for failing to include lay people and an independent lay chair, but he agreed 'to give the voluntary Press Council a chance to prove its worth, efficiency and competence to do the job to which it has set its hand. I give warning here and now that if it fails some of us will again have to come forward with a measure similar to this Bill.'[16]

The General Council of the Press met for the first time on 1 July 1953. It was an essentially negative response to a positive recommendation by the Royal Commission and the Labour Cabinet. Under Labour, the urge was to balance persuasion with the threat of action. It was Labour and Liberal pressure during 1952 that pushed the government into bringing the proprietors around to a compromise. While the delay testified to the power of the proprietors, it also helped nurture the idea that in the end statutory means might be needed to impose standards.

1953–64 – a slow start

The General Council of the Press

The General Council was set up with 25 members: eight national and provincial newspaper editors, four NUJ and IOJ representatives, and ten members from the Newspaper Proprietors' Association (NPA), the Newspaper Society (NS), the Scottish Daily Newspaper Society and the Scottish Newspaper Proprietors' Association. Between them the NPA and the NS contributed over 50 per cent of the £2500 running costs. Thus the Council had no lay members and a small budget. Its objects were:

(i)   to preserve the established freedom of the British Press
(ii)   to maintain the character of the British Press in accordance with the highest professional and commercial standards
(iii) to keep under review any developments likely to restrict the supply of information of public interest and importance
(iv)   to promote and encourage methods of recruitment, education and training of journalists
(v)   to promote a proper functional relation among all sections of the profession
(vi)   to promote technical and other research
(vii) to study developments in the Press which may tend towards greater concentration or monopoly

(viii)   to publish periodical reports recording its own work and reviewing from time to time the various developments in the Press and the factors affecting them.

Under its procedural clauses was the following:

> provided that in dealing with representations which it may receive about the conduct of the Press or of any persons towards the Press, the Council shall be required to consider only those from complainants actually affected, and shall deal with such in whatever manner may seem to it practical and appropriate.

It was able, however, 'at its discretion' to consider complaints from any source.

The differences between these aims and procedure and the 1949 recommendation were significant. Numbers (3), (5), (6) and (8) came directly from the 1949 Report. Number (4) substituted 'promote' and 'encourage' training for the more pro-active 'improve' used by the Royal Commission. The objects omitted the Commission's recommendations about a common pension scheme and common services, a sure mark of the industry's unwillingness to allow the General Council a role in the economics of the industry. Equally telling was the omission of the Commission's view that the Council should act as the voice of the press in its relation to official bodies. This would have usurped the role of the established employers' organisations. So, on the key question of economic and political co-ordination the Council had significantly less authority than the Commission had recommended.

The Commission had envisaged the Council being pro-active on the question of standards: it was 'to encourage the growth of the sense of public responsibility and public service' in the industry. The General Council turned out to have a much more passive role, 'to maintain the character of the British Press', one which implied less work than the Commission had envisaged. Connected to this more passive role was the omission from the objects of the Commission's recommendation that the Council should censure 'undesirable types of journalistic conduct', build up a code of practice and consider 'any complaints which it might receive about the conduct of the Press'. The General Council in fact was required to consider 'only those' complaints from people 'actually affected', and any others at its discretion; no mention of censure or codes.[17] Thus, at its birth, the General Council was weaker and significantly less pro-active in intent than had been recommended by the Commission.

Critical responses to the General Council of the Press

Gradually the shortcomings of the Council came under public scrutiny. In 1954 the *Observer* criticised the lack of lay membership on the Council, and in July 1955 the Labour MP Lieutenant-Colonel Lipton criticised it for condemning a newspaper without informing it in advance. He wanted 'this rather slipshod Star Chamber to be abolished and replaced by a more judicial body'. Churchill replied that he found it 'hard to see how statutory powers could be effectively arranged which did not have some effect on the freedom of the Press'.[18] In that year the rise in production costs plus competition for readers had fuelled intense rivalry between papers, and serious concerns about standards. On 31 July *The Times* attacked standards in the popular press: 'The race for mammoth circulations has led in some cases to a disgraceful lowering of values. The baser instincts are being pandered to, not only in lasciviousness ... but on social attitudes and conduct as well.'

In the following year the Earl of Selborne clearly felt things had gone too far and attempted, unsuccessfully, to set up a three-person Press Authority nominated by the Lord Chief Justice and the Lord President of the Court of Sessions (Scotland's Chief Judge). Such a rebuke from so elevated a source, coming only three years into its life, stung, and provoked a strong response from the Council, which attacked the initiative as 'misguided and reactionary'. Selborne's initiative was a mark of how the Council had failed to convince people in political circles of its effectiveness.[19]

The sense of doubt and criticism gained momentum in May 1957 when the MP Anthony Kershaw moved 'That this House, recognising the great importance of a free and independent Press, views with concern some recent examples of newspaper reporting and is of the opinion that a vigorous effort by the industry itself to maintain a high standard of conduct is desirable.'

The Labour MP Frank Allaun put his name to an amendment urging 'the strengthening of the Press Council which should include representatives of the people'. Kershaw disputed the Council's assertions that its reprimands were 'neither made nor taken lightly', pointing to the fact that one offending paper, the *People*, had its editor on the Council. 'There is therefore,' Kershaw added, 'I think, a certain amount of complacency in the Reports of the Press Council.' He went on: 'I ask, therefore, whether the Press Council is working as well as was hoped. To some extent, the answer is to be found in whether or not public concern about the state of the Press has been allayed. I think that the answer to that must be "No".' He urged the Council to establish a sub-committee to define the ethics of journalism and to exercise a power of suspension over journalists.

Frank Allaun linked the problems of the press to concentration of ownership and proprietorial power. He complimented the Council for building up 'a case law' and for dealing with questions of intrusion, but he still felt there was a need to add lay members. Others urged the Council to appoint a lay chair, create a code of ethics and form a sub-committee 'to investigate the whole aspect of newspaper costs', a topic of increasing concern in the 1950s. For the government, J.E.S. Simon took the view that there was no major problem with concentration of ownership and fielded criticism of the Council by asserting that 'it is only fair to regard it at the moment as experimental'. Standards in the popular press were, he argued, 'a reflection' of the community at large, and 'the educational progress which is now being made is the best hope of all for the future of the Press'. Kershaw's motion was, nonetheless, passed unamended.[20]

The academic Richard Hoggart accused the Press Council of holding a similar view to Simon's. In his influential book *The Uses of Literacy*, published in 1957, he argued that 'the General Council of the Press seems readier to indicate the responsibility of readers for the present quantitative and qualitative changes in the Press than to analyse the nature of Press responsibility'. His view, based on a reading of the Press Council's publications, was of sufficient weight to provoke a critical response from the Council in its fourth Annual Report for the year 1956–57.

On the other side of this coin were those who continued to think the Council should be given a chance. Francis Williams, the distinguished journalist, wrote in 1957 that during the 1940s he had thought 'there would have been great advantage in establishing the Council as a statutory body', but by now, like Allaun and Kershaw, was prepared to consider it 'possible that a voluntary Press Council may in the end succeed'. But 'possible' after four years of existence suggested doubt, and those doubts were, as has been shown, very much in the air in 1957. They were to be exacerbated by the growing crisis of economics and ownership in the industry during the late 1950s and early 1960s.[21]

Standards, economics and the second Royal Commission 1961–62

This crisis was expressed in the form of newspaper closures. In October 1960 a national morning paper, the *News Chronicle*, and a London evening paper, the *Star*, were closed. Three other papers, the *Empire News*, the *Sunday Dispatch* and the *Sunday Graphic*, all closed between October 1960 and June 1961. There were also wider concerns about concentration of ownership and by November 1960 Labour MPs were pressing the government to initiate a Royal Commission. R.A. Butler, the Home Secretary, was reluctant, claiming the issues had been dealt with by the 1947–49 Commission, that the government should 'not interfere in the sphere of the press' and that 'the only remedy is the initiative and drive of the enterprises concerned'. A major debate on the closures on 2 December 1960 included an attack on the General Council by one MP who said it was 'the prosecutor, the defender, the judge and jury. To say that it is the executioner in all cases would be a gross exaggeration, but on occasions it inflicts some light slaps on the wrists of offending newspapers and journalists.' The Labour MP Christopher

Mayhew also criticised the Council for failing to look into the economic crisis in the industry.[22]

The parliamentary pressure on the government continued into December 1960 and January 1961, and was also paralleled by concerns about the way the press paid for the stories of both witnesses and criminals involved in court cases.[23] In a Cabinet discussion on 7 February the Prime Minister, Harold Macmillan, thought that 'if the Government were to institute an enquiry ... they might appear to be giving way to pressure and they would run the risk that the enquiry would extend embarrassingly into the whole working of the capitalist system'. Nonetheless, he considered that 'there was a case on merits for an enquiry into the economics of the newspaper industry and, more particularly, into the restrictive practices of the trades unions concerned. It would, however, be preferable that the terms of reference should not make any explicit mention of the relationship between management and labour.'

Macmillan announced the Royal Commission on 9 February and was then pressed by Christopher Mayhew into acknowledging that it would be able to investigate the General Council: 'No doubt,' he said, 'when the Commission is set up, it will certainly consider calling evidence from, or the position of [sic], the Press Council'. This idea was also in part implied in the terms of reference of the Commission, which was required, when considering economic questions, to have regard for 'the importance, in the public interest, of the accurate presentation of news'.[24]

The episode illustrates the perennial link in the minds of observers between questions of standards and economics in the industry. It also shows how, unlike the 1947–49 Commission, this one was driven, in part, by a perception in government that trade unions were at the heart of the problems being experienced in the industry. Finally, the push for an enquiry had also been accompanied by a concern amongst politicians and observers that standards of press behaviour were a problem in the 1950s, in spite of the existence of the General Council.

Once the Commission was announced the pressures on self-regulation continued. In March 1961 Lord Mancroft introduced a Right to Privacy Bill in the House of Lords, offering the possibility of the public claiming damages for the 'unjustifiable publication of matter concerning private and personal affairs'. Though opposed by the government, it gained sufficient support to get a Second Reading before being withdrawn. Within the industry, tensions between the Council and the press were also apparent. The *Guardian* had held aloof from the Council believing it was only needed to police the popular end of the market. As the company chairman, Laurence Scott, wrote in March 1961: 'if the Press Council is to have any influence on the popular press, then that influence will be reduced if the Council includes more than a tiny fraction of the quality newspapers among its members'. From the vantage point of Hugh Cudlipp, Managing Director of the *Mirror* group of newspapers, the failure of the General Council was because 'as present constituted it carries little weight and does not amount to much more than an exercise in futility'. It was within this climate of disaffection with the Council, both inside and outside the industry, that the 1961–62 Commission made its recommendations.[25]

The 1961–62 commission and after

The Commission, chaired by Lord Shawcross, a former member of Attlee's government, delivered its verdict in September 1962. It argued that the General Council had not been set up with sufficient powers to monitor changes in ownership and that, overall, the industry had failed to implement, properly, the recommendations of the 1947–49 Commission:

> In our view all the interests concerned should consider as a matter of urgency the revision of the Council's constitution so as both to comply with the recommendations of the 1949 Commission as to membership and objects and to ensure that the Council would have the necessary powers, including the power to call for information about ownership and control, and funds to enable it to carry out all its objectives to the fullest degree.

The indictment was strong and the Commission followed up with a threat of statutory action which echoed the debates that had gone on during the 1950s:

> We think that the Press should be given another opportunity itself voluntarily to establish an authoritative General Council with a lay element as recommended by the 1949 Commission. We recommend, however, that the Government should specify a time limit after which legislation would be introduced for the establishment of such a body, if in the meantime it had not been set up voluntarily.

This meant having 'a lay chairman and a substantial lay membership'. It also recommended that the Council should be properly funded to allow it to do its job properly. The Commission also recognised the link between economics and accuracy by recommending that the General Council 'act as a tribunal to hear complaints from editors and journalists of undue influence by advertisers or advertising agents and of pressure by their superiors to distort the truth or otherwise engage in unprofessional conduct'.[26]

The underlying criticism in the report was of the industry's failure to take on board the spirit of the 1947–49 recommendation. The Shawcross Commission had, like the critics of the 1950s, recognised that the experiment in self-regulation was not working and felt that, whilst not the best solution, a statutory measure might be a way of achieving the goals which to date self-regulation had failed to realise.

The Times's leader on the Commission concentrated on the economic issues and did not mention the Press Council. The NUJ, in contrast, was 'pleased at the recommendation for lay membership which it had been alone in consistently urging since the 1949 Royal Commission'. The government then approached the General Council to get its views on the recommendations for reform. The Council's public response was to delay: 'It will take many months of discussion by the various sections of the newspaper profession and industry before agreement is reached upon what response should be made to the Commission's proposals.'

Whilst prepared to consider lay membership it reacted strongly to the suggestion of a statutory measure:

> Even to make such a suggestion is to tread on dangerous ground. It is true that the statutory control which the Commission had in mind would be concerned only with economic questions. But these and professional standards are sometimes mixed up to such an extent that statutory control of the industry could easily become statutory control of the profession.[27]

But the Shawcross recommendations were as much about standards as economics. The Council acknowledged this by changing its name and constitution from 1 July 1963. It became the Press Council. It dropped the sections in its constitution on recruitment and training, on the functional relations between sections of the profession and on the promotion of technical research. It included three new clauses that reflected more closely the 1949 recommendation. The most prominent was:

> (3) To consider complaints about the conduct of the Press or the conduct of persons and organisations towards the Press; to deal with these complaints in whatever manner might seem practical and appropriate and record resultant action.

This promoted the status of dealing with complaints from an aspect of procedure, in the 1953 constitution, to a key objective. In 1953 the Council was only meant to 'study' developments in the press; now it would 'report publicly on developments that may tend towards greater concentration or monopoly in the Press'. It also adopted the objective of making representations 'on appropriate occasions to the Government, organs of the United Nations and to the Press organisations abroad'. It appointed a lay chairman and made provision for up to 20 per cent of its members to be drawn from outside the industry. The constituent members of the Council increased its funding from £5287 in 1962–63 to £13,675 in 1963–64.[28]

The Press Council announced these reforms in June 1963 to a mixed reception. The Labour MP Patrick Gordon Walker welcomed the changes but queried who would appoint the lay members. Appointment by the proprietors, he argued, meant that 'there will be widespread doubts whether it has gone far enough to create public confidence in the complete independence of the Press Council'. Likewise, Jo Grimond pushed for the chairman to be appointed by Trustees.[29]

These doubts were exacerbated by press coverage of the Profumo affair. When John Profumo, a government minister, was forced to resign in a scandal that mixed sex and espionage, the press covered the story with enthusiasm. The *News of the World* paid money for the story of Christine Keeler, one of the people involved in the scandal. This payment prompted the Press Council to issue a rebuke to the paper at the end of September 1963. The editor of the *News of the World*, Stafford Somerfield, considered the rebuke showed 'a complete misunderstanding of a newspaper's duty to reveal unpalatable truths'. The Press Council, however, was responding to wider concerns about press coverage of the scandal, such as those expressed by Lord Denning in mid-September. In his report on the scandal, Denning noted that

> scandalous information about well-known people has become a marketable commodity ... It is offered to those newspapers – there are only a few of them – who deal in this commodity ... something should be done to stop this trafficking in scandal for reward. The machinery is ready to hand. There is a new Press Council already in being.

Writing in 1964, the academic Graham Martin was less confident than Denning that this machinery worked: 'Despite some good work, the Council has repeatedly failed to show that its professional ethic is adequate to the task of effective self-regulation.'[30] The effect of the Shawcross recommendations was to upgrade the role of dealing with complaints in the Council's work and to achieve both an increase in finances and an element of lay membership. These, however, were changes forced on a reluctant industry, and relied for their success on the willingness of proprietors to make the Council effective; this could not be taken for granted in 1963.

1964–72 – from Shawcross to Younger: reform and rebuke

In 1964 the Labour Party won its first general election since 1951, ending 13 years of Conservative government. Labour retained office until 1970, when the Conservatives under Edward Heath were returned to power. Heath's government lasted until 1974. In the run-up to the 1964 election, Jim Northcott of the Labour Party's research department argued that the problems of sensationalism, hypocrisy, sex, intolerance and intrusion in the press 'can probably be dealt with satisfactorily by following the advice of both Royal Commissions on the Press'. His optimism about the Council was shared by others. The Labour MP Tony Benn used the Press Council to lay a complaint in 1964 and in 1965, whilst at dinner with the chairman of the Board of Governors at the BBC, Lord Normanbrook, and Sir Hugh Greene, the Director General, he 'had a long and rather fierce discussion with them about the desirability of having some broadcasting council, comparable to the Press Council, to which people could take complaints'.

The idea of a broadcasting complaints body modelled on the Press Council also had support in the ranks of the Conservative Party in the 1960s. This was part of a wider willingness to look favourably on the work of Lord Devlin. Raymond Williams, writing in 1966, felt that 'The newly constituted Council, under the Chairmanship of Lord Devlin, is a more evidently authoritative body, and many of its detailed reports are valuable. The Council has now reported that it is now better known to the public as a resource in cases of complaint.'[31]

This revised opinion can, in part, be attributed to the influence of Cecil King, who as chairman of the Newspaper Publishers' Association 'worked hard ... to rebuild the Press Council' and, with the support of the owner of the *Sunday Times*, Roy Thomson, 'was central to a consensus against crude journalism which gave the Press Council some weight'. Devlin presided over the Council issuing high-profile declarations of principle, printing statistical information on the industry and encouraging the publication of a book in 1967 detailing the decisions taken since 1953. But this was a fragile revival of status and practice. It did not prevent the flow of criticism. In retrospect, this period seems to have relied heavily on Devlin's skills underpinned by an all-important element of consensus amongst some key proprietors. This dependence on the support of proprietors for the success of the Council was acknowledged by Devlin. Speaking on his retirement in October 1969, he asserted: 'It must be remembered that a single great newspaper, if it chose to go its own way, could gravely weaken the basis on which the Press Council rests.'[32]

Added to this problem were continuing criticisms of the press and self-regulation. In January 1964 a request by Frank Allaun MP for legislation to give the Council money so it could advertise its rulings in papers that refused to publish them was turned down by the Conservative government. In May another MP, Stratton-Mills, with support from Michael Foot, asked the Conservative Minister without Portfolio, William Deedes, for legislation to formalise Press Council procedures. The idea was to ensure that those complained about could be informed about the complaint and have a right to be represented. This was turned down.[33]

During 1965 repeated questions were put to the government by members of the Houses of Lords and Commons, decrying the practice of newspaper payments to criminals for their memoirs. The government insisted that these were matters for the Press Council. In 1966 the trial of the Moors Murderers, two people who were eventually convicted for child murder, provoked concerns about payments to a witness. The trial judge asked the Attorney General to investigate the payment of £1000 to the chief prosecution witness by, it turned out, the *News of the World*. The Attorney General decided that the paper had not been guilty of a contempt of court, but the incident generated further criticism of the press in Parliament. Devlin went to see the Prime Minister, Harold Wilson; subsequently, the Press Council issued a declaration of principle on payments to criminals and witnesses. This forbade payments to witnesses for the duration of trials, and also payment to criminals and those engaged in 'notorious misbehaviour where the public interest does not warrant it'. Whilst Devlin's chairmanship did not prevent these kinds of practices, it did show that the Press Council was willing to be seen to be acting to discourage them.

The editor of the *News of the World*, Stafford Somerfield, was less than impressed with the furore: 'Both Houses of Parliament and the Press Council criticised us, but I felt the Council was piling it on and did not intend doing much about it.' Whilst accepting the declaration's ban on payment to witnesses before the completion of a trial, the *News of the World* rejected the idea of non-payment to criminals as 'a blatant attempt to muzzle the Press'. The *News of the World* therefore called into question the effectiveness of any declaration by the Council that was unacceptable to a major paper and was, anyway, unenforceable.[34]

Somerfield's insight proved accurate. Nothing substantial had happened to stem disturbing practices by newspapers. In February 1967 complaints about chequebook journalism reappeared in the House of Commons in a debate on the economic malaise of the industry. The press coverage of the Aberfan disaster in 1966, when children were killed after a coal tip destroyed their school, provoked complaints and prompted the Press Council to publish a booklet on the topic. In March 1968 Edwin Brooks MP asked for legislation to force the publication of details of payments to witnesses, and later another MP pressed for a law to curb invasions of privacy by long-range cameras and TV equipment. Both requests were refused by the government. By April 1968 Lord Devlin felt he had to impress upon a meeting of the Guild of British Newspaper Editors the 'important role of the Press Council as an alternative to statutory control of the Press'.[35]

This was a timely warning, as the public image of the Council's effectiveness continued to be challenged by members of the industry. The

Council's lack of teeth was further illustrated in 1968 when the *Guardian* published an unfavourable adjudication with the offending article reprinted beneath it. Then, in January 1969, Rupert Murdoch bought the *News of the World*. When later that year the Council initiated an enquiry into the *News of the World*'s decision to pay Christine Keeler a further £21,000 for a new version of her part in the Profumo affair, Murdoch and Somerfield simply refused to attend.[36]

Whatever confidence existed amongst observers in the authority of the Press Council was therefore under severe pressure by 1969, if only because of the fragility of a system of self-regulation with no real sanctions. It was also under pressure from backbench MPs who by then were pressing for 'a Royal Commission to inquire into the problems of the daily national newspapers'. The intensified competition which followed on from the economic problems of the industry encouraged, according to one MP, in a reference to the Profumo scandal, newspapers to republish 'old, stale scandals, aimed at boosting circulation, which cause a great deal of injury to those who are now private citizens'. Harold Wilson turned down the request for a Royal Commission and one for 'an inquiry into the limited question of the role of the Press Council, with a view to establishing whether that much respected body should be given a little more authority to deal with the very small minority of newspapers which depart from the standards of the Council'. In January 1970, however, responding in particular to a Private Member's Bill on privacy introduced by Brian Walden and to wider concerns about privacy, the government established a Committee on the topic, chaired by Kenneth Younger, to which the Press Council made a submission.[37]

While the Younger Committee was sitting, challenges to the authority of the Press Council from within the industry continued. In 1970 and 1971 incidents occurred at the *Observer*, the *Evening Standard*, the Bristol *Evening Post* and the Southend *Evening Echo* where newspaper workers disrupted production in protest at the content of the papers. These incidents looked forward to the 1980s when print workers were to play a major role in using industrial action to secure the right of reply in the national press. At the time they provided yet another illustration of the way the regime of self-regulation was failing to win the support of all sections of the industry. Workers preferred to use their industrial power to seek changes in content as opposed to airing their grievance before the Press Council. A similar disregard for the Council was expressed by one of the key proprietors, Rupert Murdoch, who in the early 1970s wrote: 'I do not hate the Press Council. I just think they are a pussy-footing arm of the establishment.'[38]

These underlying problems of credibility and effectiveness were addressed by the Younger Committee when it considered privacy and the press. The Committee recorded the industry's defence of its practices, a defence that sought to downplay the extent to which invasions of privacy were a problem:

> The press view is that the Press Council is the best means of dealing with these transgressions and that it is better to accept that they will occur from time to time – and to deal with them when they do – than to incur the risks of legislative controls. They maintain that the problem of invasion of privacy by the press has been exaggerated by the dramatic nature of some instances that have occurred and that there is no evidence of a burning need for a change of the law.

The 'transgressions' considered by the Committee covered the use of 'objectionable means' to get information and the giving of widespread publicity to information regarded as private. The Committee was ambivalent: on the one hand it 'received more complaints about the activities of the press than on any other aspect of our subject'; and on the other 'we received no clear evidence that the press is in the forefront of people's minds as a threat to privacy'. It also recorded divisions within the industry between the NUJ and the IOJ, who had codes of conduct and the 'other press representatives', that is the employers and editors, who thought 'codes of conduct ... serve no useful purpose'.

The Committee was not prepared to recommend a general law on privacy, but it did pointedly recommend reforms of the Press Council that addressed questions of its credibility, membership, sanctions and code of conduct. The Committee could not 'see how the Council can expect to command public confidence in its ability to take account of the reactions of the public, unless it has at least an equal membership of persons who are qualified to speak for the public at large'. The public half of the Council needed to be appointed by an independent appointments commission, not directly by the Press Council.

More tellingly the Committee was 'not satisfied that the sole action which the Council can now take, that is to order an offending newspaper to publish a critical adjudication, is sufficient in its present form'. The recommendation was that in future a critical adjudication should be published with 'similar prominence, if possible, to that given to the original item of news'. It also commended to the Press Council, against the prevailing view of the editors and proprietors, 'a codification of its adjudications on privacy'.[39]

The Press Council's chairman, Lord Pearce, thought the Committee's report contained 'no evidence' to support its view about the link between the volume of lay membership and public confidence. It agreed to increase lay membership to 10 out of 30, not the equal numbers advised by Younger. Instead it made a commitment to the Council having equal numbers on the Complaints Committee. It accepted the idea of an appointments commission, was silent on giving adjudications similar prominence to the offending article and made no commitment to producing a codification of its rulings on privacy. These minor changes took effect in July 1973.[40]

By 1973 the Press Council had, under pressure, finally implemented some parts of the 1949 recommendation. After the 1961–62 Royal Commission it had altered its constitution to include handling complaints in its objectives and, theoretically, to take a more pro-active stance on questions of monitoring press economics and freedom. After Younger a third of its members were drawn from the public, more than the quarter suggested in 1949. It had taken steps towards establishing an appointments procedure that was designed to allay concerns about industry dominance of the process. It had, however, failed to produce a code of conduct, in spite of this being a key part of the 1949 and 1972 recommendations. The painfully slow pace of reform had been noted by Younger. The Committee urged the Council to implement reforms 'at an early date' as they had 'in mind the delay by the press in giving effect to the proposals for the composition of the Press Council made by the two Royal Commissions on the Press'.[41]

Delay epitomised the industry response to reform from the 1940s onwards. In spite of regularly expressed concerns about press standards and the provision by the 1949 Commission of a strong model for self-regulation proprietors dragged their feet. When the General Council of the Press was established, demands for statutory intervention had continued to be made, a testimony in themselves to the inability of the Council to convince observers of its effectiveness. The brief period of high-profile activity under Lord Devlin masked an underlying current of doubt, expressed largely in parliament but also within the industry, about the effectiveness and worth of the Press Council. The Younger Committee was, in effect, a rebuke to the industry for failing to make the recommendations of 1949 a reality. This mixture of recalcitrance and delay, public and official criticism meant that in its first 20 years the Press Council was unable to persuade enough people that, as a body, it was intended to, or could, deliver higher standards. This failure was to reap its rewards after 1973 when a new period of intensified public and political criticism led to sustained demands for statutory reform.

5

Nothing Resolved: Self-Regulation, 1972–98

The period after the Younger Report can, in retrospect, be viewed as a second phase in the history of postwar regulation. During this period assaults on the principle of self-regulation became more frequent, especially during the 1980s. The Press Council proved unable to act swiftly or effectively enough to stem demands for statutory reform.

Turbulence – 1973–79

During the 1970s the question of media policy and accountability moved to the centre of the political debate in the UK. The wider industrial and social conflicts of the period found one expression in debates about the economics of the newspaper industry, trade union rights – especially the closed shop – and ethical standards, including the role of the Press Council. These underlay the build-up to and report of the 1974–77 Royal Commission on the Press. The Commission was part of a much wider process involving the growth of public interest in questions of media accountability.[1] Many of the issues raised about media policy in this period were, however, left unresolved when the Labour governments of Harold Wilson (1974–76) and Jim Callaghan (1976–79) gave way to those of Margaret Thatcher's Conservative administrations of 1979–90.

The economic problems of the press, plus questions of bias, diversity of viewpoint and standards all came together in pressure, after Labour was elected in 1974, for a third postwar Royal Commission on the press. On 21 March 1974 the Prime Minister, Harold Wilson, responded positively to questions from MPs calling for an inquiry. He drew attention to the fact that the pro-business organisation Aims of Industry and the print trade union NATSOPA had called for an inquiry, and recognised there were 'matters to be inquired into', in spite of the expression of scepticism about the worth of such an inquiry from the leader of the opposition Edward Heath. The decision by Beaverbrook newspapers to close operations in Glasgow prompted Hugh Brown MP to call on 26 March for a Royal Commission to 'recommend ways and means not of Government control, but of ensuring a greater degree of impartiality in the Press' and to examine the long-term role of the press.

On the 11 April the Tory MP John Gorst asked Wilson to consider 'the possibility of an inquiry into the functioning of the Press Council'. Wilson accepted that 'Everyone has his own views about the adequacy of the Press Council and its relative success in dealing with some kinds of question and not with others. This would be a matter that a Royal Commission would look into.' Later that day, Gorst returned to his subject. Whilst preferring self-regulation he drew attention to the 'inadequacies of the Press Council', how it had 'fallen far behind the times in terms of consumer protection' and argued that it should be subjected to 'careful scrutiny'. When Wilson announced the Royal Commission on the Press on 2 May one of its tasks, as well as examining questions of 'independence, diversity and editorial standards', was to review 'the responsibilities, constitution and functioning of the Press Council'.[2]

This concern with the Press Council's performance ran deep. On 14 May, in a debate on the press, Edward Heath said:

> I must add, personally, I have never been greatly impressed with the activities of the Press Council. It may be that if it were provided with more resources from the industry itself it would not need to wait for complaints to come to it but could study the state of the Press as a whole and, through a body in which the Press was represented, make its views known.

Heath, however, was convinced that 'the Press must be responsible for maintaining its own standards'. For the Liberals, Clement Freud pinpointed the 'lunacy of having a Press Council with only weak powers of persuasion'. One MP attacked the practice of newspapers printing corrections 'in small type on its back page'. The Labour MP Maurice Edelman pressed for the Council to have sanctions, like the ones operated by the medical profession, 'for those in the Press found guilty of disreputable, dishonourable and discreditable conduct'. John Gorst supported this.[3]

Outside the Parliamentary Labour Party pressure had grown for major media reforms. Building on the tradition of discussion about the media that ran through Labour Party history, and feeding on a burgeoning left-of-centre academic interest in the question of media policy in the 1960s, the Party's Home Policy Committee established a working group on 'the Relationship between the People, the Press and Broadcasting' in May 1972. The group included MPs, academics, media trade unionists and journalists. Its report *The People and the Media* (1974), whilst not Labour Party policy, illustrated the extent to which concerns about the media had become a pressing issue in the wider Labour movement. The group aimed 'to devise a framework for the media that avoids the twin dangers of government and commercial control. This must centre upon making the system genuinely democratic and genuinely accountable, which is after all only fitting for an activity that is so basic to democracy.' It thought the Press Council was 'in need of reorganisation in a number of respects. Its composition is not adequately representative of the community or of occupations within the press industry; and the amount of research undertaken is inadequate.'

It argued that the Council's functions should be subsumed under a Communications Council. The Communication Council's job would be to 'keep the operation, development and interrelation of all the mass media ... under permanent review and to make its findings publicly available, in order to encourage and assist public debate'. This would have taken over the Press Council's monitoring role. The Communication Council would also have acquired the Council's complaints function, only this time with real sanctions: 'the Council would have the right to demand air time or column space for the correction of errors of fact or redress grievances'. The Communications Council would 'include elected representatives from trade unions, local or regional government and national organisations, as well as some MPs'. This clear rejection of the Press Council and of voluntary regulation was to gain widespread support in the Labour and trade union movements by the 1980s.[4]

Concerns about the question of privacy and the implementation of the Younger Committee's recommendations were voiced frequently in this period.[5] Running parallel with this was a heated controversy between the government and the press over plans to allow the NUJ to operate a 'closed shop'. This practice, common in other industries at the time, would have required all journalists to join a union, thus strengthening collective bargaining and influencing press standards by enhancing the ability of the union to enforce its code of conduct. The proprietors and editors opposed this vehemently in the name of editorial freedom and attacked the government accordingly. Delays and opposition meant the closed shop was never implemented in the media. In addition, during this period, Harold Wilson's relationship with the press became increasingly fractious and a subject of both parliamentary and press commentary. Wilson eventually submitted evidence on the topic to the Royal Commission.[6]

In February 1975 a number of papers published an inaccurate attack on the government minister Tony Benn. The General Secretary of the Labour Party, Ron Hayward, then sent a complaint to the Press Council 'but eventually withdrew it after the Council's Chairman, Lord

Shawcross, made a speech describing Benn as among those who wanted to destroy "Britain's civilized and democratic way of life"'.

Shawcross's article appeared in *The Times* on 16 May 1975, and can have done little to inspire confidence in Labour party circles in the impartiality of the Council. When asked to comment, in February 1976, on whether he had plans to meet Shawcross, in the latter's capacity as chairman of the Press Council, Wilson showed he understood the situation. Asked about whether he was aware of Shawcross's political views when both were members of Attlee's administration, Wilson phrased his reply in a manner that hinted that there was now some distance between the two men: 'I am aware of my then Right. Hon. and learned friend's political view, but I think his views have changed ... In any case, I do not want to bother my noble friend – if he still is – Lord Shawcross.'[7]

The 1974–77 Commission therefore conducted its work in a climate of heightened political controversy about the press. It received submissions from a larger number and wider range of organisations than had been the case in 1947–49 or 1961–62.[8] There was no political consensus about the role of the press in society, and its remarks and recommendations on the Press Council reflected this. The Commission did, however, identify one area of consensus: 'There is thus a consensus, shared by almost all of those who gave evidence to us, that the press should neither be subject to state controls nor left entirely to the unregulated market.'

It was establishing the implications of this for the Press Council that proved a problem for the Commission. It recognised that after Younger: 'The Press Council has increased the number of lay members from five to ten and given parity to press and lay members on the Complaints Committee though not on the Council as a whole. It has expressed the intention of codifying past adjudications although it has not done so yet.' Noting that the 'press's conduct in respect of privacy is thus still being actively debated', it expressed 'dissatisfaction both with the present effectiveness of the Press Council and with the behaviour of the press itself'. It rejected a privacy law, not on grounds of principle, but of practicality; it would have recommended one 'if there were a legal remedy which we considered likely to be effective, readily understandable and practical'. It preferred to see a reformed Press Council tackle these issues.[9]

In its specific discussion of the Press Council, the Commission mixed damning criticism with a commitment to maintaining self-regulation. It rejected as 'potentially authoritarian' the idea of 'a standing commission for broadcasting and the press, representative of all major sections of the community and responsible to a Minister for monitoring the performance of the press'. The Commission, however, registered the by now widespread sense that the Press Council was a failure:

Witnesses held strong views about the Press Council, varying from wholehearted approval to outright opposition. Some suggested that it should be abolished or replaced. The press was broadly satisfied; lay critics were unhappy to a greater or lesser extent; the most extreme charged the Council with bias in favour of the press, unwillingness to censure it and even with reluctance to consider complaints against it. It is unhappily certain that the Council has so far failed to persuade the knowledgeable public that it deals satisfactorily with complaints against newspapers, notwithstanding that this has come to be seen as its main purpose.

It attacked the Council for vehemently defending the press in 'the language of partisanship which inevitably weakens confidence in the impartiality of the Press Council'. At one point, with the example of Lord Shawcross in mind, it suggested that the chair of the Council should not be 'closely identified with party political controversy and that he should keep clear of it during his chairmanship'.[10]

The Commission also recognised that the law on right of reply in Germany 'has worked for a number of years' and 'we see no practical reason why it could not do so here'. Nonetheless it objected to the right of reply on grounds of principle, claiming that 'the press should not be subjected to a special regime of law, and that it should neither have special privileges nor labour under special disadvantages compared with the ordinary citizen'.[11]

The Royal Commission set its face against statutory regulation of press standards. It harked back to the 1947–49 Commission when making its recommendations, hoping that the Press Council would accept and act upon them 'and that it will fulfil the hopes that were held for it in 1949'. In essence the 1974–77 Commission sought to persuade the industry to establish the kind of body that the 1947–49 Commission had recommended.[12] The recommendations were:

That the Press Council should be constituted of an equal number of lay and press representatives under an independent chairman ...

That the element of independence provided by the Press Council's Appointments Commission should be retained, but that the Chairman of the Press Council should also be Chairman of the Appointments Commission ...

That nominations for vacancies among the lay members of the Press Council should be invited from any source, and not only from existing members. In making their choice, the Appointments Commission should seek to achieve as wide a range of members as possible, in age, career, background and part of the country. They should also try to obtain the services of people of quality and reputation who might thereby increase public confidence in the Council, and help to obtain more publicity for its work.

That the staff of the Press Council should include a Conciliator, whose role in the conciliation procedure would include proposing a remedy if he thought that right; and if his remedy were rejected by the complainant or the newspaper, we would expect the rejection to be taken into account by the Complaints Committee when the complaint reached them ...

That the Press Council extend its doctrine of the right of reply and uphold a newspaper's making available space to those it has criticised inaccurately ...

That, as part of the process of conciliation, the Press Council should involve itself actively in obtaining the publication as soon as practicable of counterstatements on behalf of people who have been criticised unfairly on inaccurate information, using the criteria of equal prominence and space, and limiting an editor's right of refusal to legal grounds ...

That the Press Council should draw up a code of behaviour on which to base its adjudications, which should set out in some detail the spirit, which should govern the conduct of editors and journalists; and that the Council should be free to censure conduct in breach of the spirit as well as of the letter of the code, and to decline to censure conduct, technically breaching the code, if there are sufficient extenuating circumstances ...

That the Press Council should be provided with enough funds to enable it to advertise its services in the same way as the Advertising Standards Authority ...

That the Press Council should approach the various organisations representing publishers of newspapers and periodicals, asking them to agree that their members should undertake to publish adjudications which uphold complaints on the front page of the newspaper in question, or, in the case of periodicals, with a prominence at least equal to that of the offending passage ...

That the Press Council should be prepared to undertake a wider review than it normally does at present of the record of the publication or journalist concerned in a complaint ...

That the Press Council make a regular practice of taking the initiative more frequently than in the past in investigating the conduct of the press without waiting for a formal complaint ...

That the Press Council should change its position on the two important questions of accuracy and bias, so that inaccuracy, even if subsequently corrected, should be *prima facie* evidence for upholding a complaint, and that contentious opinions based on inaccurate information should be grounds for censure.[13]

On membership the Royal Commission wanted Younger's recommendation implemented; five years had passed since Younger without this happening. It also wanted the kinds of people selected not only to be genuinely representative of the public, but of sufficient 'quality and reputation' so as to 'increase public confidence in the Council'. Neither point implied a compliment to the Council.

The bulk of the recommendations were about making the Council's procedures and sanctions work, and being seen to work. The Commission urged the appointment of a Conciliator and a more vigorous attempt by the Council to get the publication of 'counterstatements' that were of 'equal prominence and space' to the original offending pieces. The latter point here went back to Younger, and the recommendation for a code to both Younger and the 1947–49 Commission; these were to be enforced through agreement between the Council and the newspapers. Such a method of enforcement, however, left the Council without sanctions independent of the whims of editors and proprietors.

The recommendations about reviewing the record of papers and initiating complaints were intended to make the Council more pro-active on the issue of standards, but were also a testimony to the contemporary perception of its inertia on these matters. As with the recommendation on finances, which repeated the 1962 Commission's proposal, the overall thrust of the 1974–77 Commission was to try to get the spirit and the letter of the recommendations of previous Commissions and the Younger Committee implemented.

When the Commission made its recommendations there existed a strong body of contemporary scepticism, if not outright opposition, to self-regulation. Given that its criticisms were so damning and the climate so favourable for reform, its remedies seemed weak in contrast. In many ways the judgement of one contemporary that the report exhibited an overall 'conservatism and lack of imagination' was, where the Press Council was concerned, correct.[14] On the other hand, by rehearsing so publicly the shortcomings of the Press Council and pointing to the extent of the reforms needed to effect improvements, the Commission did little to improve the long-term credibility of that body. In its formal response to the report, the Labour government chose to concentrate on those recommendations that called for government action, thereby ruling out a response to those addressed specifically to the Press Council.[15]

The Press Council adopted the recommendation on equal lay and press representatives in 1978, but rejected the idea that the chair should also chair the Appointments Commission on the ground that this might compromise the Commission's independence. It agreed to seek nominations 'from any source' and also appointed a Conciliator in response to the recommendation that it 'extend its doctrine of the right of reply'. The Council asserted that it had always upheld 'the principle' that once attacked someone was 'morally entitled to and should be given the opportunity to make a reasonable reply'. This, in effect, brushed aside whether the Council operated a 'right' of reply by using different but similar language. The Council considered that drafting a code would be too difficult and so rejected that recommendation, as it did the idea that it should spend more money on publicity. It also rejected 'the Commission's suggestion that it should seek undertakings that newspapers would publish adjudications upholding complaints against them on their front page'. This was, of course, a recommendation, not a 'suggestion'.[16]

In all the Council accepted three of the recommendations, asserting that on one (extending the Right of Reply) it was already doing what the Commission recommended. It rejected in part, or in full, five and did not mention three others in its response published in the Annual Report. It therefore chose to be very selective about which of the Commission's recommendations it would implement. This response echoed the way proprietors had first delayed and then only partially implemented the 1949 report. It exhibited a confidence in the industry's ability to face down public criticism and suggested that, at the time, in spite of the criticisms levied by the Commission, the Council felt confident that no politician was about to force them to implement the recommendations. Circumstances were to change in the 1980s, when political pressure became so great that proprietors were, as will be shown, forced to dissolve the Council.

Self-regulation, 1979–93

During these years the debate over press regulation intensified. The Conservative governments under Margaret Thatcher (1979–90) had strong support in the national press, and even her successor, John Major (1990–97), enjoyed significant press support although this declined towards the end of his period in office. This was a period in which Conservative governments gave active support to the newspaper industry as it expanded into other areas of mass communications.[17] The security of the relations between proprietors and the Conservative governments was paralleled by increasing calls, inside and outside Parliament, for legislative reform on right of reply and privacy.

The push for right of reply – to 1983

In September 1979 the Campaign for Press Freedom (CPF) was created. This had its origins in widespread discontent amongst the Labour and trade union movement with developments in the media industries, especially relating to ownership, diversity and industrial democracy. It drew support from trade unions, both inside and outside the industry, journalists, broadcasters, MPs, academics, Church people and individuals. It became the Campaign for Press and Broadcasting Freedom (CPBF) in 1982. It campaigned for a reform of the Press Council, including a levy on advertising revenue to provide 'independent finance' for new ventures, the publication of adjudications on the front page of papers and the adoption of the NUJ's Code of Conduct 'as an all-industry code of professional practice'. Press Council membership needed reform to make it more representative of the workforce in the industry and 'the community at large'. Nonetheless the CPF sounded a note of deep scepticism about the likelihood of voluntary reform:

> It would be better if these Press Council reforms were introduced voluntarily. But when one examines the history of the Press Council it becomes clear how irrelevant its 'voluntary' nature has been in extending press freedom or giving the public any adequate means of redress. Newspaper proprietors preach a hatred of any government involvement but happily accept zero VAT on newspapers, beg for newsprint subsidies and co-operate with the government in 'D' Notice committees to shield certain areas of government activity from journalistic investigation.

In April 1980 the Campaign set up an independent inquiry into the Press Council, chaired by Geoffrey Robertson QC, and in June a Right of Reply Committee. By the autumn of 1980 the Campaign had won a resolution of support for its work from the Trades Union Congress.[18]

Throughout 1980 and 1981 MPs continued to raise questions about media standards: including privacy, about whether the Press Council should be given legal powers and whether payments by the media to defendants should be outlawed. In 1980 criticism of the Press Council within the NUJ reached a watershed, and it withdrew from the Council on the grounds that it was 'wholly ineffective' and 'incapable of reform'.[19] In 1981 Frank Allaun MP introduced a bill 'to give members of the public the right of reply to allegations made against them in the press, or on radio or television' in June 1981. Under the bill:

> an individual, organisation or company will be able to require the editor of a newspaper which has carried a factually inaccurate or distorted report involving that individual, organisation or company to print a reply within three days. The reply must be printed free of charge and be of equal length to, and in the same position as, the original article. If the editor refuses, the case will go to court, and the court must decide within ten days. If the complainant's right of reply is upheld, the editor will be required to print it immediately and also to pay a fine varying between £2000 and £40,000.

Allaun cited examples of similar systems in France, West Germany and Denmark, and pointed out that: 'The TUC last autumn overwhelmingly voted for a right of reply for victims of media bias or distortion. The Labour Party media study group, composed of working journalists, broadcasters and other media experts, unanimously supports the proposal.'

He felt his bill would 'draw some of the claws of the media magnates' and 'help people of all political persuasions and of none'. Allaun realised that the bill would run out of time in that session but planned to persist. He also saw it as running parallel to efforts within the CPF to gain a right of reply by 'trade union strength and action at individual papers'.[20] All of this reflected not only the long-standing political critique of self-regulation but an intensified awareness in the Labour movement that the national press was systematically untruthful and biased against the Labour and trade union movement, as well as other groups, such as the women's and peace movements and people from ethnic minorities.[21]

In early 1982 the Conservative MP Teddy Taylor pressed the government for reviews of both the remedies available to the public when the press or broadcasting organisations published 'inaccurate or misleading reports' and of the 'legal remedies' available to employers when industrial action was used to influence the content of publications. The government rejected his request, but the question showed his recognition that deficiencies in the system of regulating standards were linked to the use of industrial action to achieve redress. During 1982 industrial action continued. The print union, the National Graphical Association (NGA), pressurised managements in Fleet Street over the coverage of health workers who were then involved in an industrial dispute. Frank Allaun also continued to press his bill although it fell again due to lack of time. By the end of that year his efforts had earned him the condemnation of Murdoch's *Sun*. In an editorial on 2 October 1982 the paper attacked Allaun's speech to the Labour Party conference thus:

> Frank Allaun MP, whose whining and whinging has been such an unedifying feature of the Labour Party for many years, had his big moment yesterday. He is the leader of a campaign orchestrated by Labour's backwoodsmen to shackle this country's free press. Yesterday, putting forward his lunatic plans to force newspapers to allow what he grandly calls a 'right of reply' to aggrieved people, he let all the pent-up venom of his years as a political nonentity flood out.

Allaun moved again and, with cross-party support, presented his bill on 1 December 1982.[22]

His bill came at a time when the authority of the Press Council had been badly undermined by its inability to check excesses in the reporting of the pursuit, trial and conviction of the serial murderer Peter Sutcliffe.

For the *Guardian*, in an editorial on 4 February 1983, the problem seemed so severe that there needed to be action by the proprietors to stem abuses: 'If the Lords and tycoons and conglomerates who own so much of our press would agree to follow the Press Council to the letter, then that might just hold. But it is the final fix of free medicine in the Last Chance Saloon.'

The *Guardian*'s prediction proved inaccurate. But at the time even *The Times* recognised the seriousness of the situation, when on February 18 it commented on Frank Allaun's bill: 'His bill has eminent cross-party support, however, which should remind editors that the situation has gone beyond that hallowed tension between press and Parliament, to a point where politicians are only reflecting a genuine and justified concern that the country is not being well served by its newspapers.' It also recognised that the Press Council was not a success: 'If Fleet Street is to prevent increased pressure for statutory supervision of its methods it has to ensure that the Press Council is financed, staffed, equipped and – most important of all – respected fully by press and laity alike to do its job.' It reasoned that it was worth 'thousands more pounds of British newspaper money to equip a Press Council ... in order to avoid a statutory alternative'. The NUJ, whilst having 'reservations about certain details and aspects' of the bill, welcomed it and 'its provisions for a statutory right of reply' as consistent with the union's Code. More pointedly it recognised that the bill 'has already performed a valuable public service by focusing attention on the need for an adequate right of reply'.[23]

During the debate on 18 February the Press Council was heavily criticised. Frank Allaun attacked delays 'of six or nine months' in adjudications and argued that the Council was 'overloaded with and over influenced by press proprietors' representatives'. The Conservative MP W. Benyon pointed out that the Council was held by 'some newspapers ... openly in contempt, and others completely ignore its findings'. Roy Hattersley, the Labour Shadow Home Secretary, accused the Council of doing 'two things: the first is nothing and the second is to ask for a retraction and an apology'. He supported the bill. Sir Angus Maude, a Conservative, opposed the bill but saw that 'Unless the press is prepared to set up a body that is as effective for it as the Advertising Standards Authority is for advertisements, some legislation will be inevitable.' Another Conservative, Sir Geoffrey Johnson Smith, attacked the bill as 'badly conceived and it opens the door to many unpleasant things that will do exactly the opposite of what the bill's proponents wish'.

For the government, David Mellor opposed the bill on the grounds 'that no special laws' should apply to the press. The Press Council's judgements were 'adhered to pretty well by the press' and it was taking steps to speed up its procedures. But he did warn the media to put its house in order. The bill got 90 votes, ten short of the number it needed to proceed to its next, Committee stage, but a significant expression of political concern, nonetheless.[24]

In June 1983 the Robertson Report on the Press Council, which had been initiated by the CPF, was published. The enquiry had contacted users of the Council as well as carefully examining its record. Its findings, whilst sympathetic in many ways to efforts made by Council members and officers who 'genuinely try to maintain and improve the ethical performance of the British press' nevertheless argued that:

> the Press Council has not adjudicated public complaints speedily or effectively, its principles on cheque-book journalism, privacy and right of reply have been continually flouted, and it has been incapable of defending press freedom against serious encroachments or of making any impact in warning against press monopolies.

The solution offered was to leave the Press Council intact, but to make some major changes:

1. *Laws for the Press*: Law reform aimed at securing greater freedom for investigative reporting through specific legislation, which would include a Freedom of Information Act and relaxation of the laws of libel, contempt and breach of confidence.
2. *A Press Ombudsman*: A statutory officer, empowered to direct the publication of corrections and replies in newspapers which have failed to put right demonstrable errors of fact. The Ombudsman would in most cases replace both the law of libel and the Press Council as a method of redress for this problem.
3. *A reformed Press Council*: A body representative of both public and the press, supporting the persuasive force of its adjudications by contractual powers to direct prominent publication in offending newspapers, together with the long-term influence which could come from published codes of conduct, monitoring and auditing, reporting to the Monopolies Commission and responsibility for compulsory professional-conduct courses in training schemes for journalists.

The CPBF welcomed the report, with the reservation that it did not consider the Press Council capable of reform.[25]

By July 1983 the Secretary of State for Employment was asserting that using industrial action to prevent publication was 'unlawful'. In August the TUC reiterated its support for a statutory right of reply. By the autumn the CPBF had set up a Right of Reply unit which sought to help people gain a right of reply by working with media trade unionists. In the four years after 1979 the pressure both inside and outside Parliament had mounted considerably.[26]

Allaun's bill and the Robertson Report were rooted in the postwar scepticism about, and opposition to, self-regulation that has been described here. The bill could not have achieved so much impact had not the record of the Press Council and the behaviour of the press made the intervention plausible. But all of this activity also reflected the way the debate on press accountability had sharpened during the late 1970s, and how the Labour Party, which until the 1970s had gone along with self-regulation, in spite of doubts from MPs, had now lost confidence in it as a mechanism, as had others who were not in the Party.

1983–87 – sharper divides

The period 1983–87 was a particularly turbulent one, during which debates about media policy were forced onto the national political agenda.[27] In January 1984 the NGA secured the right of reply in the *Sun* for the President of the National Union of Mineworkers (NUM), Arthur Scargill. Debate over the future of the Press Council continued within the NUJ. In February the union's paper, the *Journalist*, ran an editorial which expressed one point of view: 'the union and the Press Council (which for all its faults, is a better body now than it was when the NUJ pulled out) should work together to find effective means of voluntary non-statutory self-control and regulation'.

The other side was put by journalist Simon Collings: 'The only thing which will cause the Council and the Press to reform themselves is the serious threat of legislation ... if satisfactory reform cannot be achieved voluntarily we should not hesitate to seek to bring about those desired changes by statutory means.' Later that year, the NUJ's ADM rejected an appeal from the TUC to rejoin the Press Council.[28]

On 5 June Alf Dubs MP pressed unsuccessfully for a measure to make a paper declare when it had paid money in exchange for the stories of witnesses or criminals. On 12 June, another Labour MP, Austin Mitchell, moved a bill 'to give members of the public the right of reply to allegations made against them or to misreporting or misrepresentations concerning them in the press, or radio or on television; to set up a media ombudsman'. He restricted this right to the public, unlike the wider remit of Allaun's proposal. He also included in his proposals the idea in the Robertson Report of an ombudsman. Again, he had cross-party support, but the intervention was, in effect, a technical manoeuvre designed to publicise the issue; it never stood a chance of progressing.[29]

Later in June print workers and journalists took action in support of the NUM, which was then engaged in a bitter dispute with government over the future of the coal industry. The NUM had been subjected to, what was considered in the Labour movement and beyond, extremely distorted media coverage. The print workers and journalists managed to get statements in support of the miners published in the *Guardian*, *The Times*, the *Daily Express*, the *Daily Star*, and the *Daily Mail*. Unions were laying claim to a right to exercise some influence over the content of the papers they produced, a claim that struck at the very heart of proprietorial power which, in turn, underpinned the ethos of the Press Council. In September the TUC passed a motion that, for the first time, stressed the importance of a legal right of reply: 'The General Council is to seek an assurance from the Labour Party that they will, upon return to Government, introduce the necessary legislation to ensure a legal "right of reply" to any person or group of persons who believe that their views have been misrepresented by the media.'[30]

The public debate about right of reply produced divisions that did not fit the left-versus-right political divide. Paul Foot was a member of the revolutionary Socialist Workers Party, as well as being an acclaimed columnist on the *Daily Mirror*. He objected to establishing a legal right of reply on grounds of practicality, but also because it was likely to hand more power to the courts on media matters, and would be used by rich people to hammer the press: 'The problem is that, in class society, law lines up with one class against another. And any attempt to right the class imbalance by "even-handed" and "fair-minded" laws usually tips the balance still further the other way.'

Mike Power, a printer, NGA member and prominent figure in the CPBF, replied that the campaign for right of reply was not a panacea for the ills of the media, but it did highlight the need for a 'fairer press': 'Paul Foot's main point is that the campaign for a legal right of reply attempts to create a balance in a class-divided society where none can possibly exist. That hopeless position can be applied to any effort to change or introduce new laws.'

On the right of the spectrum, flying in the face of the official position of the government, one of Mrs Thatcher's most vociferous supporters, the journalist Paul Johnson, argued that: 'The Press Council is useless, especially now it has chosen to wallow in the gutter itself. Broadcasting complaints bodies are equally ineffective. Members of the public ought to have a statutory right of reply.'[31]

This focus on the merits of a legal right of reply pointed to a more important political shift. During 1985 Rupert Murdoch was making secret preparations to move the production of his newspapers to the East End of London away from the area traditionally associated with newspapers, Fleet Street. Part of this move assumed a dramatic erosion of trade union bargaining power. In January 1986 he sacked his print workers and moved his production to a new plant at Wapping. There followed a year-long confrontation between Murdoch and the media unions, in which the proprietor had the full backing of the government. The outcome was a victory for Murdoch and the spread of employer-led attacks on the NUJ and print unions in the national press. This was a major shift in relations in the industry. As Kenneth Morgan has noted: 'The long, sometimes violent, dispute with the print unions over the relocation of *The Times* plant at Wapping marked a notable step both in the new financial and technological independence of the press and its ideological separateness from the union-corporate approach of the past.'

This meant that the employers had, after a long period of managing in a way that conceded substantial benefits to the print unions in particular, decided to lead from the front, and, where possible, to gain the whip hand over the unions. This was helped by changes in the laws governing strikes introduced by the Conservatives in the early 1980s. The conflict effectively removed the option of an industrial right of reply from the political agenda, and thereafter the pressure for change became centred more on parliamentary action.[32]

A peak of activity: 1987–93

The political events of these years were of major importance in the history of postwar press regulation. In this period there were three attempts to gain a statutory right of reply and two to introduce a privacy bill. There were also two more government-initiated inquiries into press self-regulation and, in 1990, the collapse of the Press Council and its rebirth as the Press Complaints Commission in 1991.

In February 1987 Lord Longford opened a debate on press standards in the House of Lords and in July the Labour Party forced a debate on the purchase by Murdoch of the *Today* newspaper from Lonrho. In October the Labour MP Ann Clywd, supported by the CPBF, introduced her Unfair Reporting and Right of Reply Bill. This was meant to 'Give members of the public the right of reply to allegations made against them or to mis-reporting about them in the press or in broadcasts; to establish a Media Complaints Commission; to extend legal aid to actions for defamation; and for connected purposes.'

The bill sought to achieve the speedy publication of a correction with equal prominence to the original error, in radio, television and the press. Failure to gain a correction gave the complainant the right to appeal to a Media Complaints Commission, which had the power to order publication and enforce the order, if needs be, by application to the High Court. The Commission, of 21 people, would be appointed by the relevant cabinet minister and would have to 'represent the diverse nature of society'.[33]

Although Ann Clywd's bill was not high in the list of Private Member's Bills and therefore stood only a marginal chance of progress, it did strike a chord, feeding into a wider debate about press standards. On 3 November the Conservative MP William Cash presented his Right of Privacy Bill to the House of Commons, and the whole subject came up again on 27 November in a debate led by Clive Soley. Soley attacked the sensationalism and unfair reporting in the press, arguing that something had to be done about right of reply.[34] The government was forced into defending the Press Council, in spite of the criticisms. Neither

Clywd's nor Cash's bill received government support, but they were important barometers of an intensifying dissatisfaction with self-regulation among MPs.

In the next parliamentary session the Conservative MP John Browne introduced a Protection of Privacy Bill, and the Labour MP Tony Worthington, backed by the CPBF, presented his Right of Reply Bill, both on 21 December 1988. Worthington's bill was focused on the press and on the question of inaccuracy, rather than the wider questions covered by the earlier bills. By now the Press Council had begun to realise the need to respond, and in 1988 had appointed Louis Blom-Cooper QC as its new chairman, thus allowing supporters of self-regulation to plead the case for a delay in any government action on the issue. This view was put by the editor of the *Observer*, Donald Trelford, in March 1989:

> I said I'd come back to the Press Council. It has a new chairman with an experienced legal mind, a good deal of energy and a highly developed sense of social justice. He has proposed a radical reform of the Press Council by the autumn, reviewing its powers, its membership and its complaints procedures. He should be allowed to complete this inquiry before any piecemeal and hack-handed action is taken in parliament on privacy and right of reply.

By then the Director of the Press Council, Kenneth Morgan, had recognised the implications for self-regulation of both poor standards in the press and the recent wave of parliamentary activity:

> We're in a climate where largely as a result of the excesses of particular national newspapers, the press as an entity cannot look for the support against repression that it could normally expect to get from the public. There is a particular danger in the government flexing its muscles to restrain the serious press at a moment when the conduct of another kind of paper alienates the public. The press is an unpopular case and that is pretty grim.[35]

Worthington's bill had its Second Reading on 3 February 1989. Then he pointed out that his bill was deliberately simple and referred only to the correction of factual inaccuracies, thereby increasing 'the Government's difficulty in rejecting the proposal'. He also drew attention to a contradiction in the Council's purposes:

> The Press Council's first legitimate objective is to defend press freedom. It cannot also be the body that defends people against the press. I could not propose the abolition of the Press Council. The Press Council has a legitimate role to defend the press or lay down decent standards of

conduct for journalists, but it cannot be the body that protects those who are abused by the press.

For the government, Timothy Renton raised the question of just how the right of reply would work, and argued that:

> The motives behind the bill can be admired, but the subject does not lend itself to straightforward or uncontroversial legislation. We shall not oppose Second Reading, as we did not oppose the Protection of Privacy Bill last week … The Government have a number of reservations about the philosophy of statutory control over the press and the procedures set out in the bill.

Like the Protection of Privacy Bill, Worthington's got a Second Reading. This allowed it to proceed to its Committee stage, in preparation for the Third Reading.[36]

Never, since the birth of the Press Council, had two bills with substantial cross-party support got so far down the road of parliamentary procedure at the same time. The bills pushed the Press Council into another bout of reform under Louis Blom-Cooper, and presented the government with a problem. It did not want to be seen to be crushing two bills, especially one from a Conservative MP, which had such clear backbench support across parties, but it was clearly unwilling to forge ahead, back the bills and thereby incur the wrath of the proprietors. So, in the end, after some hesitation, it opted for 'the time-honoured compromise. It offered a committee of enquiry.' As a result both bills fell and the Calcutt Inquiry was established in 1989.[37]

The terms of reference for Calcutt were reminiscent of the issues raised in successive postwar inquiries:

> In the light of the recent public concern about intrusions into the private lives of individuals by certain sections of the press, to consider what measures (whether legislative or otherwise) are needed to give further protection to individual privacy from the activities of the press and improve recourse against the press for the individual citizen, taking account of the existing remedies, including the law of defamation and breach of confidence; and to make recommendations.[38]

The inquiry was conducted at a time when the Labour Party was committed to creating a statutory Press Council with the powers to enforce a code of practice 'covering such matters as harassment, invasion of privacy, offensive stereotyping of women and ethnic minorities – and to provide individuals with a right of reply'. It was also a period of intense activity at the Press Council under its new chair, Louis Blom-Cooper. By the autumn of 1989 the Council had, for the first time in its history, drawn up a code of practice covering privacy, opportunity for reply, prompt correction, the conduct of journalists, and references to race, religion and colour. All the national papers also appointed their own in-house ombudsmen to handle complaints. In 1969 Murdoch had refused to attend a Press Council hearing on the payments to Christine Keeler; this time he and the editor of the *Sun* gave evidence to Calcutt and each 'argued that any new statutory machinery was unnecessary now that the tabloids had reformed themselves'. The proprietors were doing their utmost to appear contrite and willing to reform, a position that, given the long history of bouts of reform followed by relapse and failure, was not strong enough to convince the Calcutt Committee.[39]

Calcutt rehearsed the criticisms of the Press Council which were by now familiar to anyone who had an interest in the debates. These included its ineffectiveness as an adjudicating body; its perceived lack of independence from the proprietors; its tendency to reject large numbers of complaints before adjudication; the lack of clarity in the way it classified complaints; the delay in getting adjudications in contested cases; and the lack of effective sanctions. In summary, it concluded:

> We *recommend* that the press should be given one final chance to prove that voluntary self-regulation can be made to work. However we do not consider that the Press Council, even if reformed, as proposed in its internal review, should be kept as part of the system. We therefore *recommend* that the Press Council should be disbanded and replaced by a new body, specifically charged with adjudicating on complaints of press malpractice. This body must be seen to be authoritative, independent and impartial. It must also have jurisdiction over the press as a whole, must be adequately funded and must provide a means of seeking to prevent publication of intrusive material. We consider it particularly important to emphasise the break from the past. The new body should, therefore, be called the Press Complaints Commission.

The Press Complaints Commission (PCC) had therefore to deal with complaints, publish and monitor 'a comprehensive code of practice', have a 24-hour complaints telephone line, be able to recommend an apology and, where appropriate, influence the position that an apology appeared in the publication. It was to be smaller than the Press Council, with an independent chair and no more than twelve members; all members were to be appointed by an appointments commission which would be independently appointed by the Lord Chancellor; it would have clear procedures and the industry needed to 'demonstrate its commitment ... by providing the necessary money for setting up and maintaining the Press Complaints Commission'. In all of this Calcutt was repeating the demands for serious reform which had been made, periodically, since 1953. Calcutt avoided, in effect, the thorny question of the sanctions that the PCC might apply, relying on the willingness of the press to adhere, voluntarily, to the new body's adjudications.

Calcutt, however, also said that were the PCC not set up in time, or were there to be a low rate of compliance or large-scale flouting of its adjudications then the government should establish a 'statutory tribunal with statutory powers and implementing a statutory code of conduct'. This Press Complaints Tribunal would adjudicate complaints, award compensation and restrain publications in cases of privacy. It would be appointed jointly by the Lord Chancellor and the Home Secretary. This was a return to the position of the 1961–62 Commission, only this time with a much clearer statement of what should be put in the place of self-regulation. Whilst Calcutt did 'not regard a right of correction as a practical proposition' it had shifted the terms of debate. Calcutt made statutory regulation a real possibility, and had not ruled it out on the somewhat confusing grounds articulated by the 1974–77 Commission.[40]

David Waddington, the Home Secretary, made it clear on 21 June 1990 that the government accepted 'the central recommendation of the committee that the press should be given twelve months to establish a press complaints commission on the lines proposed'. He went on:

> If a non-statutory commission is established, the Government will review its performance after 18 months of operation to determine whether a statutory underpinning is required. If no steps are taken to set up such a commission, the Government, albeit, with some regret, will proceed to establish a statutory framework, taking account of the committee's recommendations.

The Labour Party backed this position. The press was therefore left with a chance to escape statutory measures in a manner reminiscent of the post-Shawcross era.

There was some resistance to the proposal to abolish the Press Council from within the industry, but by October the Newspaper Publishers Association and the Newspaper Society, amongst other press interests, set up a Press Board of Finance (Presbof) to collect funds from the industry to pay for a Press Complaints Commission. The Press Council was dissolved in 1990 and the PCC came into operation on 1 January 1991.[41]

The PCC was chaired, initially, by Lord McGregor of Durris, an academic and the chair of the 1974–77 Royal Commission. Members were selected by an Appointments Commission consisting of McGregor, the chair of Presbof and a public nominee. Thus the appointments procedure, contrary to Calcutt's recommendations, remained in the hands of the industry. In 1991 it had sixteen members as opposed to the twelve recommended by Calcutt, nine of whom were editors or managers. It operated a 16-clause code of conduct that had been drawn up by a 'committee of national and regional newspaper and magazine editors'. 'All publishers and editors committed themselves to the Code of Practice', claimed the PCC. The organisation had a slimmed-down set of objectives compared to the Press Council. These included:

(i)   To handle speedily and judge fairly complaints which raise a *prima facie* breach of the industry Code of Practice.
(ii) To give advice to editors about both the interpretation of the Code and journalistic ethics.
      ...
(iv) To secure support from the public, parliament and the Press for maintaining self-regulation of the Press by achieving recognition that the Commission is accessible to complainants and independent of Press interests in its judgements.[42]

The proprietors had, under pressure from outside, followed Calcutt, killed the Press Council and presided over its rebirth in a sleeker form as the PCC.

By 1991 public confidence in the British press was low. A poll conducted in that year showed that 'those expressing confidence' in the British press 'had dropped from 29 per cent in 1981 to only 14 per cent in 1991'. It is not surprising therefore that between 1991 and 1992, the period of probation specified by Calcutt, the PCC continued to draw fire. Complaints about the press coverage of the Royal Family were particularly prominent. The government was aware of the ongoing sensitivity of the issue and during 1991 the Home Office kept in regular touch with the PCC through meetings with Lord McGregor. In March 1992 the former chair of the Press Council, Louis Blom-Cooper, attacked the PCC for its 'cursory opinions short on factual and legal analysis' and for acting 'like the newspaper industry's protector, that may occasionally bark at its misdemeanours'. He wanted a small body that was independent from the press, appointed by an appointments commission that was not industry based, with powers to take evidence, censure, and request a right of reply. It should have its own code and be able to initiate its own inquiries without waiting for a complaint. On 10 June 1992, reflecting the continuing dissatisfaction with self-regulation, and backed by the CPBF, Clive Soley published his Freedom and Responsibility of the Press Private Member's Bill. It was against this background that in July 1992 David Calcutt was asked by the government 'to assess the effectiveness of non-statutory self-regulation by the Press since the establishment of the Press Complaints Commission and to give his views on whether the present arrangements for self-regulation should be modified or put on a statutory basis'. In the same month the House of Commons National

Heritage Committee added to the pressure by announcing an inquiry into self-regulation.[43]

So the second Calcutt inquiry was conducted during a period when through the Soley bill, and the National Heritage inquiry, the press was being exposed to another round of public scrutiny. Soley's bill replayed many of the key themes raised in previous attempts to get statutory reform. This time, however, the bill wanted to link the right to correction of inaccuracies with support for press freedom. The bill set out to establish an Independent Press Authority:

(a) to promote the highest standards of journalism in newspapers;
(b) to investigate and monitor issues relating to freedom of the press and to report to parliament on any measure it may consider desirable to protect press freedom;
(c) to investigate and monitor ethical standards of the press, distribution of newspapers, ownership and control of the media, access to information and restrictions on reporting and any related matter it may consider appropriate;
(d) to produce and promote codes of professional and ethical standards for the press.

It would also 'determine the question of factual inaccuracy' and, if necessary, enforce its ruling through the courts. The Authority of 21 members was to be appointed by the Secretary of State and have a Press Complaints Advisor to aid the public and facilitate conciliation.[44]

The bill, according to the *British Editor*, organ of the Association of British Editors, could be used by MPs 'as an excuse to retaliate against what they regard as media excesses'. Lord McGregor, in response to the mounting attacks on his organisation, defended the PCC's Code as having 'made dramatic changes' in working practices in the industry. In the autumn the President of the Guild of British Newspaper Editors attacked Soley's bill: 'I wish his bill to the devil ... It is the kind of legislation which pettifogging politicians and lawyers will love, and will achieve very little good at the end of the day.'[45]

Clive Soley held a series of cross-party special hearings in the House of Commons in December 1992, where people on both sides of the debate, from a range of organisations, expressed views on the effectiveness of the PCC. At the hearings on self-regulation held by the National Heritage Committee, on 3 December, Lord McGregor once again defended the Code and Peter Preston, Editor of the *Guardian*, argued that there had been an improvement under the PCC: 'When I talk to the editors of tabloid newspapers it is a source of complaint that they have been forced or have chosen to withdraw some of the things they had been doing.' This debate continued against a backdrop of a public opinion poll that showed that 53 per cent of the population thought tabloid newspapers were under too little control.[46]

On 12 December, in an attack reminiscent of the one on Frank Allaun in 1982, Murdoch's *Sun* asserted:

> Mr Soley, until now one of the invisible men of Parliament, espouses freedom and responsibility – worthy causes which, under his malevolent influence, become twisted.
> **FOR** freedom of the Press, read censorship.
> **FOR** responsibility read neutering.
> Mr Soley and his left-wing pals have declared war on The Sun.

A more restrained criticism was offered by the *Daily Telegraph* on the 16 December. It considered that Calcutt was likely to propose a privacy law of some sort:

> The evil that Mr Clive Soley's current Private Member's Bill is designed to tackle – the failure of a newspaper to correct a factual mistake – is today a far less serious problem than invasions of privacy. But in opposing his bill as irrelevant and impractical, the press might have to pay some other price for its unpopularity and its excesses.

The Times, another Murdoch paper, took the line that some measures might be needed to strengthen the PCC 'or some successor group, to impose fines upon papers' but repeated the view that statutory measures posed a threat to press freedom: 'A statutory body should not be under consideration. A newspaper that opposes a government can, on occasions, try to destroy it. Those occasions will be rare. But they should be there. And there should be no politically appointed panel, however representative or sincere, to hinder or abet that duty.' In January 1993 it was reported that editors appearing before the National Heritage Committee 'say privately they have been surprised by the degree of hostility they have met' and the vigour of their response to the various initiatives clearly illustrated their awareness that, once again, self-regulation was being called into question.[47]

The concerns about any statutory measure being a short-cut to censorship were expressed by investigative journalists at Clive Soley's special hearings in December and in the socialist press. These concerns reflected the suspicions, held by many journalists for generations, that the state should not have a role in regulating the press; they were countered by arguments stressing the fact that the Soley bill imposed post-publication retractions after conciliation had failed and that this was not a form of pre-publication censorship. To the concern about the fact that the IPA would be appointed by the government and could in future be used as an instrument of repression, it was argued that this was equally so of any government-appointed body in public life, such as the BBC Board of Governors, and that this was not a reason for ruling out an IPA in principle. We return to these issues more fully in Chapter 11.[48]

When Calcutt reported in January 1993 his judgement came as no surprise. He considered the PCC a failure and that there was a need for a more independent body to command public confidence, a statutory press complaints tribunal of the sort he had recommended in 1990. The whole issue received a further public airing on 29 January when Soley's bill received, like Worthington's, a Second Reading. During the debate there were calls for a privacy bill, criticisms of the effectiveness of the PCC and of employers for creating a working environment that encouraged low standards. When the bill reached its Committee stage, in March 1993, Peter Brooke, the Secretary of State for National Heritage, on behalf of the government, opposed both the idea of an IPA and Calcutt's tribunal, arguing that the government would await the outcome of National Heritage Committee's report. Soley's bill was therefore lost, failing to get a Third Reading. In fact, the government took over two years to pronounce finally on the issue.[49]

When the National Heritage Committee reported it rejected a statutory Press Commission but suggested a series of statutory measures to improve standards. Editors and journalists should be obliged by contract to comply with the industry code of practice; there should be a Protection of Privacy Law and a new voluntary Press Commission would be able to pay compensation to victims of the press. Individuals would have the right to appeal from the Commission to a press ombudsman with statutory powers to supervise the wording, position and format of corrections, apologies and retractions, and who would also have 'statutory authority to impose a fine'. By 1993 two official inquiries had backed the creation of statutory measures to improve standards, and another Private Member's Bill had gained substantial parliamentary support.[50]

The status quo, 1993–98

Between 1993 and 1998 senior politicians re-established the status quo prior to 1990. With a general election due in 1997 the Conservative government of John Major proved reluctant to undermine self-regulation. The Labour Party, under its new leader from 1994 onwards, Tony Blair, quickly moved to neutralise press hostility towards the Labour by effectively rejecting the bulk of the policies on media reform developed in the party since the early 1970s, and by the time Labour reached government in 1997 it was openly embracing a policy of encouraging both self-regulation and increases in the concentration of ownership in the media.[51]

In November 1993 the PCC failed to stop the *Sunday Mirror* publishing secretly-taken pictures of the Princess of Wales. This, and other incidents, prompted the PCC to appoint a Privacy Commissioner 'to initiate inquiries into high-profile cases' in January 1994. In March 1994 editors in the industry published an attack on the idea of a civil law of privacy, thus making their position abundantly clear to the government, which was still considering its response to the second Calcutt and the National Heritage Committee's reports.[52]

By July 1994 a shift in Labour media policy was under way. A conference in London, hosted by the Shadow Heritage Secretary, Mo Mowlam, had a platform full of figures from the top echelons of the media industry none of whom represented workers within the industry. Mowlam declared that 'There has to be a loosening of ownership rules' in the media. This gesture towards the conventional wisdom held by media industry employers was reciprocated, for, as one journalist wrote: 'If nothing else, the substantial turnout of the great and good at the Labour Party's 21st Century Media Conference ... on July 13 was proof that many powerful figures in the media are now taking the possibility of a Labour victory seriously.' This shift marked a major break with Labour party policy as it had developed since the 1970s, such that Labour was preparing for power, in part, by abandoning policies that were critical of the media. The outcome of this, as will be seen, was an abandonment of its commitments to end self-regulation in the media.[53]

In July 1995 Tony Blair made a symbolic gesture towards placating the UK's most powerful media owner, Rupert Murdoch. He accepted an offer from Murdoch of a return flight to Australia. There he addressed Murdoch's executives and, in his speech, made it clear that he wanted an 'open and competitive media market'. This visit to Murdoch was controversial and, in spite of the new direction of the leadership, concern about ownership in the media was still apparent amongst Labour MPs. In the same month the Tory government, with an eye on the forthcoming election, rejected a privacy law and supported the continuance of self-regulation. Since January 1995 the PCC had been chaired by Lord John Wakeham. He was the most experienced senior politician ever to have chaired either the PC or the PCC since Lord Shawcross and, having been a key figure in the administrations of Margaret Thatcher during the 1980s, had the confidence of the Major government, many of whom were his former colleagues. This was an act of clear-sighted political shrewdness on the part of the industry, appointing at a sensitive time a figure who could reassure the government that the PCC was chaired by someone with acute political antennae and finely honed skills of working in government and Whitehall. Wakeham's presence and stature, in a sense like Devlin's in the 1960s, gave the PCC an appearance of renewed vigour, despatch and purpose, thereby making it easier for the government to ignore the arguments of the early 1990s and back the proprietors in their desire to see self-regulation continue. Thus, by 1995, the underlying influence of newspaper proprietors in helping to set the agenda of media policy, in spite of by now almost a generation of critique of self-regulation, was very apparent.[54]

At the NUJ's 1995 ADM working journalists showed that they were not impressed by the 'new look' PCC: 'This ADM regards as ridiculous the British government's reaffirmation of confidence in "self-regulation" of the press and declares it has no confidence in the PCC's ability to exercise any serious restraint on the excesses of the popular press.' The ADM believed that the Press Commission suggested by the 1993 National Heritage Committee report 'offered hope of realising the NUJ's aim to preserve press freedom within effective self-regulation of ethical standards through a new and credible commission operating a code of conduct with disciplinary sanctions'.

It was clear that Lord Wakeham was not succeeding in his hope, expressed in October 1995, 'to put the maintenance of democratic press self-regulation where it should be: beyond the bounds of controversial political debate', because press behaviour and the PCC's adjudications continued to attract considerable controversy. At its 1996 ADM the NUJ supported dialogue with the PCC to see if the union could achieve the end of the dominance of editors on the body and the alteration of the PCC code to conform to the NUJ's code. It also hoped to persuade the PCC to take complaints about racist content in the press more seriously, and to adopt a role defending press freedom. The union retained, however, its commitment to a Press Commission with real disciplinary sanctions.[55]

During 1996 allegations about intrusions into the privacy of the Royal Family continued and prompted further criticism of the PCC. The xenophobic coverage of the 1996 European Cup football tournament, which had been staged in the UK, illustrated yet again the problem posed for an organisation that was trying to maintain standards whilst having no powers of sanction. By early 1997 the National Heritage Committee was once more attacking the PCC's effectiveness: 'Time and time again the PCC's reaction to criticism is to offer half measures when radical change is called for ... We do not accept that the PCC cannot provide itself with authority to fine or order the payment of compensation.'[56]

In spite of this continuing criticism of the PCC no evidence emerged of the Labour Party leadership being willing to act on self-regulation. Its manifesto for the 1997 election contained no reference to the PCC or press regulation. On 18 March 1997 the *Sun* announced it would be backing Tony Blair in the forthcoming election – an historic shift for that paper, which had been the cheerleader of right-wing conservatism since the 1970s. Once Labour won the election, and despite the fact that the minister who became responsible for the area, Chris Smith, had a long record of supporting statutory reform whilst in opposition, backing the

Worthington bill and acting as a sponsor on Clive Soley's bill, the new government swung firmly behind the self-regulation of the press. This was in spite of the continuation of scandals around press intrusion and malpractice. The mood amongst journalists was apparent at their 1999 ADM when they voted for 'a statutory Right of Reply to factual inaccuracies', thus keeping alive the critical attitude towards proprietorially influenced standards that had inspired delegates in the 1940s, led to critiques of the membership of the Press Council in the 1960s, and to the organisation's break with the Press Council in 1980. In a sense, the NUJ, the organisation of those who worked in the industry, indicated in its history the extent to which scepticism and opposition to self-regulation was a continuing feature of postwar history.[57]

Years of debate

This chapter and Chapter 4 have sketched the extent of political and public debate over the regulation of the press after 1945. They illustrate the continuity of debates since 1945 about standards, the nature of press regulation, and the relationship between the state and the press with debates that go back to the seventeenth century, but more particularly with those that emerged in the UK from the mid-nineteenth century onwards. They show, as does the evidence in earlier chapters, that the idea that the press should be free from state regulation is, of course, untenable. It has never been the case and is unlikely to be so for a long time to come, and this fact has long been recognised by proprietors and reformers alike.

We have also illustrated that the demands for reform of press standards, and of the self-regulation of the press, intensified in the postwar years. This was in part because of the work of those, like the NUJ in the 1940s, the MPs in the 1950s, and the CPBF and others thereafter, who campaigned for change, but also because of the argument that the statutory control of standards automatically constituted some form of censorship was decisively rejected by journalists, MPs and unofficial and official inquiries.

In a sense these debates recast nineteenth-century ideas about the importance of press freedom from governmental controls into ones focusing on the need to balance press freedom with a responsibility to the public. It was the failure of the Press Council and the Press Complaints Commission to convince knowledgeable observers of the worth of self-regulation that provided the most potent evidence for reformers. We illustrate these points more fully in Chapters 6 and 7 by examining in some detail aspects of the history of the Press Council and the Press Complaints Commission.

6

Organising and Defining Self-Regulation

> To a newspaper press which had enjoyed absolute freedom from restriction and special taxation for something like a century, the appointment of a body to safeguard its liberty by curbing its excesses was a startling and unwelcome innovation.[1]

These were the words of George Murray, chairman of the Press Council, writing in 1963. This chapter examines the way this 'startling and unwelcome innovation' developed after 1953, focusing on the dominant organisational characteristics of the Press Council and the Press Complaints Commission.

1953–98

The General Council of the Press – known usually as the Press Council – came into being on 1 July 1953, with a membership drawn solely from the industry. After the 1962 Royal Commission it changed its name to the Press Council, introduced a small element of lay membership and appointed a lay chair. It revised its constitution in response to high-profile political criticism, such as that levied by the Younger Committee (1972) and the third Royal Commission on the Press (1974–77); this amounted to increasing the number of lay people on the Council and revising and attempting to streamline its complaints procedure. At the height of the parliamentary attacks on self-regulation in 1989 it agreed a major programme of internal reform. This came too late and in 1990 it was dissolved and replaced by the Press Complaints Commission, a body charged, largely, with dealing with complaints. It is best to think of this as a continuous history, with each reform producing some changes in constitution or procedures, but with the central features of self-regulation remaining intact, most notably the dominance of proprietors in the organisation and the absence of any effective method of enforcing its rulings.

The PC and the PCC have had a series of chairmen over the years. The first three were from the industry: J.J. Astor (1953–55), Sir Linton Andrews (1955–59) and George Murray (1959–63). After the reforms in 1963 the chairs were Lord Devlin (1963–69), Lord Pearce (1969–73), Lord Shawcross (1973–78), Patrick Neil QC (1978–83), Sir Zelman Cowan (1983–88) and Louis Blom-Cooper QC (1988–90). From 1991 the Chair of the PCC was Lord McGregor of Durris, who, like Lord Shawcross, had chaired a Royal Commission on the Press. He was succeeded in 1995 by Lord John Wakeham. Devlin, Pearce, Neil, Cowan and Blom-Cooper were lawyers; Shawcross, a lawyer and politician; McGregor, an academic; and Wakeham, a politician. Thus the lay chairs were drawn from a very narrow social group.

Finance and membership

Finances

The main source of finance for the Press Council was employers' organisations. This can be seen in Table 6.1, where the proportion of Council income from different sources is represented at roughly ten-year intervals.

Table 6.1   Relative contributions by constituent organisations to the financing of the Press Council[1]

	1953–54 %	1961–62 %	1969–70 %	1981–82 %	1990 %
NPA	28	37	51	53	53
NS	24	34	26	33	33
PPA	–	–	7	7	7
SDNS	6	5	3	2	3
SNPA	6	4	2	3	3
NUJ	16	10	7	–	–
IOJ	12	6	2	1	0.2
GBNE	8	4	2	1	0.8
Total	100	100	100	100	100

1. These figures are based on material included in the Council's annual reports for the following years: *1st AR 1953–54*, pp. 35–36; *9th AR 1961–62*, pp. 84–85; *17th AR 1969–70*, pp. 126–28; *27th and 28th ARs, 1980 and 1981*, pp. 296–98; *37th AR 1990*, pp. 260–62.

The figures in Table 6.1 have been taken from the annual reports, turned into percentages and rounded to produce a clear total. The organisations are: NPA, Newspaper Publishers Association; NS, Newspaper Society; PPA, Periodical Publishers Association; SDNS, Scottish Daily Newspaper Society; SNPA, Scottish Newspaper Proprietors Association; NUJ, National Union of Journalists; IOJ, Institute of Journalists; GBNE, Guild of British Newspaper Editors.

The Council was funded in the main by the two major employers' organisations, the NPA and the NS. Their share of the funding rose from 52 per cent in 1953–54, through 77 per cent in 1969–70, to 86 per cent by 1990. The NPA moved from providing 28 per cent of funding in 1953–54, through 51 per cent in 1969–70 to 53 per cent in 1990. By the 1970s the NPA was easily the most important funder of the Press Council, and it increased its grip as the Press Council came under heavier and heavier fire in the 1970s and 1980s. The NUJ's contribution diminished from 16 per cent in 1953–54 to 1.7 per cent in 1980, when it contributed £3413 out of a total of £199, 541.[2] The IOJ's contribution fell from 12 per cent in 1953–54 to 0.2 per cent in 1990. In financial terms the Press Council had, by the early 1960s, become an organisation funded mainly by the employers.

A recurrent theme in criticism of the Press Council was that it was under-funded. This was recognised even by George Murray, who in 1961, responding to demands that the Council do work to monitor changes in the economics of the industry, wrote that the Council's 'activities are limited and confined within a total income of £4100 a year – a sum insufficient to maintain anything beyond the present exiguous organisation. The Council is well aware of the restrictions imposed on its activities by a thin purse'.[3] In fact the pattern of funding for the Press Council seems to have been linked to the ebb and flow of external political pressure, as Table 6.2 illustrates.

The Council's income came from constituent organisations. In one or two cases the figures given in the reports are not always clear or consistent with each other, from year to year, and where this has happened the nearest approximate figure has been given. The figure for 1977–78 covers the 18-month period July 1977 to December 1978; hence it shows a very big rise.

For four out of the eight years 1953–61, the Council's income remained constant. It rose from £5787 in 1961–62 to £13,900 in 1963–64, a rise of 140 per cent, after a period of no increase between 1957 and 1961. This rise was a response to the 1961–62 Royal Commission. Under the first phase of Lord Devlin's chairmanship, the income rose from £13,900 in 1963–64 to £20,112 in 1966–67, remaining static for the next three years. The next rise of 33 per cent came in 1970–71 when the Younger Committee was sitting, but income remained static then until 1973–74. Thereafter, in the climate of

Table 6.2   Press council income 1953–90[1]

Year	Income £	% Change
1953–54	2,500	
1954–55	3,000	0
1955–56	3,000	0
1956–57	3,000	0
1957–58	4,100	+37
1958–59	4,100	0
1959–60	4,100	0
1960–61	4,100	0
1961–62	5,787	+41
1962–63	5,287	−8
1963–64	13,900	+163
1964–65	14,175	+2
1965–66	19,910	+41
1966–67	20,112	+1
1967–68	20,112	0
1968–69	20,112	0
1969–70	20,112	0
1970–71	26,816	+33
1971–72	26,816	0
1972–73	26,816	0
1973–74	39,425	+47
1974–75	44,425	+13
1975–76	66,263	+49
1976–77	99,001	+49
1977–78	198,225	+100
1979	155,744	−21
1980	199,541	+28
1981	219,332	+10
1982	307,852	+40
1983	324,031	+5
1984	474,774	+47
1985	445,312	−6
1986	472,471	+6
1987	492,501	+4
1988	520,208	+6
1989	586,605	+13
1990	718,015	+22

1. Source: Press Council Annual Reports.

intensified debate, income rose regularly during the period 1974–79. In the 1980s two of the largest percentage increases coincided with the parliamentary controversies around the Allaun (1983) and the Worthington (1988–89) bills. Income rose by 47 per cent between 1983 and 1984 and by 38 per cent between 1988 and 1990. So, the pattern of Press Council finance was responsive to external political pressure, mirroring the contours of public controversy rather than a steady year-on-year pattern of increase.

Membership[4]

The figures on membership outlined below are drawn from an analysis of the details given in the annual reports. They include in the membership those non-voting officials from constituent organisations who had a right to attend but do not include named officers of the Council. The Council did not give biographical information on its members in a consistent manner, usually waiting until someone left or died before inserting a biographical notice. The figures should therefore be treated with caution, even though they are a useful indicator of the nature of Council membership and officers.

The composition of the Press Council was a source of controversy throughout its history. This controversy centred frequently on the way the industry dominated the Council until the 1970s and also on the socially unrepresentative nature of its lay membership. The Press Council's annual reports show that between 1953 and 1990 the Council had 247 members. Of these only 28, or 11 per cent, were identifiable as female. Lay members were introduced after the 1963 reforms, rising from 5 out of 25 in 1964, through 10 out of 30 from 1973, and ending up with 18 out of 36 in 1977.[5] Of the lay members 51 were men and 25 were women. The Press Council was therefore throughout its history a predominantly male-dominated institution, with only three of its female members coming from within the industry.

Fifty-two, or 21 per cent, of members served for eight or more years: 34 of these came from the employers' side; 15 from the NUJ and IOJ; and three were long-serving lay members. Some of these people served for an extraordinarily lengthy period. Barrie Abbot from the Scottish Newspaper Proprietors Association was involved from 1959 to 1984; Eric Clayson sat for the Newspaper Society from 1954 to 1972; Sir Denis Hamilton served for the NPA from 1960 to 1981. There was thus a good deal of continuity of membership across the years.

Of the 76 lay people who served on the Council, the annual reports provide details on the occupations of 61; these are summarised in Table 6.3.

The categories listed in Table 6.3 have been very broadly defined so as to accommodate the information in the annual reports and should

Table 6.3   Main occupations of lay members of Press Council

Education	12
Local Government /Public Service/Voluntary Sector	10
Military/Police	6
Church	5
TU connection	5
Non-managerial (Industry/Commerce)	5
Managerial (Industry/Commerce)	4
Local Politics	4
Farming	3
Other	7
Total	61

therefore be seen as an only an indication of the kinds of occupations that dominated membership. Education was by far the biggest occupational category, accounting for 12 of the 61; the Church, military and the police accounted for another 11. The overall bias was towards white-collar occupations and the public services. The emphasis seems to have been on appointing people from occupations that had some status in society, hence the absence of many non-managerial, non-white collar occupations. This stress on status is even more pronounced when the number of lay and non-lay members with titles or government-bestowed honours is considered. Over its existence it had 25 titled members (peers, baronesses, knights), another 34 had some form of government-bestowed honour (e.g. a CBE, OBE) and another 10 were JPs. Thus about 27.5 per cent of the total members had some form of inherited or government-bestowed title or were Justices of the Peace.

The Council had a distinct flavour of social conservatism about it. The PCC carried this conservatism over into its smaller version of the Press Council, only in a much more pronounced form. It jettisoned the less socially elevated sections of its lay membership in favour of those with a much higher profile. As John Tulloch has pointed out:

> The membership of the PCC in July 1991 consisted of five lords, two knights, one professor, a publisher, a dentist, an NHS Trust chair and seven editors from the national, local and magazine press ... The political intention behind the construction of this group is to balance its contacts with the political world and with the press ... So, in a very transparent way, it is not a body which in any modern democratic sense 'represents' the public, except as a trustee or guardian might represent an infant.[6]

Tulloch's point can be applied to the Press Council. This was always a carefully balanced institution with the power of the proprietors expressed through their historically dominant position within the membership and the careful selection of lay members. In spite of calls from the 1947–49 Commission onwards for appointments to the Council to be taken out of the hands of the industry, this never happened. Even though an Appointments Commission was set up after the 1963 reforms, ultimate control over who was on the Commission never left the hands of the industry.

The appointment of lay members to the Press Council may have been a sign of its willingness to respond to political pressure, but it was never more than a reluctantly agreed, carefully controlled concession, designed to retain power in the Council in the hands of its main funders. By the late 1990s, there was little evidence that the PCC had, in any meaningful sense, departed from this practice.

Aims and powers

Aims

In presenting its first annual report in 1954, the Council emphasised 'that it considers its prime duty to be that of preserving in full the existing liberty of the Press. A free and trusted press is the only ultimate safeguard of our democracy.' This conformed to the early constitution of 1953–63, with its emphasis on preserving the status quo. In 1958, after a sustained bout of parliamentary criticism in the mid-1950s, the Council had changed the emphasis of the way it presented its aims:

> The Council began as an experiment. 'What good can it do?' became the favourite question of our critics in the early days. Our aims were to investigate and, if possible, redress personal grievances of public and private citizens, to curb practices that would bring the Press into disrepute, and to defend assaults on the freedom of the Press.

The confident assertion of its role as defender of the press freedom of 1954 had by 1958 shifted down the publicly expressed list of aims, below that of redressing grievances.[7]

By 1960 a less ambitious tone had entered the way it described its purpose: 'The Press, like all human institutions, is liable to error. The Press Council's purpose is to do what it can to restrain excesses in the midst of excess, and to preserve minimum decencies in a free-mannered, free-thinking, loud and intrusive age.' When responding to criticisms about its failure to produce studies of the economic status of the press in the 1950s, the Council revealed how its aims and practice were heavily constrained by the competition between the members of its constituent organisations:

> Its primary function is to consider ethical questions concerning the newspaper Press and this it performs as a homogenous body. But when it comes to economic questions there is, naturally, a division of opinion among constituent bodies representing varied interests. It would be almost impossible to present a unanimous report on, for example, an industrial dispute within the industry.

In its first ten years the Council lacked clarity about its purpose. It interpreted its role, variously, as defender of press freedom, as primarily a body for redress of grievances, as a restrainer of excesses, and as an organisation whose 'primary function' was to consider ethical questions.[8]

By 1966 under Lord Devlin the 'function of the Press Council' had become 'to settle standards' and also 'to stand up for the freedom and right of the press as well as to censure misconduct ... The Council must never allow itself to become merely a tribunal which convicts or acquits.'

These aims were accompanied by an additional purpose, expressed in 1968; the Council was, in fact, 'an alternative to statutory control of the Press'. This latter purpose had, by the mid-1970s, become a prominent theme in justifications for the existence of the Council, at a time when perceptions of its failure were widespread and the third postwar Royal Commission was sitting. Writing in 1977, Lord Shawcross argued:

> And of this I am certain. That in the political atmosphere of today, unless the Council continues actively to involve itself in protecting the freedom of the press in the public interest and the concomitant of that freedom in promoting the responsibility and ethics of newspapers and is fully supported in that task by proprietors, editors and, by no means least, by journalists, something quite different will be established by law.

By 1989 the record of the Council was under sustained attack. The last chairman, Louis Blom-Cooper, implicitly acknowledged the lack of clarity in the Council's interpretation of is role when he argued for a more pro-active body. He wanted 'to construct a Press Council that responds more actively to social conditions in which the public is increasingly hostile to some of the outpourings of some sections of the press'.[9]

Thus the Council did not express a clear, consistent sense of purpose. Its understanding of its aims, as expressed in its annual reports, vacillated between defending press freedom (as interpreted by the Council) and, in various ways, intervening on questions of standards, complaints and ethics. By the late 1970s the Council had evolved, under external pressure, into a body that dealt with grievances, but not because grievances in themselves merited positive treatment, but because, as Shawcross put it, otherwise 'something quite different will be established by law'.

Powers

In 1954 the Council was confident in its powers of persuasion: 'It has no powers of sanction, but its less spectacular methods will probably be the most effective, and our appeal to conscience and fair play has rarely been in vain.' This confidence in its powers was still strong when in 1956 the chairman, Sir Linton Andrews, claimed, with no substantiation, that 'Though it has no statutory powers to impose sanctions, the Council believes that through its power of censure and publicity it is doing much good – more than may be realised by a precis of cases dealt with.' In the same year the Council asserted: 'Our reprimands are neither made nor taken lightly'; it was 'a voluntary organisation, a sort of court of honour', which '*can* do much to enlighten public opinion'.[10]

By the late 1950s the failure of the Council to monitor the economics of the industry prompted criticism about its powers. Sir Linton Andrews's response stressed the limitations of the Council's powers: 'it must be borne in mind that the Council properly concerns itself with the ethical side of the profession, and not with the economics'; no mention, here, of the 1949 recommendation about monitoring the industry. A further limitation was recognised by the Council in 1960 when discussing criticism raised in a House of Lords debate, where some peers had 'regretted it had no power to punish journalists for professional misconduct'. After asserting its position, the Council admitted that: 'All this is not to contend that the Press Council is perfect and cannot be improved. It is all too conscious of its weakness and deficiencies. Some members believe that the Council's authority would be strengthened if more of the "quality" or "class" newspapers took a more active part.' For, since the retirement in 1954 of J.J. Astor, proprietor of *The Times*, from the chairmanship 'neither the Editor nor the management of *The Times* has held membership of the Council. Nor have the Editors or manager of the *Daily Telegraph, Guardian,* or *Sunday Times* been on the Council.' So, at the end of the 1950s the Council had retreated from its earlier, breezy confidence in its lack of statutory powers, into a position where it was having to justify itself in the face of criticism of its lack of authority.[11]

By the 1960s the Press Council was issuing statements and rebukes to newspapers that failed to publish its adjudications, warning that failure to publish meant 'it is likely that some other means will be sought of giving redress to members of the public who have well-founded complaints'. It had to defend its overall position to the 1961–62 Royal

Commission, but survived without being forced to adopt effective sanctions against recalcitrant publications.[12]

Doubts about the effectiveness of the Council's sanctions remained and were reflected in the way the Council had to keep simply asserting the usefulness of its moral authority, often by conjuring up the threat of alternatives that would pose a threat to press freedom. Lord Pearce argued in 1970 that 'The Press Council (rightly, as I think) has no coercive power. Freedom of speech is so vital that any coercion is too dangerous. But the moral force is considerable.' In 1973 he praised the system in the face of examples of papers not printing adjudications, asserting that 'by a self-disciplined ordinance each individual newspaper has accepted the obligation to publish in its columns the adjudication of the Press Council on its behaviour. This is a strong sanction.' In 1975 Lord Shawcross went on the attack, throwing up a fearful image of the unsavoury alternative to voluntary sanctions: 'the only weapon available to the Council is the force of public opinion. Any further sanction such as a fine or suspension would require statutory authority and be in itself a restriction on freedom of speech.' A stronger position was put by Patrick Neil in the 1979 annual report, stronger but nonetheless consistent with earlier pronouncements:

> I see no prospect whatever of universal consent being forthcoming from journalists, editors, proprietors and publishers for the Council to be enabled to impose penalties on a voluntary basis. For the conferment of such powers legislation would be essential. This would mean direct parliamentary intervention into the way the press operates and would by itself be a highly undesirable development. But beyond that the powers that would have to be conferred would in themselves constitute sinister shadows over press freedom.[13]

During the 1980s the Council's reports reflected its increasing difficulties in making its adjudications and its declarations effective. The behaviour of the tabloid papers in their coverage of the trial of Peter Sutcliffe, a serial murderer, forced the Council to issue a series of high-profile condemnations. It censured the *Daily Mail* for 'deliberately suppressing facts during the Council's inquiry into press conduct' and condemned the *Daily Star* 'for breaking the Declaration of Principle, which forbids newspapers making payments to potential witnesses'. It also judged that the payment of money for the memoirs of a policeman involved in the Sutcliffe case was 'a deplorable example of chequebook journalism'.

Thereafter as the scandals and misdemeanours of the 1980s mounted, the tone of the Council's appeal to newspapers revealed a growing sense of the fragility of its power and influence. In 1984 Zelman Cowan stressed that the Council's '**only** authority is the moral persuasion which it hopes that its pronouncements will carry'. In 1985 the Council appealed to editors for support: 'If editors fail to play a part in promoting public awareness of, and confidence in, the Council, they will have none but themselves to blame if Parliament replaces it with something more dictatorial.' By 1987 the Council was having to lecture papers whose disregard and delay in their dealings with the Council undermined its powers and prestige:

> There must be *full* compliance with the rules relating to publication of adjudications. It is simply *not* compliance to publish in an obscure place in the paper, in minuscule type ... The editors and those working with them must respond quickly to Press Council procedures on complaints. There are too many cases of delayed response ... It is a central principle that newspapers must not pick and choose, electing to comply with those principles derived from rulings of which they approve, but declining compliance with those with which they disagree.[14]

Thus, the 'appeal to conscience and fair play' of 1954 had, by the late 1980s, become demands for compliance with Council processes and adjudications. In the intervening years the Council had continually to repeat the virtues of self-regulation without sanctions because recurrent evidence of failure kept calling the system into question. The most common way the Council dealt with this problem was by invoking the idea that the alternative to the Council was statutory control and further restraints on press freedom. In effect the absence of effective sanctions allowed a great deal of editorial freedom to newspapers to pursue profits through methods that defied the Press Council, such as the chequebook journalism of the 1960s and 1980s.

Procedures

Press Council procedures evolved from 1953 to 1990 as a consequence of the political pressure on the organisation to make its practices more transparent and to respond more quickly to complaints. The Council became an organisation driven by its complaints function, such that when the PCC arrived in 1991 its main purpose was to deal with complaints and the wider goals of the 1949 recommendation had, in effect, been lost.

At its first meeting in July 1953 the Council agreed that it would 'at its discretion, consider complaints reaching it from any source'. This allowed it the flexibility to handle protests from people not directly affected by a report, whilst at the same time not committing the organisation to handling all such complaints. The Council held closed meetings as 'while it remains unprotected against legal proceedings it feels that it cannot operate in open session'. The Secretary of the Council had the job of redirecting complainants to the editor of the paper, and on more general issues the General Purposes Committee recommended action to a full meeting of the Council. The Council rarely allowed parties to appear before it mainly because of the volume of work this would entail. Its rather patronising view of complainants was hinted at when, in its first report, it asserted that 'The establishment of the Council opened the door to many with chips on their shoulders, axes to grind, or bees in their bonnets.'

The Council issued statements of its decisions after each quarterly meeting. From the beginning, its procedures were vague and left enormous powers of rejection in the hands of the Secretary. There were no published criteria against which decisions could be judged. It also had the power from the start to allow complaints from people not affected, known as third party complaints. The Press Council used this power to consider 'at its inaugural meeting certain newspaper publicity about Princess Margaret, though no specific complaint had been received'.[15]

This relatively casual manner of proceeding was expressed in the Council's attitude to the ordering and publication of its adjudications. Although its system of classifying complaints was always unclear, before the 1963 reforms there was no system at all. In 1957 Linton Andrews indicated that much of its complaints work was not recorded in the annual report, and in the following year the Council declared: 'Scores of cases, though important to those concerned, are of little general interest and find no place in the Council communiqués or its annual reports.' According to Linton Andrews the number of cases dealt with by the Council in his four-year chairmanship was in the hundreds. Nonetheless the actual numbers recorded in the annual reports in the 1950s were low (see Chapter 7).[16]

By the late 1950s the Council was continually stressing that its main function was to steer complainants away from itself towards newspapers; its procedures were designed to achieve this. For example, in 1958 it asserted:

It should be realised that only a tithe of the subjects which are raised by the public ever come before the full Council, for the procedure of sifting which was laid down by the Council in its early days has worked out extremely well. If it was required to deal with all the subjects which are raised, the Council would certainly have to meet monthly instead of quarterly and even then its meetings would be protracted.

Complaints, by this time, were rising and the Council insisted that they were first dealt with by the editors of papers. In spite of this rise the Council felt under no obligation to analyse or tabulate either the complaints or the adjudications. Complaints may have increased but, according to the chairman, George Murray, writing in 1960, the blame for this lay with the public's ignorance of Council procedure: 'Many people still write to us first. They fail to understand that the Council is primarily intended not as a receptacle for individual grievances but as an investigating body.' Thus the early Council was essentially a minimalist body, reluctant to engage in a systematic manner with the issues raised by the public.[17]

After January 1959 the Council met five times a year in response to an increasing workload. In 1961, in response to this situation, the Council published a statement on 'How to Make a Complaint', which sought to clarify and justify its procedures. It continued to publish this in various modified forms thereafter. The 1961 version was as follows:

More than 99 per cent of cases dealt with by the Press Council under its constitutional obligation to maintain the highest professional and commercial standards are allegations of specific breaches of the recognised code of newspaper practice.

It is open to any member of the public to initiate a case against a newspaper for such breaches whether they are due to publication of statements or the conduct of official representatives.

The procedure is simple. Initially, the aggrieved person must complain to the editor of the newspaper concerned. This rule is strictly enforced because it serves two valuable purposes. It eliminates the illogical position of the Press Council serving both as accusers and as adjudicators and it allows the 'accused' to take whatever action he may deem to be desirable before the complaint is lodged with the Council. In some instances a complainant has been wrongly informed, or has misinterpreted the facts. In others there is discovery of inadvertent error which the editor is only too ready to rectify.

Assuming that the case is to go forward, the complainant's second step is to send the Secretary of the Press Council ... (a) A statement of complaint; (b) Copies of the correspondence with the editor; (c) Enough of the page of the newspaper containing the alleged offensive matter to show date of publication; (d) Names and addresses of witnesses if this is applicable, and (e) Any other evidence which may support the case.

From this point the Press Council takes over and pursues its own investigations.[18]

On the positive side, the publication of this guidance was an advance on previous practice, where no such guidance had been published in such a concise and relatively prominent manner. There were, however, problems. The Council did not adopt a code of conduct until 1989 and never endorsed the NUJ's code of conduct as the industry's own. The 'code of newspaper' practice referred to in the guidance was, at best, an unwritten code, the expression and interpretation of which was a matter for the Council. The reference to a code was, therefore, ambiguous at best, at worst, misleading. The Council reiterated its view that it was not the proper body to receive initial complaints. But the reasoning was peculiar. It did not want to be accuser, judge and jury, and so it directed people firstly to the newspapers; but, using this line of reasoning, it did act as accuser, judge and jury when it initiated complaints inquiries in the 1950s, such as the one relating to press coverage of Princess Margaret. Simply requesting that a newspaper respond to a complaint, rather than insisting that the complainant go through the roundabout procedure described, need not in itself have placed the Council in an invidious position.

The system also left a great deal of discretion in the hands of editors. The reference to the shortcomings of complainants in the guide, whilst possibly true, implied a less than welcoming attitude on the part of the Council. The procedures, especially after the complainant had received an unsatisfactory reply from the newspaper, placed a great deal of emphasis on her or his ability and resources, both to marshal the appropriate evidence and to persist in the complaint. This system was therefore essentially one for filtering out, not for addressing, complaints.

The 1963 reforms promoted dealing with complaints as one of the Council's objectives. At the same time the Council saw the introduction of lay members as a way of dampening public criticism because 'it ought to satisfy the public that the Press is not acting simply as a judge in its own cause'. Nonetheless it had to restate that it did not usually hold oral hearings, in the light of 'some misunderstandings about its method of adjudication'. When Lord Devlin took over he defended these procedures against critics, appearing in the process to imply that, contrary to the statement in 'How to Make a Complaint', there was no code of ethics. These were the words of a man aware of the Council's procedural short-comings, but anxious all the same to defend them:

> The task of the Press Council in dealing with complaints is not always easy. There is no settled code for it to administer. Press ethics are still in the formative stage ... The procedure for hearing complaints is flexible. Some critics would like to see greater formality as a protection to journalists whose reputation may be injured by an adverse finding. Others fear the danger of a legalistic approach. Procedure as well as substance is in a formative stage.

This was a major advance on the attitude towards procedure expressed in the 1950s. Under Devlin the misleading nature of the reference to the code was eliminated. By 1964 'the recognised code' had become 'the recognised ethical code'.[19] By 1966 the opening statement in the guidance on complaints had become 'It is open to any member of the public to initiate a case against a newspaper for breach of the unwritten ethical code of newspaper practice.'[20] This ambiguity had remained embedded in the Council's public statements throughout the 1950s and into the second half of the 1960s.

In 1967 the Council complained of delays by the public in the presentation of complaints, declaring that 'where there is unreasonable delay it may decline to entertain them'; it gave no indication of what constituted an unreasonable delay. It also pressurised editors to respond to its inquiries more swiftly.[21] In 1968 it produced a more comprehensive guide to complaining, which repeated the warnings about delays but replaced the judicial explanation for directing complaints to editors given in 1961 by a more positive one: 'The rule is necessary because it acquaints the editor with the identity of his accuser and the details of the complaint and allows him an opportunity to deal with the matter at first hand.'[22]

The 1967 official history of the Press Council contained a section on procedures that pointed out that the Council would not deal with cases that were the subject of legal proceedings. A complainant about to embark on such proceedings would be required to abandon them or await their completion before pursuing the matter with the Press Council. This requirement became known as the 'legal waiver' and was attacked by the 1974–77 Royal Commission. The Commission felt that the Press Council was not an alternative to the courts and should be willing to adjudicate on complaints in spite of the possibility of legal action. It asked the Council to re-consider the waiver 'with a view to giving up the requirement' and regarded the refusal to adjudicate because of possible legal proceedings as 'strange'. The Robertson Report in 1983 asserted that 'questions of legal liability are irrelevant to the task of maintaining professional standards'.[23] For our purposes, the waiver is best viewed in the context of the development of procedures within the Council, which by the late 1960s, although more positive towards the receipt of complaints than had been the case in the 1950s, still had the effect of discouraging, rejecting or redirecting most complaints. In fact the guidance on complaints, issued in the 1960s, made no mention of the waiver. The waiver's real function appears to have been to act as a further disincentive to complainants on top of those provided by the published guidance.

In the wake of the scrutiny exercised by the Younger Committee, the Council altered the tone of its advice to complainants. Until 1974 it had stated that 'the aggrieved person must complain to the editor'. From then on it offered a choice, which carried with it the promise, for the first time, that the Council might be of assistance to the complainant in the initial stages of the process:

> Initially the aggrieved person may complain to the editor of the
> newspaper concerned. Most people appreciate, particularly in the case

of inaccuracy, that this is a good way of seeking the prompt publication of a correction. Alternatively, if a complainant chooses to send full particulars of the complaint by letter to the Secretary of the Press Council he will forward it to the Editor, without commenting on the merits of the matter, so that he has the opportunity of dealing with the matter direct and taking any action he thinks fit.[24]

This was, after over 20 years of existence, a formal, if partial, recognition that one function of the Council ought to be to help complainants. But, like the constitutional changes discussed in previous chapters, the sheer length of time this development took testified to the unwillingness of the Council in adopting a positive attitude to dealing with the questions of standards raised by public complaints about the press.

The pressure on the Council to make its procedures even more user-friendly continued until its demise in 1990. In the 1970s, however, the sense that the public misunderstood the purpose of the Council, so evident in the 1950s, was still evident in public statements, most strikingly in the utterances of Lord Shawcross. In the 1974–75 annual report he noted how 'most complaints whilst naturally of great importance to those who make them (and we deal with them on that basis) are usually of little significance from the point of view of the public interest'.[25] Nonetheless, in January 1978, in part because of the stance taken by the 1974–77 Royal Commission, the Council appointed a Conciliator to speed up the complaints process. This did not, however, go far enough to build confidence in the Council. The withdrawal of the NUJ from the Council in 1980 clearly called into question its validity as an industry-wide body, and there continued to be persistent criticisms about the inadequacies of its procedures, many of which were aired during the debates on Frank Allaun's Private Member's Bill in 1983.

From January 1984 the Council set up a 'fast track' complaints procedure, in response to these criticisms, yet at the same time it started printing in the annual report its demand for a waiver where 'legal action' was threatened. Printing this demand took some of the force away from the positive gesture of 'a fast track procedure' and, anyway, was a public rejection of the spirit if not the letter of the 1974–77 Commission's line on the waiver.[26]

The PCC was designed with the experience of the Press Council in mind, and therefore carried within it elements of continuity and change. The Commission was established to 'handle speedily and to judge fairly complaints which raise a *prima facie* breach of the industry's Code of Practice'. The PCC was thus a complaints body, unlike its predecessor which had also had objectives connected with the defence of press freedom. This was a retreat from the grand vision of 1949, but a logical outcome of the way the Press Council had developed after the 1960s. The Commission also made it a point to react quickly and in a high-profile manner to criticisms, such as when it aided the production of a revised code of practice in 1993 and appointed a Privacy Commissioner in 1994. It also put great stress on publicising its activities and trying, unlike the Press Council for much of its history, to make itself appear an accessible organisation. In a speech in May 1998 Lord Wakeham asserted:

> Self-regulation can therefore pass the test of accessibility – which is central to the work of the PCC. Indeed, we do everything we can to ensure our service is as [accessible] and as well known as possible – for instance by publishing our literature in a range of minority languages, setting up a Textphone service to assist deaf or hard of hearing persons in making complaints, and operating a Helpline to give advice to members of the public on how to use the PCC.

In a sense the industry showed, through the way the PCC was projecting itself, that it had learnt some of the lessons of the 1980s. It had to be seen to be running a form of self-regulation with accessible procedures if it was to stave off further pressure for statutory reform. In another sense the continuities ran deep. The early Press Council's procedures were designed to filter out complaints and minimise adjudications. In his May 1998 speech Lord Wakeham claimed that in 1997 of 3000 complaints to the PCC only 80 went to adjudication. These kind of figures could be viewed, in Wakeham's words, as a testimony to the PCC's role in 'calming a dispute down and sorting it out'. They could equally be viewed as evidence that, in spite of changes in the nature and visibility of its procedures, the PCC in the 1990s managed to exclude the vast majority of complaints from the adjudication process. Making procedures more accessible to the public did not alter the extent to which complaints reached adjudication. The PCC therefore, in part, reinvented self-regulation as a streamlined, user-friendly, public-relations-conscious body, placing procedural accessibility at its heart in a way the Press Council never did. Nonetheless the procedural progress made by the 1990s had been wrung, very slowly, out of a reluctant industry.[27]

Attitudes

The early Council's reports contain evidence of the way it thought of itself as addressing not the public at large, but a small, well educated section of the middle classes, to whose reason and shared assumptions it could appeal when defending itself. It did not seem to be addressing a wider conception of the public. In 1954, for instance, it addressed its readers as if they were reasonably well informed about classical and modern literature, and appealed to this knowledge in its argument:

It has often been suggested to the Press Council that this or that report is in bad taste and for that reason should be condemned. This is difficult and disputable ground. Classical literature is full of reminders that we have as many thousands of tastes as there are persons living and that what is right and joyous to some is poisonous to others. In our own day Shaw has spoken of 'A man of great common sense and good taste' as meaning 'without originality or moral courage'.

When it defended the right of one paper to publish the memoirs of a valet in the Royal Household, it did so by asserting that 'English literature is enriched by the writings of Royal servants'.

Whilst it defended the Press against accusations of pornography, it took the view in its first year 'that there is unwholesome exploitation of sex by certain journals'. It therefore positioned itself as a realistic upholder of conventional values, but not so conventional as to discourage the coverage of all morally controversial material in the press. The 1950s and the 1960s were a time of shifting cultural and moral values in the United Kingdom, a period which saw the gradual emergence of more open attitudes to questions of taste and sex in public life. The Press Council addressed these issues in order to defend the press, but in a tone designed to register with a middle-class, educated readership. It clearly did not feel the need to address a wider body of opinion.[28]

As early as its second annual report, for the year 1954–55, the Council claimed, without providing supporting evidence, that it was 'becoming an institution widely accepted in our national life', exercising 'a healthy and much needed influence in relations between the public and the Press'; at the same time it claimed that the Council 'has no complacent belief that its methods are already adequate'. But a year later the tone was altogether more confident: 'Our first and second annual reports described the Press Council as an experiment. It has become an institution. No one expects it to give up.' Not only was it an institution: 'After three years the Council believes it has justified its purpose. It has done something significant to improve the tone of the Press and it has had an increasingly sound and healthy effect on public opinion.'[29]

In 1958, again without providing supporting evidence, the Council claimed that:

the number of complaints of alleged invasion of private life by the Press has, we believe, decreased, possibly because so much attention has been directed to this subject through the Press Council and through the correspondence columns of some of our leading papers ... The Council has been in many ways a restraining and moderating influence and has reason to be proud of its public spirit and fairness in examining the many cases submitted to it.

By 1959, however, Sir Linton Andrews felt he needed to address the charges that the Council was too self-satisfied:

'Complacent' is another term of prejudice occasionally used about my faith in the Press Council, the members of which have spent so many hours in trying to disentangle the truth from censorious complaints and do justice towards all who feel aggrieved by some statement in the Press. If it is complacent to believe in the dominant public spirit of our journalism and in the work of those who try to keep it worthy of its freedom, then I must plead guilty to being complacent. But that is not the word that I should choose for such a faith.[30]

The annual reports of the 1950s have plenty of examples of self-satisfied comments like those quoted above. Linton Andrews was responding to critics who did not share the Council's estimate of its own worth. As the 1950s drew to a close, demands from politicians that the Press Council act to monitor the economic problems in the industry, which were part of the push for a Royal Commission, led to the Council's work coming under closer scrutiny. After the report of the 1961–62 Royal Commission the retiring chairman, George Murray, noted the changed situation. Whilst still expressing approval of the Council's work, his remarks registered a recognition that the Council had to address and respond to a much wider audience than the educated middle classes to whom the remarks of the 1950s were addressed:

What I must now call the 'Old Council' formed a link between the time the Press was subjected to no outside restraints (apart from those provided by the law) and today when the public, whom it serves, will help to keep an eye on it. By its mere survival the Council has accustomed newspaper editors to the existence of a body constantly on the watch to see that they maintain the standards expected of a decent and responsible Press.[31]

Nonetheless, in spite of criticism of the press and the Press Council that continued in the 1960s, the self-satisfied tone persisted. In 1967 the official chronicler of the Council claimed: 'The Press Council is manifestly restoring the relations between the Press and the public which had been so seriously damaged by the events associated with the names Vassall, Profumo, Keeler and Ward. It has virtually dissipated the apprehension its creation caused in newspaper circles.'

In 1969, Lord Devlin was much more emphatic. Referring to George Murray's remarks quoted above he claimed: 'My predecessor in his foreword six years ago claimed no more for the Press Council in 1963 than that, in the *mot* of the Abbe Siyes, it had survived. He put it too modestly. Drawing on his period of office as well as my own, I think I can now claim on behalf of the Council that it has succeeded.'[32]

These comments were premature, coming as they did on the eve the 1970s, a period of inquiries into the Council and of a shift in opinion about self-regulation within the Labour Party. Claims such as Devlin's persisted thereafter, but, because of the intensification of the debate in the 1970s and 1980s, were overshadowed by the institution's need to respond organisationally to the successive bouts of public criticism. Even so, after 1991, the tendency to self-praise, some might argue inordinately complacent self-praise, was evident in the pronouncements from the PCC. In 1995 Lord Wakeham described the establishment of that body as a 'logistical and political triumph' and that it was 'undoubtedly the most effective self-regulatory system in existence'.[33]

Claims such as this served as propaganda for self-regulation; but the need to keep reasserting how successful self-regulation was implied a sense that out there, beyond the four walls of the Council and Commission's offices, were too many people who needed convincing of this fact. The other side of this coin was that the Council was harsh and dismissive of both its critics and critics of the press.

In 1955 the Council attacked critics of the coverage of sex, sport and gambling in the press: 'Like many old-fashioned puritans they would like the lustier and more violent aspects of life to be hidden from the general view'; it also condemned papers that 'declined to answer' a complaint as 'merely childish when it complains that we have not verified the facts'. It mounted a spirited defence of the popular press against an attack in *The Times*, pointing out that accusations of inaccuracy, falsehood and poor writing were long standing and that 'the Press has always been indicted on these counts – and "always" means for at least three centuries'.[34]

In 1956 the Council implied that demands for higher standards were unrealistic:

It has been complained that some papers cast a glamour on law-breakers and tempt the morally immature to believe that plunging into crime can be a thrilling and profitable gamble. In fact, newspapers in general report both crime and punishment, and they show that the way of a transgressor is hard and that crime does not pay. This attitude does not satisfy all critics, but it would be impossible to formulate regulations that would satisfy everybody.

By 1957 Linton Andrews was reacting quite sharply to the level of parliamentary and public criticism. During 1957 the Council had come under scrutiny in a debate in the House of Commons on 17 May, and had been criticised in Richard Hoggart's *The Uses of Literacy* (see Chapter 4). In response, Andrews's tone was highly defensive, sarcastic and belittling:

No one is better aware than members of the Press Council how often Press tendencies excite scornful attack and how often well-meaning mentors blame the Press Council because it has not brought about, presumably by edict, the complete transformation that minority reformers would like to see in the tone and methods of all or some newspapers.

He rejected outright Hoggart's criticism that the Council 'seems readier to indicate the responsibility of readers for the present quantitative and qualitative changes in the Press than to analyse the nature of Press responsibility'. Hoggart was suggesting that the Press Council was laying the blame for poor standards in the press on the demand for that material from the public, rather than addressing the ways in which the press could raise standards. Andrews, however, chose to misinterpret and ridicule the criticism at one and the same time: 'this seems to mean that Mr Hoggart thinks the Press Council believes a newspaper must give the public what it wants regardless of restraint. The Council does not hold this doctrine.'[35] In 1958 Andrews argued that 'Some of our opponents clearly do not take the trouble to read our annual reports ... My view, after much experience, is that many would-be reformers of the Press are in need of the curbs they propose for others, since they themselves are guilty of the offences they allege – wild exaggeration, distortion of the truth, and the unproved assumption that they speak for the nation.'[36]

When, in 1960, the Council responded to attacks on its lack of powers, it retreated into arguing that the main factor underpinning press standards was not the Council's powers or lack of them, but the force of public opinion which 'is in the end decisive. It is the climate of community thought and feeling on religion, morality and taste which determines what is acceptable from platform and pulpit, on stage screen and radio, and in the newspapers.' In defending the craft of the journalist as one in which it was 'less important for a newspaper writer to know the facts himself than to know where to get them', the Council aimed a blow at its parliamentary critics: 'One imagines that Members of both Houses of Parliament discuss topics about which they are not especially well informed. This very debate in the Lords contained a good deal of erroneous and inaccurate information about the Press.'

In 1961, in response to parliamentary demands for the Council to take action and inquire into the economics of the industry, it made its preference for a Royal Commission clear whilst belittling the views of those who had wanted the Press Council to do the job:

If a new inquiry had to be made, a Royal Commission was undoubtedly the best way of doing it. Had it been undertaken by the Press Council, the objection that this was an interested body would at once have been raised, and, indeed would have been justified ... Those who have demanded an inquiry into Press closures by the Press Council appear to have given small thought to what they were asking.[37]

One of the changes brought about by Lord Devlin was a less acerbic tone and a readiness to respond more positively to criticism. In his first annual report he welcomed criticisms of the Council's procedures as they were still at 'a formative stage' and 'criticisms of these points, whether of the substance of any decision or of the way it is arrived at, is immensely valuable'. Nonetheless, whilst welcoming criticism, he was worried that criticism from the press might 'give the wrong impression to the public ... an impression which is perhaps unconsciously emanating from the critic himself – that the Council is an alien body whose activities the Press can survey from a position of detachment'. The public tone may have shifted, but the sensitivity to criticism remained. The attacks on the Council intensified in the 1970s and then, under Lord Shawcross, the aggressive, dismissive style of response returned. Commenting on the critics of the Council, Shawcross made it absolutely clear that the critics were really attacking press freedom:

> The attack on the Press Council ... emanates from those who would like to see it as a stick with which to beat the Press, to secure its conformity to an imposed code of conduct and principle, rather than as an instrument to 'preserve the established freedom of the British Press' ... every attack on the Council, every attempt to destroy its credibility, is directed against the free Press as a whole.

After Shawcross this kind of dismissive approach to criticism, so much a feature of the Council's history to that point, was never quite repeated, except by newspaper leader writers and some MPs. This approach to criticism belied, as did the other aspects of the Council's history and organisation, the fact that Council conceived of itself as an organisation which defended the press against its critics by staving off threats to self-regulation. This underlying defensiveness was embodied in the PCC. In 1991 its 'immediate aims' made it explicit that the Commission was designed to protect the press from threats to self-regulation. Aim (iv) of the PCC in 1991 was: 'To secure support from the public, Parliament and the Press for maintaining self-regulation of the Press by achieving recognition that the Commission is accessible to complainants and independent of Press interests in its judgements.'[38]

In seeking to 'secure public support' for self-regulation the proprietors were in a sense effecting a return to the ideas that underlay the period of Devlin's chairmanship. The PCC showed that sections of the industry had at least recognised what was not the case in earlier periods; that is, that the attitude of the Commission needed to be one of building positively political support for self-regulation, rather than, as had been the case for much of the Council's history, helping to fuel the flames of controversy by complacency and a dismissive attitude to criticism.

Self-regulation in the UK therefore remained a form of proprietors' organisation structured and run to protect the interests of the industry as defined by Press Council from attack. Positive changes in finance and membership were largely achieved as a result of outside pressure. Membership was, like finance, dominated for the first 20 years by the industry; thereafter the Council's lay membership appears to have been chosen to ensure it represented white-collar, middle-class occupations. It also had the aura of respectability that titles and government honours bring to an organisation. The evidence is that the PCC's membership was chosen with a much more focused sense of good political connections, and in that sense was a much less broad-based body than its predecessor. Until the late 1980s Press Council interpreted its aims variously, rarely, in a clear, simple, positive way. Its procedures were, for most of its history, either unclear or slow and burdensome for complainants, more like an obstacle course than anything else. Self-regulation in the UK after 1953 was organised, ultimately, to defend the press, and by extension the proprietors who funded it, against its public and parliamentary critics.

7

Self-Regulation at Work – An Overview

This chapter explores the way self-regulation worked in practice. Self-regulation in this sense meant the Press Council and the Press Complaints Commission promoting actively the interests of the industry as defined by them and dealing with the growing number of complaints they received about press conduct.

Lobbying

The Press Council was at its most positive when monitoring or intervening in the political process, acting in effect as a high-profile extension of the organisations that funded it. In its first year the Council gave support to an industry-wide initiative to lobby the government and promote Private Member's Bills, designed to change the law governing the access of the press to local government meetings. The Council claimed that it was 'the one body that can claim to speak for all sections of the Press, and its influence will be important when, next session, it is hoped, the bill is introduced'. The bill became the Public Bodies (Admission of the Press to Meetings) Bill, which was drafted by the industry and was introduced eventually in August 1956 with all party backing. The bill proceeded no further, due to lack of government support, but the Council continued to support further attempts to pass similar legislation. In 1955 it noted its opposition to an attempt to restrict the publication of the contents of wills, a move it described as 'censorship'. In 1955–56 it lobbied the government successfully and prompted the Home Secretary to remind law officers of their power to, if they wished, prohibit the naming of children who were witnesses in court cases. In April 1957 the Council lobbied the government-appointed Tucker Committee against attempts to hold preliminary hearings in magistrates' courts in private. By the time of the 1961–62 Royal

Commission, whilst not publishing clear accounts of its activities as an adjudicator of complaints, it was well enough organised to submit evidence to the Commission and to respond at length to the Commission's recommendations.[1] In addition, from the outset the Council monitored and responded in its annual reports to parliamentary discussions of the press, a practice which by the early 1960s had become an extensive feature of these documents, covering parliamentary concerns about the Profumo affair, chequebook journalism, criticisms of the Press Council and attempts to reform the libel laws.[2]

By the time of the 1963 reform the Council was well organised as a pressure group for the industry. Devlin, in a sense, made this part of the Council's work more high profile, making sure that the Council was seen to be an important player in the counsels of government. Taking up the baton of the nineteenth-century proprietors, Devlin, 'with the approval of the Press Council' and with the help of the large newspapers, began work on reforming the libel laws. In his view the libel laws 'hampered newspapers ... in their legitimate activities'. The obstacles to reform were lack of parliamentary time and 'the fear, which I believe still to be quite widespread, of Press irresponsibility. It is this fear of irresponsibility that the Press Council endeavours to remove.' During the year 1965–66 the Council persuaded the Minister of Health to take 'action in encouraging hospitals to share in the development of good relations between themselves and the Press'. Later the Council intervened and got the Home Office to issue guidance to clerks to Justices of the Peace on procedure relating to the naming of defendants in open court, and in 1967 it made an extensive intervention on behalf of the press in the wake of controversy over coverage of the Aberfan disaster. By 1967 this role was well enough established to have become a source of pride. In that year the official historian of the Council wrote:

> As the Press Council grew in strength and prestige its recognition was more widely accepted and its authority more firmly established. Complaints in Parliament about the conduct of the Press came to be regarded by the Government as matters for the Council. Government departments and other organisations, official and unofficial, at home and abroad, have come to regard the Council as the authority on matters relating to the Press.[3]

If the Devlin era achieved anything, it was the development of the Council's role as an organised lobby, in the tradition of the employers' organisations of the nineteenth century.

This activity continued through the period of the late 1960s, the Conservative government of 1970–74 and into the more turbulent mid–1970s. The range of lobbying activities in which the Council was involved was, in part, a recognition of the fact that the political process was by then intervening frequently in matters connected with the press. By 1969, at a time when the Council perceived the 'gap between Parliament and the Press' had 'widened considerably', it decided to formalise its lobbying by setting up 'a small Parliamentary Sub-Committee to study pending legislation on behalf of its general purposes committee'. This was because where legislation that might affect the press was concerned it was 'important for the Press to be vigilant and when it knows legislation to be in the offing, to make its representations at the drafting stage'. By 1971 the pace quickened considerably:

> The Press Council, in common with other Press interests, has submitted or is in the process of submitting, written evidence to all three Committees – the Inquiry into the Official Secrets Act 1911 ... chaired by Lord Franks ... the Inquiry into the Law of Defamation in England, Wales and Scotland, under the chairmanship of Mr Justice Faulks; and the Inquiry into the Law of Contempt of Court, under the chairmanship of Lord Justice Phillimore. In addition the Press Council has submitted evidence, both written and oral, to the Committee on Privacy set up by the previous government, under the chairmanship of Mr Kenneth Younger.[4]

This activity also reflected the growing pressures from outside the industry, often exercised through the Labour and trade union movement, for reform; pressures which by the mid-1970s were not welcomed by the Council:

> Relationships between Parliament and the Press when the year 1974 gave way to the year 1975 were at a low ebb. Seldom in the history of Free Speech in Britain have they been any lower. The year 1974 saw two general elections; the establishment of a Royal Commission into the Press; the publication of a 'near green' paper on the Labour Party's outline proposals for reorganising the mass media; and a statement in the Commons by the Prime Minister that the Government was considering legislation affecting the Press in relation to the laws of contempt, defamation, official secrets and privacy.

Nonetheless the Council worked to influence the outcome of the Royal Commission.[5]

The Press Council's attitude to the law could involve agreement to use the law, in appropriate cases, to secure pre-publication censorship; by 1975 the Council had concurred in the then widely accepted view that rape victims should have the benefit of anonymity which could be achieved by 'the trial judge exercising his right in Common Law to order anonymity'. The Council never implied that the use of the law in these kind of cases was a threat to press freedom but it did selectively attack

those proposals for state intervention that it did not like, often charac-
terising them as threats to press freedom.

The Council also, tacitly, endorsed the self-censorship of editors in their
handling of the war in Ireland in the 1970s, between the British
government and the Provisional Irish Republican Army. There was considerable controversy about the role of the British press in reporting the
conflict, which was related to the sensitivity of the British state to critical
coverage of its role in Ireland. A government committee, the 'Gardiner
Committee on Terrorism in Northern Ireland ... suggested that the Press
should closely examine the reconciliation of the reporting of terrorist
activities with the public interest'. In its statement on this the Council
accepted the conventional view that the government was dealing with
'terrorists' and 'criminals' without considering the underlying causes of
the conflict and the complexity of the issues for journalists raised by the
situation:

> The Council is confident that in publishing reports about terrorist
> activities Editors will continue to have regard to overriding consider-
> ations of the public interest, the dangers of glamorising such incidents
> in a way which may encourage support for them and of providing a
> platform for propaganda in favour of criminal or subversive acts.

A year later, using a more liberal tone , the Council was decrying the
delays in the way the government was dealing with the question of law
reform as it affected the press:

> In the year now reviewed [mid-1976–77] there was no joy: only
> continued frustration in the three areas where alleviation of legal
> restraints has long been sought. It is nearly 12 years since JUSTICE
> recommended changes in the laws of contempt, defamation and
> official secrets. The recommendation of Franks (official secrets, 1972),
> Phillimore (contempt, 1974) and Faulks (defamation 1975) still rest
> in Whitehall pigeon holes or dormant in departmental in-trays.[6]

During the 1980s the Council continued to lobby on behalf of the
industry, but increasingly in situations where it was having to defend
itself against initiatives, such as the right to reply and privacy bills, or
the Calcutt Inquiry. As the decade progressed it was also having to deal
with attacks on its authority from important sections of the press which,
in case after case, ignored the 'the unwritten ethical code of newspaper
practice'. The annual reports reflect all of this, with detailed accounts of
inquiries into high-profile cases of unacceptable behaviour by the press.[7]
The extent to which the Council was increasingly concerned with its own
authority by the late 1980s and mindful of the lack of support, even in
the quality press, for its work, was illustrated in the press coverage in

1988 of the Council's appointment of Louis Blom-Cooper as chairman. The outgoing chair, Sir Zelman Cowan, half hurt, half angry, wrote revealingly:

> I cannot think of anything more calculated to damage the morale and authority of a Press Council than the formidable body and volume of criticism recently directed against the existing Press Council. This focused on the procedures and steps to name a new chairman ... It has been a difficult period, damaging to the morale of the Press Council which has the limitations which arise from its voluntary character. It was particularly regrettable that sections of the press which pride themselves on their respect for the standards which the Press Council is required to maintain, should have fallen short of expected standards.[8]

The Council's capacity to lobby successfully on behalf of the industry was therefore weakened as its authority was called into question in the 1980s, both inside and outside the industry.

Codes and declarations

The NUJ had had a code of conduct since the 1930s and the 1947–49 Royal Commission had recommended the development of 'a code in accordance with the highest professional standards' for the whole industry. In the early years the Council stalled, as in 1955 when it argued: 'The Press Council can only hope to establish a code of sound practice slowly by its decisions on the specific cases.' By 1956 it was offering 'suggestions' on how to facilitate relations between the press and royalty, arguing that 'Royal news should at all times be handled with discretion'. But in 1958 it insisted it 'is impossible to lay down in any code of conduct rules' on how to cover royalty.[9]

In 1959 Sir Linton Andrews argued that the Council 'By its decisions ... is building up a code of ethics' but also added that in fact the Council was not building up a code but 'In the absence of a code, the Press Council is slowly building up its case law.' 'Slow' was the operative word. Under Devlin, by 1965, the rejection of a code became quite explicit, and was couched in a mystical appeal to nationalist sentiment:

> Indeed, the British mind has always been allergic to written codes. It prefers to work by means of a general understanding about the sort of conduct that is to be expected. The decisions of the Press Council over the last decade now amount to quite a considerable body of 'case law' and I think that the time has come when some analysis of them would be useful.

This 'analysis' turned out to be Harold Levy's study, published in 1967, which, although detailed, contained such a variety of different cases and rulings that it amounted to a compilation rather than a systematic codification.[10]

The demand for some form of codification was, in effect, set to one side. In its place came a number of sonorous declarations of principle. In November 1966 the Council issued a declaration on payments to witnesses, but carefully qualified its import by saying: 'No code can cover every case. Satisfactory observance of the principles must depend upon the discretion and sense of responsibility of editors and newspaper proprietors.' It extended the declaration in 1975 to allow for indirect payment to witnesses, and again in 1983 to include payments to associates of criminals. In 1976, during the politically sensitive period when the Royal Commission was taking evidence, it issued a declaration on privacy, which allowed for publication of private information 'if there is a legitimate public interest overriding the right of privacy'. Finally, in 1984, it issued another declaration, this time covering the area of financial journalism.[11]

These were clearly inadequate as guides for the public on what constituted the 'unwritten ethical code', let alone for journalists, as they were selective in their focus and few and far between. The longest-standing one, on payments to people involved in trials, was ignored in the 1960s and 1980s when it suited editors. The 1974–77 Royal Commission, echoing its predecessor in the 1940s, was clearly not convinced that declarations were adequate, and so recommended the Council develop a code of behaviour. In response to this the *Financial Times* thought it 'questionable whether the idea of a written code of correct behaviour is either desirable or practical. It would not be easy to base a useful code on past adjudications if these are as arbitrary as the Commission alleges.' The Press Council agreed with this, refusing to implement a code because it 'would be too rigid in operation and lead to evasions of the spirit of the rules by those who adhered to its letter'.

The code would also 'need frequent amendment' and the Council wanted to 'remain free to adjudicate on new cases which involve issues not previously covered'. When, in 1985, the Council finally published a guide to its rulings, the argument for the consistency stemming from a code was rejected, as was the quasi-legalistic view of Council practice evolving around precedent that had been used in earlier presentations of the argument:

the primary concern of the Council is to make its decisions in the light of contemporary opinion ... its members are not appointed to perform the legalistic function of applying a code to the various issues laid before them but are expected to reflect current views on ethical issues, amounting in aggregate ... to an expression of the climate of public opinion. Certainly the Council takes account of precedent but it is not bound by it.[12]

This attitude did not last long. The relative force of political pressure in the late 1980s, compared to the mid- to late 1970s can, in part, be judged by the fact that the Royal Commission of 1974–77 could not make the Council implement a code, but the sequence of Private Member's Bills and the existence of the Calcutt Inquiry did. The editors adopted their own code on 27 November 1989 and the Press Council issued another on 13 March 1990. The fact that two codes were produced testified to the extent of the lack of confidence that existed by then between the Council and editors. As the chairman, Louis Blom-Cooper, argued, it also had deeper roots:

> the tide of public opinion was running fast towards an articulation of ethical principles for journalists and editors, as it has done in respect of the professions and other occupational groups. The fact that the national newspaper editors themselves felt impelled to enunciate on 27 November 1989 ... a less ample code than the Council is proffering is testimony itself to the recognition of that public demand.

Given that the Council had spent 36 years without a code, resisting all the way, it was significant that the PCC should be founded principally to administer the industry's code of practice. It was, in fact, the employers' code, as the NUJ was not party to its creation. This was a realisation, on the part of the industry, that it could no longer resist calls for a code of practice, especially as this had been a central part of the proposal made in the Calcutt Report.[13] In effect the employers avoided having a code, in spite of repeated recommendations from official inquiries, until the political situation made it virtually impossible for them to do so.

Privacy

The Council and the PCC waged a much more successful campaign against the introduction of legislation protecting privacy. Early on, the Council implied that, because invasions of privacy were not common, the problem was not that serious. For example in 1954 it asserted that 'The alleged invasion of private life is often mentioned in a general way by speakers with a desire to censure the Press, but exceedingly few specific cases have come before the Council.'

It somewhat timidly suggested that newspapers should moderate intrusions into privacy by agreeing on 'methods to cut down the number of reporters putting their questions to a harassed victim', and by 1955 it was negotiating with the British Medical Association over press practice in hospitals. The troubles between the press and royalty were, in 1956, put down to the problem of where to draw the line between the public and private world of the royals. But the Press Secretariat at Buckingham Palace was also blamed:

> The comment is sometimes heard from news editors that the Secretariat neither understands nor gives the news they want, or the necessary guidance on what is, or is not, likely to become news. The Council records this with regret, but it would be lacking in candour if it pretended that dealings between the Press and the Press Department in the Royal Household were always happy or harmonious.

The problem of the press and royalty was never permanently resolved by the Council or its successor the PCC, and it flared up again in the 1960s, 1980s and 1990s.[14]

At the end of the 1950s the Council was still able to minimise the general problem. By 1958 it believed it had helped provide a deterrent to invasions of privacy and that 'the number of complaints of alleged invasion of private life by the Press has, we believe, decreased'. It also chose to belittle those who demanded redress for breaches of privacy by implying they had misunderstood the nature of the public and that, anyway, a refusal to answer questions about your private life was in itself, suspicious:

> It has been contended that damages should be recoverable at law when a person's privacy has been invaded by newspaper representatives. The suggestion seems completely unnecessary, since it calls up a picture of the homes of Britain inhabited by a sensitive, timorous race of people who dread the reporter's knock on the door, and that picture is false. Those who resent polite inquiries have often something to hide. It might well be a danger to the public to wrench from the Press those powers of investigation which have made it so good a watchdog for the public safety.[15]

At this point the Council seemed unshaken by the idea that criticisms of invasions of privacy could result in legislation. During the 1960s, however, attempts by Lord Mancroft, Alex Lyon MP and Brian Walden MP to get something done about privacy changed the situation. The Council had to respond to real pressure for change.

In 1970 its response to Brian Walden's bill was sharp: 'Although it had been frequently said in preliminary discussion by its supporters, before the bill was published, that there was no intention on the part of its sponsors to "pick on" the Press, it was soon clear that this was the effect.' It urged caution and 'a proper and wide inquiry by some committee of high calibre set up by the Government'. This committee, the Younger Committee, received evidence from the Council in which it stressed the importance of striking the correct balance between public and private rights where privacy was concerned. But it also used the same argument it was to use against the right of reply, equating legislation on privacy with the threat of state interference with press freedom: 'There is an additional danger. A time when intrusion by the State and its agencies into the private life of the individual is steadily increasing under the guise of serving the public interest is not the time to diminish the independent public scrutiny that only a free, vigorous and confident Press can ensure.'[16]

In spite of the genuine problems posed by legislation on privacy, the Council still felt it needed to adopt an argumentative strategy designed to link a much canvassed reform, based on real concerns about the rights of individuals to privacy with the idea that reformers might have sinister designs on press freedom.

Along with demands for a right of reply, it was the pressure for privacy legislation to control press intrusions into private lives that triggered the demise of the Press Council. Scandalous examples in the early 1980s, including allegations linking the suicide of one person with press harassment and intrusions into the privacy of grieving parents, one of whom was the parent of the victim of a serial murderer, set the tone for what followed. We touch on other examples in Chapters 8, 9 and 10. After Calcutt had reported, the proprietors, in an effort to stave off legislation, called for the Press Council to dissolve itself in September 1990. The Council, in its final annual report, criticised Calcutt's proposals for legislation on privacy, using the same kind of argument it had used in evidence to the Younger Committee 18 years earlier:

It is not necessary to approve of any example of the conduct in question to be profoundly worried at the close definition which such penal laws would demand, and at the likelihood that they would sooner or later be put to a use not envisaged by the Calcutt Committee, unlikely to be envisaged by parliament in enacting them, and resulting in a journalist – very likely the wrong journalist – being sent to prison.[17]

The force of this argument was strong, but the fact that the Press Council had had 37 years in which to take action that both supported legitimate investigative journalism and protected the aspirations of ordinary citizens to freedom from harassment and invasion of privacy made it an essentially negative posture.

Right of reply

From the early years the Council asserted its willingness 'to intervene whenever a complainant thinks a newspaper has treated him badly and he has not obtained redress'. In an early adjudication it asserted the necessity of providing a visible right to correction:

> It should be accepted as a journalistic principle that where a mis-statement of fact is made and a person or group of persons likely to suffer by it calls the editor's attention to it there should be a frank correction and apology on a page where the correction and apology are likely to be seen by those who read the original mis-statement.[18]

This did not mean, however, that the complainant had a right to have a correction displayed with the same prominence as the original. In keeping with the Council's tendency to allow itself and its editors the maximum latitude of discretion, it refused to develop a clear rule on this. In 1976 it was asserting: 'There is no rule that the adjudications of the Press Council must be published on the same page or given identical prominence.'[19]

This approach was a way of protecting the autonomy of editors, and by implication proprietors, to have the final say in what went into newspapers. Editors and the Press Council resisted and criticised attempts by printers and journalists to undermine or encroach on their power by equating their autonomy with the maintenance of press freedom. In 1971 the Council condemned industrial action in the industry as 'inter-ference with the production of newspapers by workers in circumstance amounting to censorship'. In January 1977 print unions at *The Times* stopped production in protest at an article that criticised them. The Council pointed to the existence of its own complaints machinery as an alternative, and condemned the action: 'What they in fact did was censorship which is totally unacceptable in a country which enjoys freedom of expression and freedom of the Press.'

It also condemned as 'blatant and inexcusable instances of press censorship' action by printers at the *Observer* and the *Sun* in support of a group of workers involved in the Grunwick dispute over union recognition in London. This kind of action not only challenged the authority of the Press Council, it also called into question the right of editors and proprietors to control content and explicitly challenged the assumption that workers had no right to decide what went into the product they made. In the late 1970s these kinds of challenges made editors worried. In June 1977 the editor of the *Guardian*, Peter Preston, was at a reception in the United States Embassy in London, where he met the government minister Tony Benn. Benn recorded how Preston was:

> tortured by the increasing pressure on him from the trade unions, whenever they think the paper is being unfair, as for example in the Grunwick case. I said, 'Don't you think it would be a good idea if complaints were channelled through the printers?' That idea absolutely

terrified him. I continued, 'Well, I would never go to the Press Council or the courts in these matters. Surely it would be better to discuss it with the printers.' 'Oh, it would interfere with editorial freedom.'[20]

The future fierce opposition to a statutory right of reply owed a good deal to this assumption by editors and proprietors that their control over content was the same thing as 'freedom' of the press.

When during the early 1980s the pressures for an industrial right of reply were combined with the legislative initiatives of Frank Allaun, the Council remained implacably opposed to both. In 1982 it condemned the action taken by print workers in support of workers in the National Health Service, and condemned the way the train workers' union, ASLEF, tried to prevent the distribution of the two Murdoch-owned papers, the Sun and *The Times*: 'over the *Sun* splashing allegations about "Aslef men paid as they drink, sleep and disco" ... The Press Council announced that the right answer to unpalatable reporting and hostile comment could never be the blacking of papers by those who distributed them.'

To the legislative challenge posed by Frank Allaun in 1983, it took a more ameliorative line. This time it attacked the bill but also indicated a willingness to acknowledge that its own procedures had been inadequate:

> The Press Council stressed that newspapers had an obligation to give those they attacked an opportunity to respond but opposed the bill as undesirable and impracticable. It was concerned to distinguish between inaccuracy and distortion. The Council approved a new 'fast track' procedure to give a small panel power to give speedy rulings in cases based on straightforward inaccuracy.[21]

With the right of reply established as 'official Labour Party policy' the Council discussed the issue in its 1985 report. If a right of reply became statutory, it argued, then 'it is at least arguable that the Council's major function in hearing complaints and publishing adjudications would become redundant'. The Council had introduced a 'fast track' procedure which had 'been virtually unused'. It then went on to combine an attack on MPs with an admission that some form of statutory redress was potentially acceptable:

> It is regrettable that, despite the publicity given to this aspect of the Press Council's work – a development introduced for the express purpose of allaying criticism that it could not act swiftly – MPs display a remarkable ignorance. They continue to urge the statutory estab-lishment of a system to give people immediate aid in securing published corrections to published errors. That is precisely what the Council's 'fast track' procedure provides.

In fact the press could hardly object to a statutory right of correction. A statutory right of reply is a very different matter, for it would involve opinion rather than fact.[22]

By the time of the 1987 bills on privacy (William Cash) and right of reply (Ann Clwyd) the Council recognised that 'there seems to be increasing appeal in such measures to politicians of all parties'. The appointment of Louis Blom-Cooper as chairman in 1988 reflected a willingness to take the demand for a right of reply and the criticisms of press behaviour more seriously. While defending the press and the Press Council from attacks, Blom-Cooper recognised that support for Tony Worthington's bill had its roots in press behaviour 'some of it incontestably outrageous'. This did not, however, mean translating the idea expressed in 1985 that the press could 'hardly object to a statutory right of correction' into support for such a statutory measure. The outcome was for the Council, in the tradition of previous responses, to urge reform on the industry; out of this process came an internal review, the creation of in-house ombudsmen for individual papers and the production of two codes of practice, one by the editors and one by the Council.[23]

Throughout its history the Press Council refused to support either a voluntarily policed, but enforceable, obligation on papers to give a right of reply, or a statutory right of reply. It came near to supporting a statutory right to correction in 1985, and, in so doing, implicitly conceded that such a measure was not, in principle, a threat to press freedom, or unworkable. Yet it neither followed this up, nor was it able to rebuff the torrent of political criticism that had been unleashed during the 1980s. The position adopted by the PCC in 1991 was, in effect, no different to the one held by the Council at its demise: 'Whenever it is recognised that a significant inaccuracy, misleading statement or distorted report has been published, it should be corrected promptly and with due prominence.'

Like its predecessor, the PCC failed to address the problem of enforcement, for in the event of an unfavourable adjudication by the PCC the offending publication had nothing to fear, as it was only 'duty bound to print the adjudication ... in full and with due prominence'.[24]

Adjudications

The annual reports of the Council and the PCC give only a selective account of these bodies' activities. From 1953 until 1961 these reports made no attempt to record the total number of cases dealt with and published only selective examples of those considered with no accompanying criteria for their inclusion. From 1961 until 1990 the reports carried more systematically presented information in terms of the numbers of cases dealt with, but did not provide any equally clear tabulation of the types of complaints that were made. This was consistent with the Council's refusal to give system to its work through the use of a code of practice. The vagueness and minimalism of Council practice in the analysis of its adjudications accorded with its attitude to editors, giving them the maximum latitude in determining what went into their publications, and allowed the Council considerable leeway when making adjudications. The PCC, because it uses a code, has been able to categorise the types of complaints it receives (see Table 7.6 below).

The reports of these two bodies have used a range of different terms to describe the process of categorisation, terms that usually affected the description of why complaints did not reach the stage of adjudication. Also, the figures for the complaints dealt with by the Council were not consistently presented, and at times were not consistent from year to year. Some illustration of these points is provided in the notes to the tables in this chapter. Using the annual reports to construct a picture of trends in the adjudication process is therefore not an easy exercise. Nonetheless the figures presented here provide us with an indication of just what happened when the Council and its successor handled complaints from the public.

In the 1950s the Council did not see itself as having any obligation to record the full extent of its work in this area. The selection of cases published in these reports appears to have been relatively arbitrary, depending on what the Council deemed to be significant at the time of compilation. Table 7.1 provides a summary of the adjudications recorded in the annual reports for the period 1953–61.

The reports did not present clear statistics on the numbers of cases processed. Table 7.1 reflects those recorded as having been processed.

Table 7.1   Numbers of adjudications recorded in Press Council Annual Reports 1953–61

Year	Total of cases reported in Annual Report	Not adjudicated	Adjudicated	Complaints upheld	Complaints rejected
1953–54	16	–	16	9	7
1954–55	26	–	26	12	14
1955–56	15	–	15	10	5
1956–57	9	1	8	7	1
1957–58	11	–	11	8	3
1958–59	17	–	17	9	8
1959–60	17	1	16	10	6
1960–61	28	1	27	15	12
Totals	139	3	136	80	56

Table 7.2   Number of adjudications recorded in Press Council Annual Reports 1961–90

Year	Total	Withdrawn or not pursued	Disallowed	Conciliated	Total adjudicated	Upheld	Rejected
61–62	140	67	15	–	58	35	23
62–63	215	75	75	–	65	26	39
63–64	273	103	84	–	86	39	47
64–65	314	149	62	–	103	49	54
65–66	429	192	158	–	79	41	38
66–67	412	223	107	–	82	35	46
67–68	384	220	76	–	88	35	53
68–69	391	277	53	–	61	25	36
69–70	492	394	53	–	45	20	25
70–71	370	267	65	–	38	13	25
71–72	398	299	52	–	47	20	27
72–73	413	324	55	–	34	17	17
73–74	376	267	68	–	41	14	27
74–75	425	296	74	–	55	32	23
75–76	507	353	75	–	79	34	45
76–77	665	480	117	–	68	30	38
77–78	1023	693	208	24	98	45	53
1979	542	364	100	17	61	27	34
1980	753	538	137	14.5	63.5	32	31.5
1981	753	538	137	14.5	63.5	32	31.5
1982	702	487	122	12	81	46	35
1983	979	678	148	29	124	62	62
1984	912	617	142	20	133	72	61
1985	1107	752	188	28	139	79	60
1986	1162	686	321	37	118	57	61
1987	1269	712	352	46	159	80	79
1988	1377	921	276	36	144	60	84
1989	1479	960	332	45	142	72	70
1990	1639	959	478	28	174	92	82

Notes

The 'Total' column reflects cases dealt with in that year and does not include cases received but held over to following year. The figures and the categories used in the reports are not always clearly presented or consistent over time. This, and other tables, have been adjusted in places, as described here, to account for this.

The 1961–62 figures have been adjusted to account for the fact that the number of complaints received for adjudication is five less than the number of adjudications. This is because some complaints related to a number of papers, which were then disaggregated for adjudication.

1966–67. In this year, of the 82 adjudications, the Council described one as 'Unclassified', hence the totals in the 'Upheld' and 'Rejected' columns do not add up to 82.

1970–71. The Council said that a postal strike in that year affected the number of complaints it received and accounted for the drop in the total.

Notes to Table 7.2 continued

The 'Disallowed' columns for 1972–73 and 1973–74 each contain one case that the Council declined to adjudicate, which have been classified as disallowed.

The 1973–74 annual report failed to deduct the 15 cases carried forward from the previous year when calculating its totals; this has been taken into account.

The 1977–78 annual report covered an 18-month period, from July 1977 to December 1978. This was in order to bring the PC's report into line with the calendar year. The totals for this year, and the percentages in Table 7.3 reflect this.

Delays in publication of annual reports led to the 1980 and 1981 reports being published in one volume, which did not disaggregate the figures for each year. The total for the two years has therefore been halved to produce an annual figure. Also, the number of cases adjudicated is given as 127, but the number of cases for adjudication after the 1378 non-adjudicated cases are subtracted from the 1506 cases dealt with in that year is 128. One case has been added to the 'Withdrawn' category so as to round off the figures.

From 1986 onwards the Council sub-divided the 'Disallowed' category to include one called 'Not in Press Council ambit'. As this was effectively disallowing the complaint, this sub-division has not been followed here. Also the 'Withdrawn/Not pursued' category was divided into 'Withdrawn' and 'Not pursued', but, again, this has not been followed here as it does not significantly alter the nature of the material tabulated here. In addition an 'Upheld in part' category was introduced, but this has not been shown in order to maintain consistency of presentation of the figures.

In P&P 34th AR 1987, p. 15, the figures do not add up. The total of 'Disallowed' should be 1111 not 1110. Here the 1110 figure has been retained, and the category of 'Not pursued' reduced by one from 684 to 683, to round off the figures.

Where a case has been upheld in part it has been counted as 'Upheld', which is consistent with later practice by the Council. In its first eight years the Council's reports covered only 139 cases. Of these, 80, or about 58 per cent, of the total were complaints that were upheld. As the later tables show, this rate was slightly higher than that for complaints that went to adjudication and were upheld between 1961 and 1990. It was much higher than subsequent figures for cases upheld as a percentage of all cases dealt with. These figures tell us little, except that the early Council, as has been shown in other instances, was not too worried about how it presented its handling of complaints, and was anyway, as is clear from its constitution, not obliged to consider complaints.

Tables 7.2 and 7.3 are based on the annual reports from 1961 until 1990 and reflect the fact that the advent of the Shawcross Commission forced the Council to take its role in relation to handling complaints much more seriously than it had done so before. They show a number of things. Firstly, the number of cases dealt with in each year increased from 140 in 1961–62 to 1639 in 1990. This increase was slow, around, on average, 51 cases per year over a 29-year period, with no clear pattern of annual increases until the mid–1970s when political debate about the press and the Council became more intense. The figures, as do those for the PCC in Table 7.4, suggest a growing awareness on the part of the public of the complaints machinery.

The categories of 'Withdrawn', 'Not pursued', or 'Disallowed' absorbed the vast majority of complaints after 1961, with the number of cases which reached adjudication always remaining a very small proportion of the total number of cases dealt with. During the period 1975–90 the percentage of all cases dealt with that were not adjudicated on never fell below 83 per cent. Under Lord Devlin the percentage of all cases dealt with that reached adjudication hovered between 15 and 23 per cent. Thereafter this figure remained in a range of between 15.58 and 8 per cent. Thus the Press Council became more efficient, over time, in preventing cases reaching the adjudication stage, in spite of the increase in the numbers of complaints dealt with.

Looked at in terms of cases upheld as a percentage of all cases dealt with, the figures are startling. Under Devlin the highest figure was 15.61 per cent. Thereafter it was always well below 10 per cent, with most figures in the 4–6 per cent range. A complainant had a better chance of having a case upheld in 1964–65 than in 1989–90.

But a complainant also had a far better chance of having a complaint upheld under the Press Council than under the PCC – see Table 7.5. In fact the PCC was much better at rejecting complaints than the Council. Between 1995 and 1998 the percentage of all cases dealt with that were not adjudicated never fell below 96 per cent! Interestingly, the percentage of all cases that reached adjudication under the Council tended to show increases during times of heightened political controversy about self-regulation, such as 1975–76, 1983–84, 1987 and 1990. For the PCC in its first year the percentage of cases reaching adjudication was 6.68 per cent; but as the political pressure subsided in the 1990s this figure dropped to between 2 and 3 per cent.

The Council and the PCC became efficient mechanisms for rejecting complaints. It might be argued that cases which were withdrawn, disallowed, not pursued or conciliated were not, strictly speaking, rejected and that the low percentage of cases adjudicated was evidence of success in resolving complaints prior to adjudication. But the Council and the PCC never published in their annual reports even summary details of the cases under these headings nor the criteria underlying the action taken, and in the absence of a considered, clearly presented analysis of this information, it is reasonable to classify these kinds of cases as having been, in effect, rejected. After 1991 the PCC did publish summary details of the cases it failed to adjudicate in its *Report* series, published at intervals during the year. The PCC's annual reports, however, carried only cursory statistical summary of these cases. For this information to be of value to the public, the reasons for rejection needed to be grouped under headings, totalled and tabulated. This kind of information would then have provided a much more transparent picture of the PCC's reasoning when it rejected cases for adjudication.

Until 1978 the Council did not publish in its annual reports the number of cases conciliated. But the percentage of cases conciliated under the Council never reached more than 4 per cent of all the cases

Table 7.3   Analysis of Press Council adjudications in Press Council Reports 1961–90

Year	Upheld as % of total	Upheld as % of adjudications	Rejected as % of total	Rejected as % adjudications	Concilated as % of total	Cases not adjudicated as % of total	Cases adjudicated as % of total
61–62	25	60.35	16.43	39.65	—	58.57	41.43
62–63	12.09	40	18.14	60	—	69.77	30.23
63–64	14.29	45.35	17.22	54.65	—	68.5	31.5
64–65	15.61	47.57	17.2	52.43	—	67.2	32.8
65–66	9.56	51.9	8.86	48.1	—	81.58	18.42
66–67	8.5	42.68	11.17	56.1	—	80.1	19.9
67–68	9.12	39.77	13.8	60.23	—	77.08	22.92
68–69	6.39	40.98	9.21	59.02	—	84.4	15.6
69–70	4.07	44.44	5.08	55.56	—	90.85	9.15
70–71	3.51	34.21	6.76	65.79	—	89.73	10.27
71–72	5.03	42.56	6.78	57.44	—	88.19	11.81
72–73	4.12	50	4.12	50	—	91.77	8.23
73–74	3.72	34.15	7.18	65.85	—	89.1	10.9
74–75	7.53	58.18	5.41	41.82	—	87.06	12.94
75–76	6.71	43.04	8.88	56.96	—	84.42	15.58
76–77	4.51	44.12	5.71	55.88	—	89.77	10.23
77–78	4.4	45.92	5.18	54.08	2.35	88.07	9.58
1979	4.98	44.26	6.27	55.74	3.14	85.61	11.25
1980	4.25	50.39	4.18	49.61	1.93	89.64	8.43

1981	4.25	50.39	4.18	49.61	1.93	89.64	8.43
1982	6.55	56.79	4.99	43.21	1.71	86.75	11.54
1983	6.33	50	6.33	50	2.96	84.37	12.67
1984	7.89	54.14	6.69	45.86	2.2	83.22	14.58
1985	7.14	56.83	5.42	43.17	2.53	84.91	12.56
1986	4.91	48.31	5.25	51.69	3.18	86.66	10.16
1987	6.3	50.31	6.23	49.69	3.63	83.85	12.52
1988	4.36	41.67	6.1	58.33	2.61	86.93	10.46
1989	4.87	50.7	4.73	49.3	3.04	87.36	9.6
1990	5.61	52.87	5.00	47.13	1.71	87.68	10.61

Table 7.4 Adjudications of Press Complaints Commission – a sample[1]

Year	Total	Withdrawn or not pursued	Disallowed	Conciliated	Total adjudicated	Upheld	Rejected
1991	1363	153	732	387	91	43	48
1992/1993	3177	436	2169	419	153	61	92
1995	2470	413	1994	–	63	28	35
1996	2752	393	2278	–	81	27	54
1997	2631	614	1935	–	82	34	48
1998	2285	546	1662	–	77	36	41

1. Sources as in Table 7.5.

Notes
The 'Withdrawn' category listed here incorporates the 1991 reports category of 'Not pursued'. Under 'Disallowed' these figures include the PCC categories of outside remit, unjustifiable delay, no prima facie breach of code, and third party complaints. In the 1995 report the Commission amalgamated its 'Withdrawn', and 'Resolved' categories. This has been followed here. In this report, pages 6–7, there is a discrepancy of 9 between the figures for the total of cases processed (2479) and the total of the figures in each category (2470). The latter figure has been used here.

The 1996 report does not list the 271 cases carried over to 1997. The 1997 report gives 2944 complaints 'dealt with'. But the total of cases processed in the year adds up to 2631. The latter figure is used here.

Table 7.5   *Analysis of Press Complaints Commission adjudications – a sample*[1]

Year	Upheld as % of total	Upheld as % of adjudications	Rejected as % of total	Rejected as % of adjudications	Conciliated as % of total	Cases not adjudicated as % of total	Cases adjudicated as % of total
1991	3.15	47.25	3.52	52.75	28.39	64.93	6.68
1992/1993	1.92	39.87	2.9	60.13	13.19	81.99	4.82
1995	1.13	44.44	1.42	55.56	–	97.45	2.55
1996	0.98	33.33	1.96	66.66	–	97.06	2.94
1997	1.29	41.46	1.82	58.54	–	96.88	3.12
1998	1.56	46.75	1.79	53.25	–	96.63	3.37

1. Sources are all from the PCC: *First Annual Report 1991*; *Press Complaints Commission Review* (London: PCC, 1994); *Annual Report 1995* (London: PCC, nd); http://www.pcc.org.uk/annual/96/review.htm; http://www.pcc.org.uk/annual/97.htm; *Reports* (London: 1998; nos. 41–4).

dealt with; under the PCC this category was dropped from the figures presented in annual reports. Had the Council or the PCC been committed to show the different ways in which complainants received satisfaction, this would have been reflected more fully in their annual reports, both statistically and qualitatively. Once the PCC began publishing statistics of the type of complaints (Table 7.6), it became evident that the main kind of complaint was about inaccuracy; the one area where the Council had in 1985 conceded there was possibly a case for statutory action and the subject of the Soley bill. It was never, however, possible to tell exactly how many of the cases sent to the Press Council that did not reach adjudication were complaints about accuracy, or any other topic, and the annual reports of the PCC did not provide this information either. In essence the picture provided by the statistics given in the annual reports of the Council and the PCC remained woefully deficient in relevant detail.

The way the Council simply got better at rejecting cases suggests it became more and more selective over time; more, not less inclined, to reject cases before adjudication. Indeed the obstacles and lack of clarity

Table 7.6   Types of complaints as a percentage of all complaints investigated by the PCC – a sample[1]

Clause	1991–93	1995	1996	1997
1. Accuracy	73	68.9	54.5	52.9
2. Reply	1.9	3.3	3.6	3.6
3. Comment	1.6	2.2	10.5	12.8
4. Privacy	8.7	12.4	14.9	13
5. Listening Devices	0	0.9	0.3	0.1
6. Hospitals	1.2	0.7	0.1	0.3
7. Misrepresentation	1.6	2.9	2.9	2.4
8. Harassment	0.4	4	2.3	3
9. Payment	1.4	0	0.2	0.2
10. Grief	2.8	1.4	1.3	2
11. Relatives	2.9	0.3	0.3	0.6
12. Interviewing Children	0.7	0.2	1	1
13. Children in Sex Cases	0.4	0.9	0.8	0.3
14. Victims of Crime	3.2	0	0.2	0.3
15. Discrimination	0.1	1.7	6.8	6.2
16. Financial Journalism	0.1	0	0.1	0.2
17. Confidential Sources	0	0.2	0.2	0.1

1. Sources are all from the PCC: *Press Complaints Commission Review; Annual Report 1995*; http://www.pcc.org.uk/annual/96/review.htm; http://www.pcc.org.uk/annual/97.htm The 1997 figures add up to 99% in the original.

in the complaints procedure, as discussed in Chapter 6, and as carefully documented in the 1983 Robertson Report,[25] adds to the evidence here that, as far as complaints from the public were concerned, self-regulation became an elaborate mechanism designed to avoid systematic consideration of cases brought by the public.

Holding the line

The evidence therefore points strongly in one direction. The Council did lobby to improve the rights of the press on question of access to local government, libel, official secrets and other questions relating to the rights of journalists to acquire information. The Council issued adjudications that gave some, albeit unsystematic, substance to the unwritten code of newspaper ethics it proclaimed to be at the heart of its complaints procedure, and it did produce some compilations of its rulings as well as a few declarations of principle. The PCC in this respect adopted a code of practice produced by the industry, and both organisations, in one way or another, managed an increasing number of public complaints, which was in turn a reflection of an increasing public awareness of both its right to complain, and of the existence of the self-regulatory mechanism.

The Council's lobbying was an extension of the kind of lobbying done by the proprietors' organisations that funded it: essentially self-interested. The Council's response to the demand for a code of practice was to resist it, for 36 years; it took a similarly negative attitude to right of reply and privacy legislation and never offered anything that allayed successfully the concerns underlying the demands for these measures. The Council and the PCC, refused, again and again, to impose effective sanctions on the industry it was supposed to regulate. The Council's attitude to government intervention was selective: supporting measures that involved pre-publication censorship, be it statutory or voluntary, when it so pleased, and unleashing a torrent of emotive rhetoric about the threat to press freedom proposed by measures it did not like. It sought to defuse pressure for reform by piecemeal measures. The PCC's aims were essentially defensive: to use the complaints procedure as a device to 'secure support from the public, parliament and the Press for maintaining self-regulation'.[26]

A critical evaluation of the evidence therefore provides powerful support for the view that self-regulation in the UK was not a positive institution designed to promote high standards, deal effectively with complaints and protect press freedom. It was there to defend the proprietors, who funded it, from the encroachments of politicians, journalists and members of the public who wanted the press to be more responsible than the owners were prepared to allow. In so doing, the proprietors missed a major opportunity to raise standards in the press.

PART II

Cases and Issues

Clive Soley

The Problem of Accuracy in the UK Press in the 1980s and 1990s

Accuracy: why is it so important?

Newspapers provide readers with information about the world. It is therefore important that the information in newspapers is accurate, in so far as this is reasonably possible, because accurate information is a pre-requisite for arriving at informed political and social judgements. The accurate reporting of information is important also because of the need to protect the public from the damaging consequences of the dissemination of inaccurate information. Although differences exist in academic circles about the extent of media influence and the exact mechanisms whereby information in the media influences people, there is a strong body of opinion that considers that the media have a range of effects on beliefs and opinions.[1]

The law in the UK recognises the role of accuracy in the decision-making process. For example, the Sale of Goods Act 1979 protects the customer from being misled by traders. A description of goods has to be accurate because the sale of 'corrupted' goods can be dangerous.[2] The need for accuracy has also been enshrined in the statutory framework under which broadcasters work. The Broadcasting Act 1990 required the Independent Television Commission, the body that licenses commercial television, satellite and cable services in the UK, to ensure that news is 'presented with due accuracy and impartiality'.[3]

So there is, and has been for many years, a consensus within and without the media industries that the accurate reporting of information is important to the healthy exercise of decision-making in society. This consensus has been embodied in the codes of practice of the Advertising Standards Association (ASA), the NUJ[4] and, in the 1990s, of the Press Complaints Commission. The ASA in its British Code of Advertising

Practice, 1988, declared that 'no advertisement, whether by inaccuracy, ambiguity, exaggeration, omission or otherwise, should mislead consumers'.[5] In 1992 the NUJ's Code of Conduct asserted that a journalist 'shall strive to ensure that the information s/he disseminates is fair and accurate, avoid the expression of comment and conjecture as established fact, and falsification by distortion, selection or misrepresentation'.[6] By 1997 the Press Complaints Commission's Code of Practice likewise asserted that 'Newspapers and periodicals should take care not to publish inaccurate, misleading or distorted material.'[7]

The general acceptance of the desirability of accuracy in the media does not involve advocating that pre-publication censorship by the state is needed to enforce accuracy. Nor does it imply that newspapers should not express their opinions on any topic they choose. The point we illustrate in this chapter is that self-regulation, in the form of the Press Council and the PCC, was an inadequate tool for dealing with the problems that arose from inaccurate reporting in the 1980s and 1990s.

Labour councils and the press

Inaccurate reporting in the tabloid press has been, at times, politically motivated. The tabloid press in the UK during the 1980s was generally highly critical of the Labour Party and of initiatives by Labour-controlled local authorities to promote equal opportunities.[8] Inaccurate reporting was used during these years in an attempt to discredit these initiatives.

On 15 February 1986 the *Daily Star* carried a story claiming that Hackney Council had banned the nursery rhyme 'Baa Baa, Black Sheep' from use in educational environments on the grounds that it was racist. The paper did not quote an authoritative source, but instead cited an unnamed spokesman as saying that the singing of the nursery rhyme should be discouraged.[9] On 20 February the *Sun* took up the story, headlining it 'Lefties Baa Black Sheep'. The council asserted that the story was inaccurate.[10]

The basic idea behind the story was, however, picked up and used against another Labour-controlled council later in the year. In the *Daily Mail* of 9 October 1986, under the headline 'Baa baa, green (yes, green) sheep', the paper claimed that Haringey Council had insisted that children sing 'green sheep' instead of 'black'. They also claimed that playgroup leaders had been ordered to attend a racism awareness course. In this case the source of the story was an anonymous playgroup leader.

A study of these stories was made by academics based at Goldsmith's College, at the University of London. On the *Daily Mail* story about Haringey Council they found that 'the facts of the story, slow to come out and never reproduced outside the black press, were that the course had been requested by playgroup leaders in Haringey, that attendance was not compulsory and that the Council had issued no such ban. It remains unclear as to whether the rhyme was even mentioned.' This was similar to their findings on the accuracy of other stories about so called 'loony left' Councils: 'Our conclusion is that not one of these stories is accurate. A few appeared to have been conjured out of thin air; the rest, although loosely connected with some basis of fact, have got important details wrong and are misleading.'[11]

Inaccuracies were therefore, at times, seemingly deliberately printed to generate misinformation about the actions of democratically elected local authorities during the 1980s.

Race and the press complaints commission – third party complaints

The PCC was established in 1991. Unlike its predecessor, the Press Council, the PCC was for most of the 1990s reluctant to deal with complaints under its Code of Practice from anyone not directly involved in the story. These kinds of complaints were called 'third party complaints'. According to Baroness Hollis, a former member of the Press Council, up to 50 per cent of all Press Council adjudications were on third party complaints, even though the press 'hated them'.[12] In 1992 Mr Bob Borzello, who since 1984 had been bringing third party complaints to the Press Council and the PCC, commented:

> In theory the PCC will accept third party complaints if they involve 'significant issues of public interest'. But in practice you must be directly affected by a code violation before your complaint will be considered. You must be the clearly perceived 'victim'. This denial by the PCC of a fundamental democratic right – the right to complain – effectively excludes all newspaper readers from the process of self-regulation as virtually all of us are third parties and rarely direct victims of Press code violations.[13]

The inadequacy of the PCC's policy on third party complaints where questions of accuracy were concerned was illustrated by the case of the *Daily Star*'s treatment of the black American preacher Al Sharpton. On 30 April 1991 the *Daily Star* ran a story under the headline 'Boot Out Bronx Beast', which started:

> Angry MPs last night demanded that the rabble-rousing American preacher be booted out of Britain ... The 23-stone Sharpton – dubbed the Beast of the Bronx – said he had teamed up with the London-based Pan African Congress Movement during his one-week British visit.

Mr Borzello complained to the *Daily Star*'s readers' ombudsman, and to the PCC, on the grounds that his knowledge of New York politics and journalism led him to believe that no such description of Al Sharpton was used in the United States. He was supported in this by a New York journalist, Robert Fleming, who had studied press coverage of Sharpton in the US and followed Sharpton's work. Mr Fleming had never come across the phrase 'Beast of the Bronx' to describe Al Sharpton.[14] Mr Tony Fowler, the *Daily Star*'s ombudsman, initially accepted this complaint, writing: 'I regret to say that I cannot trace the source of the phrase "Beast of the Bronx" which you complained of and suspect therefore that it was the brainchild of someone in the office wanting to emphasise the displeasure which the Daily Star expressed towards the visit of the Rev Al Sharpton.'[15]

Having accepted that the description of Mr Sharpton was a fiction, Mr Fowler then went on to explain further its presence in the paper: 'I cannot therefore justify it, beyond the nature of the newspaper and the acerbic stance it took towards a man whose visit to Britain had been billed as having the intention of stirring up racial discontent.'[16]

Mr Borzello continued to pursue the matter and received a response from Mr Fowler's temporary replacement Max Davidson, Readers' Representative of the *Sunday Express*, which was owned by the same company as the *Daily Star*. Mr Davidson effectively dismissed the complaint saying, 'I regard the matter as trivial and best forgotten.'[17] Here was a case of inaccuracy admitted by one part of the *Daily Star*'s complaints procedure and rejected by another. The inadequacy of this response was not remedied by the PCC. Mr Borzello wrote to the PCC and got a reply, dismissing his complaint thus: 'In the Director's opinion, this proposed complaint would be unlikely to be entertained by the Commission from a third party.'[18]

The seriousness of the inaccuracy in the *Daily Star* has to be contextualised to be appreciated. The UK tabloid press, of which the *Daily Star* was an example, had been frequently criticised for its unfair, racist and inflammatory coverage of ethnic minorities in the UK.[19] The alarmist, derogatory and inaccurate reporting in this example can only have fostered rather than lessened social divisions. The absence of an appropriate method of redress, in the form of a swift, effective complaints procedure, encouraged a climate in which the editors of some papers had few inhibitions about distorting the reporting of events in the interests of sensation, with scant regard for the damage such reporting might have caused.

Hurting 'third parties'

Inaccurate reporting can also affect 'third parties' who were not the subject of a story. Distress caused to 'third parties' by inaccurate reporting was compounded by the unwillingness of papers to put the record straight and the absence of an independent mechanism for securing a swift resolution to complaints. The case of the *Daily Mirror*'s coverage of research into muscular dystrophy illustrates this point. Mr and Mrs McKeever had a four-year-old son who suffered from Duchenne Muscular Dystrophy (DMD). They had been told that it was incurable and that by the age of ten or eleven their son would be in a wheelchair and that his life expectancy was into his early twenties. Two months after receiving this shattering news the family were out shopping and met a friend who told them that a cure had been found for their son's condition. The source of this information was the *Daily Mirror*.

The article, a short one, appeared in the paper on 29 August 1991, headlined 'Mice Give Doomed Kids Hope'. The story claimed that 'Thousands of terminally ill boys will get the chance to live normal lives thanks to mice' and went on to quote Professor Frank Walsh of Guy's Hospital as saying: 'We expect to have a cure for the most common form of the disease, DMD, within a year.'

According to the McKeevers, 'This news story threw us into complete confusion – half hoping, half believing, yet not wanting to hope or believe too much.' But their hopes were shattered when the Muscular Dystrophy Group told them it was untrue and that the group was intending to complain because a number people had contacted them about the story. Reflecting on the incident later, the McKeevers said that, 'Words cannot fully express the desolation we felt on finding the *Mirror* article was untrue.'[20]

As a result of the story, Professor Walsh received a large number of letters. In his reply to these letters he stated: 'We are very upset by the statement in the *Daily Mirror* which is a total misrepresentation of the situation ... It is premature to make statements about how long this line of work will take.' The roots of the story were in a 45-minute interview conducted by a *Daily Mirror* reporter with Professor Walsh. More accurate accounts of the interim report of Professor Walsh's research appeared in other papers on the same day. The space devoted to the story in the *Mirror* was very limited. Trying to squeeze such a complex issue into a very short story may have, in part, been at the root of this problem.[21]

The victims of this kind of inaccuracy were the parents and relatives of DMD sufferers as well as the readers of the *Daily Mirror*. In this case, the PCC's attitude towards the acceptance of third party complaints would have been of little comfort to anyone save the *Daily Mirror*.

Fact and opinion

During the 1990s, when reporting politics and race, some papers seemed to have combined inaccuracy with racist scaremongering whilst at the same time representing opinion as if it were fact. On 4 April 1992, a matter of days before the General Election, the *Sun* ran the following story under the headline 'Human Tide Labour Would Let In'.

> Tens of thousands of immigrants will be let into Britain if Labour wins the election. Experts warn it will cost hundreds of millions in social security payments, put added strain on the health service and make it harder for our young people to find jobs ... Shadow Home Secretary Roy Hattersley has vowed to axe the crucial Asylum Bill which the Tories want to plug the biggest loophole in our laws. Labour would let in a flood of migrants – including many bogus refugees and scroungers – by relaxing the checks ... Estimated bogus political asylum seekers for 92–93 if Labour wins (does not include genuine immigrants): Zaire 2250, Somalia 8000, Uganda 4700, Angola 2500, Sudan 1250, Ethiopia 1500, Ghana 2000, Iran 1800, Iraq 1500, Lebanon 800, Turkey 11000, India 2800, Pakistan 2200, Bangladesh 1900, Sri Lanka 6000, former USSR 5500, Hungary 1000, Romania 1200.[22]

This story replayed the racist themes for which the *Sun* was well known.[23] It was clearly intended to argue, on the highly contentious assumption that immigration controls were necessary to protect services and jobs, that the Labour Party's policy against the proposed Asylum Bill would lead to a 'flood' of migrants. Labour was committed to maintaining immigration controls and had no intention of letting in a 'flood' on immigrants. The story was inaccurate and inflammatory, designed to stimulate racially motivated sentiment amongst the electorate and thereby to damage Labour's electoral chances.

On the 6 April the Tory Home Secretary, Kenneth Baker, issued a press release in which he said, 'I have warned for months about this rising tide.'[24] On 7 April the *Daily Express* picked up Baker's press release and repeated the inaccuracy about Labour's policy. Under the headline 'Baker's Migrant Flood Warning' it ran the sub-heading 'Labour "set to open doors"'. The reference to Labour in the sub-heading had not appeared in Baker's statement.[25]

In this case the stories rested on inaccurate assertions about Labour's policy on immigration. Its critical position on the Asylum Bill got translated as the date of the election neared into an inaccurate representation of its policy. An opinion, expressed in the *Sun*, that Labour's position on the Asylum Bill might lead to an increase in immigration, had been represented as a fact in its headline. This 'fact' was reproduced in other papers that were, at the time, politically hostile to the Labour Party. In addition the papers utilised appeals to racist sentiment to sustain their story.

The right of a paper to express an opinion is uncontentious. Whether this right should extend to allowing a paper to print as fact what is an opinion is another matter. Indeed, by 1997 the PCC's Code of Practice ruled this practice out, asserting in Clause 3 that 'Newspapers, whilst free to be partisan, should distinguish clearly between comment, conjecture and fact.'[26] Politically motivated inaccuracy that presented 'comment and conjecture' as fact does a disservice to democracy by encouraging electors to form views about policy on the basis of inaccurate information. Throughout the 1980s and 1990s this kind of inaccuracy occurred, in part, because of the absence of a culture of high standards within the industry.

Inaccuracy and justice

An example of inaccurate reporting conflicting with the principles of justice occurred in 1993 when the *Sun* covered police investigations into the murder of a two-year-old child, Jamie Bulger. On 17 February 1993, three days after Jamie's body had been found, the *Sun* ran the headline 'Boy 12 is Held for Jamie Murder'. The words practically covered the whole page. They were accompanied by a picture of Jamie and the following text (emphasis added):

> A boy of 12 was **arrested** last night over the murder of tot Jamie Bulger. Detectives were also questioning three youths – **who are not suspected of killing** two-year-old Jamie.
>
> Police took the 12-year-old from a house **a mile from the shopping centre** where Jamie was kidnapped last Friday.
>
> **A 100-strong mob** gathered outside the home in Snowdrop St, Kirkdale, Merseyside, as the youngster was led away, **covered in a blanket**.
>
> The furious crowd yelled, '**Murderer**' and '**You deserve to die, scum.**'
>
> The boy's parents and their other son and daughter were also driven away in police vans.
>
> The boy was being **questioned** last night at St Ann's police station, Liverpool.
>
> **Dozens** of officers were involved in the swoop. They took articles from the house in plastic bags.

The headline suggested that the boy was Jamie's murderer. The impression was reinforced by the use of the word 'arrested', and by the contrast with the fact that in the next sentence other boys are described as being 'not suspected of killing' Jamie. The description of the 'mob' outside the boy's house adds weight to the idea that the boy murdered Jamie by suggesting that local people believed this to be so.

This version of reality was contradicted on page 5 where, without the benefit of screaming headlines, a police officer was quoted as saying, 'We have not got the murderer in these cells at this stage.' The story ended by reporting a series of verbal attacks on the boy's family made, allegedly, by local people, who called them DSS claimants, 'gypsies', 'low life', and people who 'lowered the tone' of the area.

At the very least, by constructing the story in a manner which inaccurately implied the boy's guilt, and by reporting 'mob' action, the *Sun* may have fed a local conviction that the boy was guilty and contributed to making it difficult for him to return home.[27] As one complainant put it to the PCC: 'truth in small print cannot excuse lies in two-inch headlines ... The *Sun* must bear a share of responsibility for the mob fury vented on this innocent boy and his family.'[28]

Implications and inadequate remedies

Whilst there was general agreement in the media that newspapers should be accurate, it is clear from our examples that in the 1980s and 1990s there were damaging instances of inaccuracy in the press. The absence of an effective remedy for victims of inaccurate reporting in these cases fostered a climate where inaccuracy was widely accepted in the industry.

Our examples, although selective, illustrate problems that have recurred with depressing frequency since the Press Council was established in 1953. The causes of these inaccuracies are clear, and could with more care and responsibility be dealt with. Political motives led to the 'loony left' stories of the 1980s and the immigration scare story of 1992. The use of race to sensationalise a story based on inaccurate reporting, as in the Sharpton case, can reasonably be attributed to a cynical desire to promote sales by aggravating anxieties about race that existed in UK society in these years.

Economic motives played a part in the reporting of the Bulger 'arrest'; sensationalising crime stories at the expense of accuracy was clearly seen by the controllers of papers like the *Sun* as a device to sustain circulation. The McKeever story illustrates the way the twin pressures of economics and tabloid form influenced reporting. The *Daily Mirror* stressed the dramatic aspect of the story, a characteristic device of papers determined to boost circulation. But there was no drama. The story was inaccurate. The form of the tabloid – short stories, bold headlines, simplistic presentation – generally militates against such stories doing justice to the complexities of many issues.

Our examples illustrate how a mix of politics, economics and questions of space and form, combined with human error, led to the publication of inaccurate reports in newspapers. The consequences of inaccurate reporting were important. In the 'loony left' stories and the immigration scare stories electors, at a local and national level, were fed inaccurate information, designed to promote a particular political position. The stories that used race to sell papers, such as the Sharpton case, were clearly in breach of the PCC Code of Practice[29] and could only have had a negative impact on community relations. Some inaccuracies can clearly affect the lives of innocent people, causing unnecessary distress, as in the McKeever case, and fostering prejudicial attitudes towards innocent people who may be drawn into a criminal investigation, as in the Bulger story.

The inadequacy of self-regulation as a medium for dealing with these kinds of issues was apparent in the 1980s as the Press Council failed to deter newspapers from continuing to publish inaccuracies such as the ones discussed here. The PCC's Code was clearly breached in all of the cases we have described from the 1990s. The PCC's habit of disallowing third party complaints functioned as a way of avoiding the investigation of serious allegations of breaches of the code. The Commission's approach to third party complaints could easily have made any approach from the McKeevers irrelevant.[30] The newspaper ombudsman system, established in the late 1980s by the industry, as illustrated in the Borzello case, was open to the charge of lack of system: papers could simply dismiss complaints if, in the end, they so wished, without any proper method of securing a mutually agreeable outcome. In addition, although the PCC's Code encouraged accuracy, like its predecessor the Press Council it had no sanctions with which to enforce accuracy. This meant that papers could continue to publish inaccuracies during these years with little fear that the Press Council or the PCC could do anything that would cause them any serious distress.

9

The Distorting Mirror. The Problem of Misrepresentation in the Press in the 1980s and 1990s

In our discussion of inaccuracy in reporting we focused on factual inaccuracy, its causes and consequences. But frequently inaccuracies form part of a more wide-ranging problem. This problem is that of reporting that systematically misrepresents the subject of the story or stories to the public; stories, in which opinion is represented as fact, and which have many causes and a range of consequences.

Misrepresentation and distortion

By 1997 Article 1 of the PCC's Code of Practice contained the following:

1. Accuracy
i) Newspapers and periodicals should take care not to publish inaccurate, misleading, or distorted material.
ii) Whenever it is recognised that a significant inaccuracy, misleading statement or distorted report has been published, it should be corrected promptly and with due prominence.
iii) An apology should be published whenever appropriate.[1]

Thus, by this date the idea that the press could mislead or distort was accepted by the industry's regulator. What, in general, did this mean? A dictionary definition of 'misrepresent' is to 'represent wrongly, give false account'. Likewise, 'to distort' is given as to 'misrepresent (motives, facts, statements)'.[2] Selective presentation of some of the facts in a story may have the effect of misrepresenting an event or events and of drawing the reader towards believing a false account of those events. This selectivity might involve omitting or minimising the presentation of an alternative perspective on a story. Misrepresentation and distortion might also occur when facts are ordered and emphasised in such a way as to lead the reader towards believing the paper's preferred interpretation of a story. The point to note is that misrepresentation and distortion mix up, in different combinations, selective presentation of facts and partisan ordering and emphasis, with the result that the paper can mislead readers by presenting opinions to a reader as if they were fact.

Homelessness

The treatment of homelessness provides an example of how newspapers can misrepresent the plight of a minority in order to mislead readers and promote a particular political perspective. During the late 1980s the numbers of homeless people reduced to begging on the streets of major cities in the UK increased. There were two main reasons for this, both consequences of policies implemented by the Conservative governments that were in power during the 1980s. The first was that changes in the law resulted in housing benefits being withdrawn from young people under the age of 18. This meant many young people who had left or been forced to leave home could not afford accommodation. The second reason was related to the collapse in the amount of cheap rented housing stock. About 1.9 million homes were lost from the public and private rented sectors between 1979 and 1989.[3] The most visible manifestation of these policy changes was the increase in teenage beggars. Thus government policy helped lead to an increase in homelessness, a situation that demanded sympathy and appropriate public intervention. Unfortunately this was not how some of the newspapers in the UK chose to view the problem.

On 9 May 1994 the *Daily Express* ran a story under the headline 'Beggar Who Pulls in £18,000 A Year'. It claimed to have discovered one homeless person on £18,000 per year, who stayed in a good hotel and spent 'a fortune on the dogs'. The paper argued he was 'just one of many homeless who aren't nearly as desperate as they seem' and that 'across London where some 2000 people sleep rough every night, both charities and the homeless themselves agree no-one is forced to starve ... soup runs, special kitchens, day centres to wash and shave, handouts of new clothes and shoes – every basic necessity is provided for'.

By selectively focusing on one controversial case, and by implying that this person was undeserving of sympathy, the paper implied that all homeless people who begged should be treated with suspicion. The story reinforced this misrepresentation of beggars by asserting, as fact, the paper's opinion that 'many homeless ... aren't as desperate as they seem'.

It further undermined the idea that beggars were genuinely needy by suggesting that enough facilities existed in London to make begging unnecessary. The story was therefore constructed around the assumption that beggars were dishonest and undeserving of public sympathy and it selected and presented its material accordingly.

This misrepresentation was developed further in the paper's treatment of one homeless person, Dougy. Dougy, the story asserted, 'makes' so much money from begging he planned to open a bank account. According to the *Daily Express*, this boy, who was 16 years old, epileptic and schizophrenic, had attempted suicide and had been beaten up by his mother's boyfriend. Later in the story the paper conceded that a survey had revealed that 'more than half of young homeless people suffered from psychiatric disorders ... nearly 40 per cent of homeless suffered sexual or physical abuse'. But this information did not influence its presentation of Dougy, which as well as suggesting he was dishonest by making claims about his affluence, went on to suggest he would become an alcoholic, even though the story said he was not drinking: 'if he's not in prison, the chances are Dougy will have a slurred voice and a bottle in his hand – his road to ruin paved by the generosity of Londoners'.[4]

This misleading picture of the homeless was compounded the next day, 10 May, when one story asserted that 'Cheeky beggar Dougy Hall complained last night after we revealed how he makes so much money he plans to open a bank account.' Dougy had, apparently, complained that he had not given permission to use his picture or the information that the paper had printed. The *Daily Express* justified its action by asserting that at no stage did Dougy say 'he did not want anything printed', and again used the fact of the complaint to encourage people to pass by the likes of Dougy: 'our investigation in the streets of London showed Dougy is not quite as desperate as he might appear to the generous passer-by'. The purpose of this way of representing Dougy like this, and through him other homeless beggars, can be linked to a campaign that was being run at the time by the *Daily Express*. This campaign was designed to deal with the problem of begging, not by a reversal of government policy on benefits and housing, but by making begging with menaces a criminal offence. The paper asserted that 'MPs who want to make begging with menaces a criminal offence were backing the *Express* campaign last night'. Peter Butler MP was quoted as saying, 'I fully back the *Daily Express* moves on this and I hope the Government will seriously consider the problem.'

Thus the *Daily Express* wanted to encourage the government to adopt a punitive policy towards beggars and to help achieve that goal the paper misrepresented the issue of homelessness by focusing on two, contro-versial, individual cases, rather than on the general situation. It questioned the honesty of the two beggars whose story it covered, by suggesting that they had enough money not to have to beg. It also suggested that beggars in London did not really need to be out on the streets begging, as there were plenty of places for them to go for food and shelter. It encouraged its readers, therefore, to think that beggars were undeserving of sympathy. It omitted to outline or discuss the political causes of homelessness, and solutions to the problem that were at variance with its own punitive approach. Where it did include important material that provided a context for the problem, such as the details from the survey on the mental health of homeless youth, it failed to draw out the implications of this for Dougy's case or for the problem in general.

The next day, 11 May, it left its readers in no doubt about how it felt they should react to beggars. Jonathan Cooper, one the paper's columnists, advocated the very course of action by the public so clearly suggested in the stories published in the previous two days. Under the headline 'Tell Them To Beggar Off For The Good of Everyone', this paragon of insight, humanity and understanding wrote: 'It is difficult to walk by. But walk on you should. You should cast aside your natural feelings of wanting to help those worse off than yourself.'[5]

The homeless, the subject and victims of such coverage, were afforded little comfort by the system of redress in the industry. Dougy's complaint was given short shrift by the *Daily Express*. Homeless people are rarely in a position to launch a complaint to the PCC under their code, and the refusal of the Commission to accept third party complaints would have made any other individual's attempt to secure redress for this kind of misrepresentation fruitless.

The *Daily Express*'s behaviour towards the homeless was matched in 1996 by the *Sun*'s. The *Big Issue* is a magazine sold by the homeless to raise money to help re-establish themselves in accommodation and work. Note that the aim of selling the magazine is to encourage people to make and use money, and is not regarded by the *Big Issue* organisation as a form of begging. On 28 October 1996 the *Sun* ran a story headlined '"Beggar" Makes £1000 per Week Selling Big Issue'. The *Sun* had obtained the story by allegedly detailing a reporter to watch one Mark Harris, a *Big Issue* seller in Kingston. The story alleged that Mr Harris lived in a 'posh suburb' in a 'comfy flat', and that he made his £1000 per week by selling 200 copies a day of the magazine. The source for the £1000 figure was an unnamed, and therefore uncheckable, 'friend' of Mr Harris, who was quoted as saying, 'He started flogging the *Big Issue* when he was in a squat. But now he is taking the p***. If he gets less than £1000 a week he moans.'[6]

A number of things made this story misleading. Firstly, selling the *Big Issue* was not begging, yet the story uses the word 'beggar' in the headline. This kind of inaccuracy also implied, as did the stories discussed from the *Daily Express*, that some beggars were earning a lot of money and that beggars in general were therefore deceiving the public who were giving them money. Secondly, the £1000 per week seems to be an exaggeration. At the time the *Big Issue* sold at 80 pence per copy, with 35 pence going back to the organisation that published it.[7] Even if the figure of 'about 200 copies per day' was accurate, this would have given Mr Harris £90 per day, or £450 per week for his pocket. Even if we add on tips averaging, for the sake of argument, 10 pence per copy sold, his daytime income would have risen to £110 and his weekly to £550 – still well short of the £1000. We must also remember that these were the reporter's unverified figures, not Mr Harris's.

Thus the focus on Mr Harris as an example of a *Big Issue* seller raised serious questions. Even if the figures given about his income in the article were true, they were not balanced by any assessment of the general level of income for most *Big Issue* sellers at the time and could have implied that other sellers were as undeserving of support as the paper suggested Mr Harris was. Another way of looking at the information in the story might have been to praise Mr Harris for achieving what the *Big Issue* project set out to do, that is, to move people from the streets and 'squats' to 'comfy' flats by their own exertions.

Overall the story implied a fanciful account of the real situation of people who sold the *Big Issue*, and encouraged *Sun* readers to question the credentials of those homeless people who were trying to make a living through this means. One consequence of this misleading story was that sales of the *Big Issue* fell and vendors were subjected to abuse and assault.[8]

Homelessness is a serious issue. There was plenty of information on the causes of homelessness available to journalists in the 1990s, but the two papers in our example were intent on misrepresenting the issues and this information was not used to balance their accounts. They were intent on representing beggars and *Big Issue* sellers as undeserving of public sympathy. Opinions were represented as fact in what can reasonably be understood as a deliberate attempt to misrepresent the issues to readers.

Mental illness

Unfortunately the homeless were not the only victims of this process. A similar process went on where questions of mental illness were concerned. In its April/June 1997 *Report* the PCC issued guidance notes to editors about dealing with stories about 'Patients detained under the Mental Health Act 1983'. The guidance stated that editors should take care not to create a 'climate of public fear or rejection' by injudicious use of terms such as 'basket case' or 'nutters'.[9] The *Sunday Mirror*, however, published a story on 17 August 1997 that, in the scale of its misrepresentation of issues around mental illness, suggested that the editor of the paper had paid little, if any, attention to the PCC's guidance.

The story was headlined 'It's Madness', under which was written 'They're selling off Broadmoor to build a housing estate and moving crazed killers to an old folks' home.' To add to the effect, the paper printed pictures of two infamous killers, Peter Sutcliffe and Kenneth Erskine, who were confined to Broadmoor. During the article it emerged that the patients would not be moved to an old folks' home but to a former old folks' home that had been converted to a 'secure' unit. In addition, tucked away in the final column of a five-column, two-page spread, was the information that 'if Broadmoor was closed, Sutcliffe and Erskine would not, however, be moved there'.[10]

The story misrepresented the issues in a number of ways. Firstly, its headlines were inaccurate and alarmist. Secondly, by printing pictures of well-known killers the paper implied that these two people would be involved in any move. Thirdly, it inaccurately implied that the authorities were threatening to mix severely mentally ill people with the occupants of an old people's home. This implication was alarmist. The paper misrepresented the true circumstances of the story which, contrary to the PCC's guidance, seems to have been calculated to foster a 'public climate of fear' in relation to questions of mental illness. As in the case of homelessness, the story demanded a rounded, sensitive approach, with facts dominating the presentation of the story, but the temptation to mislead proved too attractive for the *Sunday Mirror*. In this case the motive can reasonably be assumed to have been economic – that is, an attempt to boost circulation by the sensational treatment of a story involving the mentally ill.

Ethnic minorities

In the United Kingdom it is an offence to publish material intended to incite racial hatred.[11] In the PCC's code of 1997 there was also a clause relating to discriminatory reporting:

15. Discrimination
i) The press should avoid prejudicial or pejorative reference to a person's race, colour, religion, sex or sexual orientation or to any physical illness or disability.
ii) It should avoid publishing details of a person's race, colour, religion, sex or sexual orientation unless these are directly relevant to the story.[12]

In spite of the existence of anti-discriminatory legislation, Press Council statements and the PCC's code, the press in the UK has a long, well-documented history of misrepresenting ethnic minorities, be they Irish, Afro-Caribbean, Chinese, Asian or from the Middle East.[13]

In 1990 Mr Bob Borzello complained to the Press Council about coverage in the *Daily Mail* of the trial for rape of a dancer with the Ballet Rambert. He felt that the *Mail*'s description of the defendant as the 'Ballet Rambert's First Black Dancer' was objectionable. The Press Council, in one of the last adjudications of its kind before it was dissolved and transformed into the PCC, upheld the complaint with these words: 'a description which reveals a person's race or colour in a prejudicial or pejorative context should be avoided, even if the description itself is highly favourable'.

In an editorial of 12 April 1990, the *Daily Mail* made its opinion of the Press Council clear by asking: 'What kind of Alice in Wonderland adjudication is this?' and went on to describe it as 'illiberal, oppressive and potentially anti-democratic'. The *Mail* claimed it was simply presenting newsworthy facts and suggested that it would have incurred equal censure for criticising a poor performance by a black actor, or for reporting a black cleric getting a parking ticket.[14]

The colour of the defendant was an irrelevance and this would not have been highlighted had the defendant been white. This kind of misrepresentation was part of a wider pattern in the national press during the 1980s and 1990s in which non-white peoples were frequently represented as being associated with crime.[15] Also, to suggest, as the editorial did, that the Press Council's ruling implied that people who were not white could not be criticised was to distort deliberately the ruling so as to imply that its intention was to encourage unjustly favourable treatment of non-white people. This kind of reasoning is also used by racist critics of anti-discriminatory initiatives who suggest that steps taken to protect ethnic minorities from discrimination are, in fact, intended to discriminate directly, or indirectly, against whites. To compound the problem, the *Daily Mail*'s editorial showed that it did not take the Press Council seriously.

Equally, the PCC's Code of Practice does not appear to have had a very strong restraining influence on papers in the 1990s. As we have indicated, Clause 15 (ii) of the code in operation between 1993 and 1997 stated that the papers should avoid publishing details of a person's race, colour or religion, 'unless they are directly relevant to the story'.[16] This was clearly breached in 1994 by the *Daily Star*, the *Sun* and the *Daily Mirror* in their reporting of a National Lottery win of £18 million by a person who had, as the rules of the UK Lottery allowed, requested anonymity. On 14 December 1994 the *Daily Star* ran the headline 'Vindaloot: Indian Dad Winner of £18 Million Takeaway'. The text reported that 'the happy chap-ati – who requested no publicity – is believed to have carried away the vindaloot with the only winning ticket in last Saturday's draw'.[17] On the front page of the *Sun* of the same day, the winner was identified as an 'Asian factory worker'[18] and the headline across pages 2 and 3 was 'What A Rich Chap ati'.[19] The *Daily Mirror*'s headline was '£18m Win's a Sin'. It claimed the winner came from India and carried the sub-headline 'Moslem's jackpot angers Mosque leaders'.[20] The stories in the *Sun* and the *Mirror* both quoted praise from neighbours for the family, but the *Mirror*'s stressed that 'the parents of the man's wife are believed to be on state benefits. Neither of them work.' Both the *Sun* and the *Mirror* printed enough information about the winner and his family to make them easily identifiable, in spite of the request for no publicity and the Lottery organiser's use of a court order to prevent the papers naming the winner.

These stories were misleading and distorted and were breaches of the PCC's code. By stating that the man's parents were on state benefits, without explaining why, the *Mirror* implicitly promoted the racist view that people from the Indian sub-continent exploit the UK benefit system. The focus on the winner's race and religion in the *Daily Star* and the *Daily Mirror* was irrelevant to the fact that he had won the Lottery and promoted the view that individuals should be categorised in terms of their race and religion. The only details relevant to the story were that an unnamed person, who had sought no publicity, had won £18 million. The code also prohibited 'Intrusions or inquiries into an individual's private life without his or her consent', the only exception being when such stories were 'in the public interest'.[21] Thus a further article of the code was breached by the papers, as the winner's consent to this invasion of his privacy was not requested and the public interest was in no way furthered by the stories about him and his family.

The pitfalls of complaining

In the 1990s the press continued to mislead the public, distort issues and misrepresent people thereby breaching the PCC's Code of Practice. Homeless people, the mentally ill, or ordinary people fortunate enough to win a prize in a public lottery were not in a strong position to launch a complaint using the PCC code and were unable, or unwilling to use, or prolong the issue by using, the courts. Yet even when more organised and powerful individuals used the system to complain, the outcome was likely to be very unsatisfactory.

In 1993 the *Daily Express* carried a story about Labour-controlled Merton Council, accusing it of trying to ban the story of 'The Ugly Duckling' from playgroups because it was racist. The intention seems to have been to deride the council for its general attitude to anti-discrimi-nation policies through the use of an inaccurate story. In fact, a council officer had expressed a personal view that the story had racist overtones and consequently the playgroup members decided to remove it from their reading material. When this decision was brought to the attention of senior officers it was over-ruled. The leader of the council, Tony Colman, complained to the *Express* and as a result a correcting letter was published.[22] The Associate Editor of the *Daily Express*, Bernard Shrimsley, wrote to Tony Colman stating that 'we regret the headline, although the text made the position clear'.[23]

The *Sun* printed the story: 'Left Wing Councillors ...want to ban the story of the Ugly Duckling' on 16 November 1993. Michael Toner, the leader writer responsible, wrote to Tony Colman on the paper's behalf. 'I see no cause to apologise', he wrote; 'you should understand that the verb "to want" expresses desire, not intent. If you read the leader again you'll find no claim that the Council had banned the book.'[24] This defence equated the action of a junior officer with the 'desire' of the council as a whole and, in so doing, repeated the inaccuracy in the report. In this case both papers misrepresented the position of the council, on the basis of an inaccurate and misleading story. Additionally one paper's response to criticism of the story differed markedly from the other's and both seem to have been intended to belittle anti-racist initiatives by local authorities.

A similar mix of inaccuracy, misrepresentation, the illegitimate play on race, and an unsatisfactory outcome to a complaint occurred in 1996. This example centres on an article written by the Prince of Wales in the architectural magazine *Perspectives*. In the article the prince put forward the view that public celebrations of the millennium should adopt a spiritual dimension:

> I would hope, for example, that a start might be made to help those faiths, growing in Britain but struggling to create places of worship, to erect buildings of real quality. This, surely, must be one of those instances where millennium money may be able to build bridges across some of the divisions in Britain's society ... But no one has come forward, for example, with plans to erect a great religious building such as the new Hindu temple in Neasden which was completed last year.[25]

The headline in the *Daily Mail* of 25 January 1996 was 'Charles: Let Lottery Money Go To Mosques', and in the *Daily Star* on the same day 'You Mosque Be Joking'. Although the Prince's article had not contained a reference to mosques, the *Daily Mail* printed a comment from an MP that implied that he had. Michael Fabricant, MP for Mid-Staffordshire, was quoted as saying: 'I would have thought there are plenty of wealthy Arabs who can fund mosques.'[26]As well as being inaccurate on two counts – the Prince did not ask for Lottery money to be spent on anything specific, nor did he mention mosques – the story misrepresented the Prince's views, misled the public and invoked questions of religion in a manner calculated to imply that the Prince was favouring Islam even though, were he to become king, he would be head of the Church of England. In addition, by focusing on Islam in this way the papers were reiterating a well-established tradition of associating Islamic and Arabic peoples with negative story lines.[27]

A complaint was lodged with the PCC by Clive Soley about the coverage of the Prince's article in the *Daily Star* and the *Daily Mail*. In its adjudication, published in June 1996, the complaint was rejected: 'The Commission considered that the ... publications had expressed their opinion on the views expressed by the Prince.' Given the fact that the stories misrepresented the Prince's views and were also very misleading the PCC's response was thoroughly inadequate. Indeed, not only did this adjudication sanction the conflation of fact with opinion, when Article 3 of the code then in force urged newspapers to 'distinguish clearly between comment, conjecture and fact', it also illustrated the fact that the PCC had difficulty in maintaining a critical distance between itself and the industry.[28]

A failure of standards and redress

Misrepresentation is more than a mistake. It involves, often, identifiable motives and the conscious use of techniques of presentation that, individually, or collectively, are calculated to mislead readers. These practices can involve the use of inaccuracy to whip up controversy, as in the Merton and Prince Charles stories. It can involve selective presentation of material, as in the case of the *Express*'s coverage of the homelessness stories and the Rambert case. It can involve presenting material in a way that fits the assumptions of the paper on politics, as in the Merton case; on race, as in the Rambert case; or on social policy, as in the stories about the homeless. Misrepresentations may foster anti-social attitudes towards ethnic minorities, the homeless, the mentally ill or particular religious groups or they may invite unjustified public criticism of elected bodies.

Recourse to the law courts only applied in limited cases, such as libel, which was both a narrow area of law and too costly a course of action for most people. Even when the courts were involved, as in the Lottery organiser Camelot's attempts to use a court order to protect the privacy of the winner of £18 million, the papers were able to circumvent the order in fact, if not in law. The victims of misrepresentation may be powerless people, like the homeless or the mentally ill, for whom complaints to newspapers or the PCC are out of the question due to lack of resources or ill health. When people did complain to newspapers the responses could be inconsistent, as in the Merton case. They could be dismissive, as in the *Sun*'s response to the Merton complaint; or the complainer ran the risk of being pilloried in the paper, as happened to the homeless teenager Dougy.

When there was a clear breach of the code in the 1990s, as in the inaccurate and misleading reports about Prince Charles's views, the PCC was quite capable of taking a decision that appeared to run counter to the facts of the case, defending stories which were in breach of the code. Adjudications such as the one in the Prince Charles case suggested that the PCC was not serious enough about enforcing high standards in the press during the 1990s.

The Press Council and the PCC were not taken all that seriously by sections of the national press in these years either, as our examples illustrate. The *Daily Mail* derided the Press Council's decision in the Rambert case. The *Daily Mirror* seems to have ignored the PCC's guidelines on covering stories about mental illness. The stories about homelessness, the Lottery, the Prince of Wales and Merton Council breached the PCC code on accuracy. The story about the Lottery breached the code on discrimination and privacy. These kinds of reporting, which misrepresented individuals, issues, groups and public bodies, and in so doing contrived to mislead readers, remained strong elements in the UK national press in the 1990s. The methods available for people to gain redress – that is, writing to the paper or complaining to the PCC – were deeply flawed and of little use to the citizen.

10

Privacy and Self-Regulation

Article 4 of the PCC's Code of Practice 1997 read as follows:

4. Privacy
i) Intrusions and enquiries into an individual's private life without his or her consent, including the use of long-lens photography to take pictures of people on private property without their consent, are only acceptable when it can be shown that these are reasonably believed to be in the public interest.[1]

Whilst the code might be criticised for lacking a precise definition of 'public interest', it did at least recognise that there was a conflict between the personal lives of individuals and the aims of newspapers. The problem was, as we will illustrate, that this recognition did not get translated into effective action in the 1990s by either the PCC or the newspapers. In addition the question of invasion of privacy by the press, although an old complaint,[2] was one which during these years attracted a high degree of publicity. This occurred in spite of the fact that amongst that section of the community able and willing to make a complaint to the PCC, the issue was of less concern than accuracy. In 1995, for example, only 12.4 per cent of complaints adjudicated by the PCC concerned privacy, whilst 68.9 per cent related to accuracy.[3]

Privacy and the public interest

The question of how to balance the relationship between the right of the individual to live a private life and the right of the media to breach that right in certain circumstances has been a source of recurring controversy in the twentieth century and in the 1980s and 1990s it attracted the interest of academics and journalists as well as politicians.[4] Here we focus on some of the issues raised in these debates.

The problems of establishing a clear definition of the issues have recurred, as has that of finding an appropriate remedy.[5] What constitutes 'privacy'? Is the sex life of anyone his or her private matter, or is the sex life of a public figure public property? Are the private financial affairs of individuals always sacrosanct, or does the need to expose fraud, exploitation and hypocrisy over-ride privacy? Is it in the public interest to expose the sexual preferences of a public servant, or is it only in the public interest when that person's sexual or financial affairs conflict with their public role?

The idea that the press has a duty to balance the act of informing the public against the legitimate right of all people, including public figures, to privacy, recurred in official literature on the press throughout the 1980s and 1990s. In 1990 David Calcutt's *Report of the Committee on Privacy and Related Matters* expressed this concern:

> We have reservations about how the term 'public interest' is used in the context of intrusions into privacy. In many cases what appears to be meant is that which is merely interesting to the public rather than that which should be brought to the attention of the public in order, for example, to expose crime, impropriety or hypocrisy. The distinction between the two lies at the heart of our deliberations. The argument that it is essential to protect serious investigative journalism loses much of its force if it is cited in defence of stories that might better be attributed to prurient curiosity.[6]

In 1993 the Lord Chancellor's department and the Scottish Office published a consultation paper on the *Infringement of Privacy* which stressed the delicacy of the issues and the need to find some kind of balance between the rights of the press and the rights of individuals, warning that 'Unless the balance can be found, one right or the other is in danger of being neutralised.'[7] In 1995 the Conservative government under John Major issued a document on *Privacy and Media Intrusion*.[8] This document concluded that there was no case for a statutory right of privacy, but that improvements to the industry's system of regulation could be made. The government said it had been unable to come up with a workable criminal instrument and there had been no consensus, amongst those it had consulted, about the need for a new civil remedy.[9]

Thus, although the issue exercised the minds of government during the 1990s, it remained unresolved (see Chapter 5). A further complexity arose from the absence of a Freedom of Information Act in the UK. The Labour government elected in 1997 had a manifesto commitment to introduce a Freedom of Information Act. There remained, however, controversy about the extent to which the measures proposed by the government would result in an effective piece of legislation.[10] Journalists and the public have not, historically, had the ability to fully investigate the way the UK is governed. The climate of secrecy and restraint in the UK was encouraged by the Official Secrets Acts of 1911 and 1989,[11] which imposed severe penalties on civil servants or journalists who investigated and revealed unauthorised information about the UK government. The problems caused by absence of laws that protected journalists engaged in serious investigations were exacerbated by the way powerful people were able to use the threat of libel to gag investigations before they got into print.[12] It is unsurprising therefore that journalists, socialists and libertarians have recoiled from supporting legislation that grants a right to privacy in the context of a legal system and climate of governmental secrecy that encompass a variety of devices for preventing the exposure of malpractice and hypocrisy.

Sex, sensationalism, politicians and royalty – sales or public interest?

The motives for intruding into someone's privacy have historically been linked to the desire of proprietors to compete economically by producing sensational stories that sell newspapers.[13] It is therefore fortunate for proprietors when their papers get hold of stories that combine sensation and sex with politicians or royalty. However, these kinds of stories can and do raise questions about the balance between the public interest and the rights of individuals to privacy.

David Mellor had cut his ministerial teeth as a loyal acolyte of the Conservative governments of the 1980s. Having been appointed to the Cabinet of John Major as Secretary of State for National Heritage, it fell to him to respond to recurring criticisms, often from his own backbenchers, about the behaviour of the national press. On 9 July 1992 Mellor announced that he was asking David Calcutt QC to look again into the question of the self-regulation of the press, for the second time in three years. On the 19 July the *Sunday People* ran a story under the headline 'David Mellor And The Actress' which gave intimate details of his affair with an actress, including details of conversations he had had with her that had been taped without his permission.[14] There followed a media onslaught on Mellor. He clung to office for a few more weeks, buffeted by an unremitting campaign in the press.

In July 1992 the PCC's code on privacy was as follows:

Intrusions and enquiries into an individual's private life without his or her consent are not generally acceptable and publication can only be justified when in the public interest. This would include:
(i) Detecting or exposing crime or serious misdemeanour.
(ii) Detecting or exposing seriously anti-social conduct.
(iii) Protecting public health and safety.
(iv) Preventing the public from being misled by some statement or action of that individual.[15]

Mellor did not complain to the PCC, but the case was of such notoriety that the Commission's chairman, Lord McGregor, issued a statement saying, 'in the case of politicians it is right for the public to be informed about private behaviour'.[16]

Initially the *Sunday People* had justified this invasion of privacy on the grounds that the minister had said in a taped conversation that he had not been able to write two speeches because of tiredness. He was quoted as saying, 'You have absolutely exhausted me. I feel seriously knackered. I had a wonderful time with you last night and I've felt really positive all day.'[17] Whilst this justification suggested that a tired minister unable to do his or her job is a legitimate target for investigation, it is a point that could apply to any minister who gets tired for whatever reason, even being tired because s/he had had energetic sex. It was not, on the face of it, a matter of burning public interest.

More to the point was that Mellor had used pictures of his family in his election address during the 1992 General Election campaign.[18] In so far as he was prepared to use his image as a family man to promote his political career – not at all unusual in UK politics – and then go out and commit adultery, he laid himself open to the charge of hypocrisy and, in terms of the PCC code, the *Sunday People* was 'Preventing the public from being misled by some statement or action of that individual'. In this sense his exposure was decidedly in the public interest. Lord McGregor's defence of the story, that the public should be informed about a politician's private behaviour, however, simply left the question of where the line should be drawn between the private and the public life of a politician unanswered. The statement was so general in its phrasing and import that it almost seemed to sanction the publication of any details about the private life of a politician.

Additional considerations were related to money and politics. A reasonable interpretation of the story might be that it had all the ingredients of a traditional political scandal, guaranteed to boost the sales of a paper like the *Sunday People*. In this case, as in others, there appears also to have been a wider political framework within which the story played an important role. Mellor was the minister responsible for framing the government's position on the self-regulation of the press. The fact that he laid himself open to attack provided an opportunity for newspapers to signal their opposition to fundamental reform of the system of self-regulation by exposing the very politician whose job it was to deal with the issue. Had he survived in office, and had he recommended a major reform of the system of self-regulation to the Cabinet, he would have been open to the charge of allowing his personal experience to influence his judgement. The exposure would have had the added effect of showing other politicians the likely personal consequences of tampering with the self-regulation of the press.

Similar sets of issues were raised by the furore surrounding the death of Diana, Princess of Wales, in 1997. Prior to her death in a car accident in Paris she had been part of long-running controversies about the extent to which the press should be allowed to intrude into the private lives of the royal family. When it emerged that prior to her car accident a number of photographers had been in pursuit of the car she was in, the whole issue of the responsibility of the press on questions of privacy came to the fore again. Her brother, the Earl Spencer, articulated this by accusing editors of having 'had blood on their hands'.[19]

Diana clearly provided material for the press, in her carefully managed personal appearance and involvement in high-profile issues such as AIDS and landmines, her readiness to discuss her bulimia, and her willingness to use the media to further her ends in her disputes with her husband and the Royal Family. The press could not get enough of it; here was a story that offered everything their marketing managers could have wished for – wealth, fame and sex – far exceeding anything in a television soap opera.

To live your life in the glare of such intense publicity creates stresses, even if you benefit a great deal from that publicity, and few can emerge unscathed from the process. Clearly, Diana and the Royal Family must accept responsibility for much of the publicity they got, and any assessment of the situation must take account of the fact that large sections of the public showed a clear interest in purchasing sensational material about the royals. But what is the responsibility of the press in situations like this?

The justifications sometimes offered for breaches of the Royal Family's privacy were that they were public figures, financed out of the public purse, who occupied a key place in the UK's unwritten constitution; as a result they were objects of legitimate public interest. But does receiving money from the public purse and having a constitutional role mean that you forgo any right to privacy? The most obvious reason for the saturation coverage of the royals was the commercial rivalry between papers, each seeking to outbid the other in the race for circulation.

Faced with a history of breaches of the PCC code on the reporting of Diana's private life and with the Royal Family reluctant to lodge a formal complaint, the PCC seemed unsure about how to react following her death. Lord McGregor, chair of the PCC, had had his fingers burnt in 1992 when he had intervened to try and stop speculation about the marriage of Diana and Charles, Prince of Wales. On 8 June the PCC had 'issued a statement condemning "intrusive", "odious" and "prurient" reporting which in tone and manner, it said, had been in breach of the PCC's industry-wide code of conduct'.[20] Later it emerged that the couple had been briefing the press separately.

Because of Prince Charles's position in the line of succession it was impossible to argue that the future of the marriage was not of legitimate public interest. The constitutional implications, however, were almost an afterthought in stories that focused on the sensational aspects of a celebrity relationship. The PCC in the end updated its code in November 1997 to strengthen the rules around the reporting of the lives of minors; a clear attempt to protect the privacy of the children of the marriage. Nonetheless, the tangled tale of press and Royal Family relations revealed the way in which the PCC was unable in the 1990s to set workable boundaries between the public interest and rights to privacy, especially where the commercial interests of proprietors were at stake. It also further illustrated the need for a clarification of the whole issue and some way of balancing public interest and the right to privacy. This was clearly something self-regulation proved unable to achieve.

Who is a legitimate subject of intrusion?

In October 1991 the then Director of Public Prosecution, Sir Alan Green, resigned, having been caught approaching a prostitute near King's Cross railway station in London.[21] After the exposure, a photograph was taken of Lady Eva Green entering her house. Beside her in the photo was a young woman, Nicola Evans, the prostitute in Sir Alan's case: she was resting on the front railings of the house. Lady Green had her hand in her bag, presumably in search of her keys, and was, apparently, ignoring the woman and the photographer. After the exposure of Sir Alan Green, he and his wife separated and, sadly, on 31 January 1993, it was announced that Eva Green was dead. She had committed suicide.

On the next day, 1 February 1993, the *Daily Mirror* carried the photograph on its front page. Underneath was the caption stating that Nicola Evans 'came to say sorry'. The article said that 'Nicola Evans tried in vain to say she was sorry ... the prostitute was rebuffed when Lady Green, 47, made it clear that she did not want to know.' It is reasonable to surmise that the photograph was set up for financial reasons with a view to selling it to a newspaper. It is also reasonable to argue that the taking of the photo amounted to harassment of Lady Green who, at the time, must have been under stress generated by the exposure of her husband's activity. Indeed, Lady Green was an innocent party in the affair, one whose privacy was invaded by the photographer.

The editor of the *Daily Mirror* should have realised all of this. Instead the photograph was used on the day after the announcement of Lady Green's death, in a manner calculated to add an element of sensation to the story. The picture was of no relevance to the story and can only have provoked distress amongst Lady Green's bereaved relatives and friends.[22] It is very difficult to see how this kind of intrusion into Lady Green's life, and into the grief of her family and friends, could be justified in terms of the public interest.

The privacy of ordinary people

Just as the families of politicians, innocent of any misdemeanour, were dragged into stories by having their privacy invaded, so in the 1990s, as before, innocent members of the public had their private lives dragged through the press. In 1993 a story broke about an Asian woman and her white husband who had had their application to adopt a black child turned down by Norfolk Social Services. This kind of decision remains controversial. It is a sensitive matter, which needs handling with care in the interests of the children, potential adopters and community relations. The decision of the Norfolk Social Services Department had been investigated and then backed by the Department of Health.[23]

On 13 September 1993 the *Daily Mail*, under the headline 'My Years With the Gay Social Worker' declared 'social worker Terry Dunning and his gay lover Phillip Smith had achieved their happiness at the expense of the family Mr Dunning walked out on'. Mr Dunning was the social worker in the adoption case, whose private life the *Daily Mail* saw fit to publicise. The following two pages highlighted Mr Dunning's sex life, with only passing references to the adoption story. The article ended by quoting Mrs Dunning, 'now living alone in a cottage a few miles outside Norwich. Her Christian forgiveness still holds firm.' She was quoted thus, in reference to the consequences of the media coverage of the adoption case: '[A]ll this started as a social work thing. Terry was blamed for it all, which was absolutely ridiculous. Our life has been open, anyway. Nothing about it was hidden. All this has been awful for my family. But I think the whole thing has been great for the gay movement. We are all pleased about that.'[24] The quotation reflected Mrs Dunning's awareness of the damaging effect of publicity on her family. What could have been the justification for putting Mr Dunning, his ex-wife and their family under such a searching spotlight?

The PCC's code at the time made it clear that invasions of privacy were only acceptable if they were in the public interest. In addition, it made it clear that sexual preference should not be included unless relevant to the story: 'It [the press] should avoid publishing details of a person's race, colour, religion, sex or sexual orientation unless these are directly relevant to the story.'[25] It is hard to see how the public interest could have been served, in any of the senses listed in the code then in force, by this intrusion into Mr Dunning's private life. Nor is it easy to see why Mr Dunning's sexuality had any direct relevance to the story. The case exemplified the willingness of the press to invade the privacy of an individual with scant regard to the effect on his or her personal or professional life, the vagueness of the 'public interest' defence in the PCC's code, and the inability of the Commission to stop this kind of activity.

A further example of the 'public interest' defence being stretched to extremes, and in the process breaching the privacy of an innocent child, occurred in 1998. In May 1998 the *Daily Mail* ran a story concerning a woman who had been imprisoned for drugs. Accompanying the story was a very large front-page photograph of the woman's four-year-old daughter.[26] The PCC code in force at the time had this to say about children:

Article 6
(1) Young people should be free to complete their time at school without unnecessary intrusion.
(2) Journalists must not interview or photograph children under the age of 16 on subjects involving the welfare of the child or of any other child, in the absence of or without the consent of a parent or other child who is responsible for the children.
(3) Pupils must not be approached or photographed while at school without the permission of the school authorities.
(4) There must be no payment to minors for material involving the welfare of children nor payment to parents or guardians for material about their children or wards unless it is demonstrably in the child's interest.
(5) Where material about the private life of a child is published, there must be justification for publication other than the fame, notoriety or position of his or her parents or guardian.

Also relevant were Article 10, which asserted that 'the press must avoid identifying relatives or friends of persons convicted or accused of crime without their consent', and the general public interest requirement, which covered the whole code, that 'in cases involving children editors must demonstrate an exceptional public interest to over-ride the normally paramount interests of the child'.[27]

When Clive Soley complained to the *Daily Mail* about the use of this photograph the paper replied that its use was justified because the child's grandmother had given permission while the mother was jailed. The paper implied that parental rights are somehow suspended during a jail sentence, saying that the mother was 'unable to have care and control of the child'. Public interest lay, apparently, in the fact that the grandmother had been so concerned for her grandchildren's welfare that she had informed on her daughter to the police. The paper denied that there had been any breach of the code, yet it hardly demonstrated 'exceptional public interest', nor any justification 'other than the fame, notoriety or position' of the girl's mother for breaching the girl's privacy.[28]

Clive Soley contacted the PCC, and on 13 May 1998 Lord Wakeham acknowledged his letter, noting that 'you raise an important case, I will be interested to see the editor's response'.[29] Lord Wakeham gave a fuller reply on 1 June, having seen a copy of the paper's response to Clive Soley's complaint, quoted above. With his reply he enclosed a speech he had made earlier in the year, which had this to say on the rights of children: 'in the recent changes to code[30] we established a new test of "over-riding" public interest in cases involving children. In other words, the interests of a child are paramount – and editors need an extremely strong public interest defence to over-ride them.' This position did not however prompt any strong response to the *Mail* story, about which he simply wrote, 'where it is necessary, I will act proactively'.[31]

On 1 December of that year a Court of Appeal judgment directed that the identity of children in cases should be withheld, whether or not a specific direction had been given to that effect. This referred, of course, to the reporting of court proceedings and did not apply to the media alone. Clive Soley wrote again to the *Daily Mail* and to the PCC asking whether 'the spirit of this judgement embraces the kind of case I raised with you earlier this year'. Neither organisation responded.[32]

A weak system

Invasions of privacy can have consequences for the innocent as well as the not so innocent; children and partners can get dragged in. Invasions of privacy can amount to a form of harassment, as in the case of Lady Green, and result in the publication of material that can cause distress to relatives, as in the Dunning case. The motives behind the publication of such stories were not always high minded. They could be a mix of the economic and the political, sometimes driven by a circulation-boosting motive, sometimes by a concern to undermine a particular decision (as in the Dunning case). The fact that stories could emerge falsely claiming a public interest that were clearly not in the public interest, and that at times innocent people were dragged into them, illustrates the ineffectiveness of the Commission in the 1990s.

Indeed an awareness in the industry of the PCC's laxity created a climate in which stories such as those on Eva Green, or Terry Dunning, could be run in the full knowledge that there would be no serious punishment inflicted on the perpetrators by the Commission. The breaches of the code in relation to privacy were, as in the Dunning case, sometimes accompanied by breaches of other articles – in this instance the article on reporting people's sexuality. These kind of cases, when juxtaposed with the Commission's failure to act effectively on matters of inaccuracy and misrepresentation, illustrate the extent to which the

Press Council and the Commission were unable in the 1980s and 1990s to foster and enforce a culture of high standards in the UK national press. By the end of the 1990s, therefore, there had developed an urgent need for a radical overhaul of the system of self-regulation of the press in the UK.

PART III

Reforming Regulation

Tom O'Malley and Clive Soley

11

Rights and Responsibilities: The Need for Reform

In this book we have tried to place the problem of self-regulation of the press in the United Kingdom in historical perspective. We have also tried to show that the relationship between the state and the press has changed over the centuries and that the question of whether or not there should be some form of statutory regulation of standards is neither new, nor easily resolved by appeal to the idea that such a development would constitute a threat to press freedom. Here we review themes developed in the book and explore some of the options that we think would help promote press freedom and responsibility.

An ongoing debate

There has clearly been a 'long argument' about the role of the press in society. Its terms have varied, sometimes stressing the need for freedom from overt state control, and more recently, in the twentieth century, the need to distance the press from both the state and the priorities of big business. Embedded in this 'argument' have also been debates about the nature of truth and accuracy and about the obligations of journalists. A further layer of complexity is added by the fact that there has never been, even since the press reforms of the nineteenth century, a blanket acceptance that the state has no role in regulating the industry. Employers, journalists, politicians, trade unionists and academics have been amongst those who have judged state intervention according to the issue involved; condemning, at times, the Official Secrets legislation, whilst soliciting privileges from the state, such as tax relief or libel reform. Questions of legal intervention have rested on the issue and the circumstances at the time, as much as on questions of principle.

The growth of a mass commercial press after 1900 in the UK brought to debates about the press the added dimension of concerns about the way intense competition for mass audiences led to objectionable journalistic practices. Journalists' organisations tried to tackle this as part of their efforts to give a sort of professional status to their work. By the 1930s these concerns were widespread, but so too was a more specific critique of the power of proprietors to influence the political process. All of these issues fed concern in the Labour Party about the press and helped to create the 1947–49 Royal Commission.

Whilst this Commission was part of a general effort by the Labour government to tackle other areas of media policy, including film and broadcasting, the Commission brought into play a new dimension by making the press a subject of public, official scrutiny for the first time since the 1860s. This allowed issues of press regulation to be discussed and political pressure for reform brought to bear on the industry, without the pressure automatically being seen to be, by all participants, a form of government interference with press freedoms. Thereafter, until the 1990s, inquiries into the media in general and the press in particular became frequent, thus opening the door to more intense and focused debates about accountability than had been the case prior to 1947.

The constant factor in these debates after 1947 was the reluctance of proprietors to reform practices voluntarily. From 1951 onwards, until the 1990s, the cycle of debate centred on self-regulation was one of criticism, political pressure and partial reform, followed, eventually, by more criticism. Political criticism forced the proprietors into having a Press Council that involved lay people who, monitored, to some extent, press standards, and dealt with complaints. By 1991 the pressure had brought about a more streamlined complaints system, operating a code of practice. But these changes were wrung out of an industry that had proven painfully slow to act unless threatened with statutory intervention. Self-regulation proved, in the end, as the departure of the NUJ from the Press Council in 1980 illustrated, too closely allied with the sectional interests of employers and the Press Council, and the PCC lacked both the powers and the will to work positively to improve standards.

Running parallel with this process was an ongoing political critique of the effectiveness of self-regulation that dates from the early 1950s and continued into the 1990s. This critique drew support from all the major political parties and intensified as the years moved on. It involved the work of successive Royal Commissions, government-appointed inquiries, criticism from outside the industry, from the NUJ, the Labour Party and the trade union movement, and the public at large. Within this range of criticism there was plenty of support for statutory regulation as a tool for improving standards. The constant use by employers, editors, some journalists and some politicians of the argument that statutory regulation posed a threat to press freedom therefore remained unaccepted by significant groups of people during the postwar period. Why therefore did self-regulation survive into the 1990s? This question requires a much more detailed consideration than we can offer; there is a clear need for more research into the topic. We can, however, make some tentative suggestions.

The notion that the press should be free from state control has remained a powerful influence on the minds of those involved in the debates.[1] It was held by all sides of the debate. But the idea could be made to mean different things: proprietors and defenders of self-regulation invoked the fear of state control of the press when faced with measures that were not intended to have that effect. Proprietors and editors tended to equate press freedom and freedom of speech with their right to publish what they wanted, thereby excluding the public and workers in the industry from having a role in setting standards or achieving redress. The fears of state control of the press were amplified by the Press Council's and the Press Complaints Commission's call at times of crisis for self-regulation and clearly helped frame the nature of many of the arguments. The repressive nature of many UK laws, such as the official secrets legislation and the laws of contempt, helped fuel these concerns. Few politicians in the postwar period wanted to be tarred with the brush of being in favour of state control of the press. Those politicians like Frank Allaun and Clive Soley who did take steps to initiate reforms were subjected to formidable abuse by the *Sun* and more measured critique by other parts of the press, all of which raised, or hinted, at the idea that their reforms would lead to state control of the press.

The various government-sponsored inquiries were also inconsistent in their approach to this issue. All accepted the idea that some form of statutory regulation of standards was possible, but then ruled out different proposals, sometimes on grounds of principle, sometimes on practical grounds.[2] The internal politics of these bodies, especially those of the three Royal Commissions, awaits further investigation and comparison. It is arguable that the Shawcross and McGregor Commissions allowed, in the end, deference to the general fear of state control of the press to provide a reason for doing little other than to suggest reforms in the system of self-regulation, whilst suggesting, most significantly in the case of the Shawcross Commission, that they did not necessarily rule out statutory measures. Had the post-1949 inquiries been prepared, as Calcutt became, to take a more robust attitude, then things would arguably have been different. We await, however, further studies of the Royal Commissions and the other inquiries into the press before it is possible to reach a more satisfactory set of conclusions on these issues.

The Press Council proved adept at showing its willingness to reform when under high-profile political pressure, and this clearly gave politicians a way out of the dilemmas posed by the manifest inadequacies of self-regulation in the 1950s, 1960s and 1970s. When Calcutt did not provide this option in the 1990s, senior politicians in both the Conservative and Labour parties proved unable and unwilling to bite the bullet.

Governments were made up of politicians for whom the reform of self-regulation was not on the top of the agenda. The growth of Labour movement pressure for media reform in the 1970s and 1980s reflected the contemporary perception that the national press was biased against Labour. Labour's adoption of the right of reply in the mid-1980s reflected this perception. The power of the press to influence politics was therefore a real factor in Labour thinking about media reform in the 1970s and 1980s. In the 1980s the Conservative governments of Margaret Thatcher were exceptionally close to national newspaper proprietors. When real parliamentary opportunities for change came in 1989 and 1993, with the Worthington and Soley bills, the Conservative government acted, using delay, to buffer and effectively secure the continuation of self-regulation. Prior to Labour's return to power in 1997 the party made it clear that it was not intending to act against the proprietors, either on questions of ownership or of regulation; this was in part the result of a fear of stirring up the kind of virulent hostility to Labour that was a feature of the national press in the 1980s and early 1990s. The evidence therefore suggests that by the 1980s and 1990s self-regulation survived because, at the end of the day, politicians who were about to be, or were, in government, were unwilling to act against the wishes of proprietors, regardless of public and parliamentary opinion. Our overall purpose has been to outline the developments in debates over these issues; much more detailed work is needed on the reasoning employed by politicians and civil servants for their consistent refusal to use statutory measures to improve standards in the press.

Real concerns

The opposition to a statutory Press Council or Independent Press Authority administering some form of post-publication correction or redress and having also the function of monitoring press freedom has provoked genuine concerns.[3] Freedom of expression in the UK is constrained by various provisions in a range of statutes including the Obscene Publications Act 1964, the Contempt of Court Act 1981, the Video Recordings Act 1984, the Official Secrets Act 1988 and the Criminal Justice and Public Order Act 1994, to name but a few. According to Collins and Murroni, in 'too many cases the interests of the state or its agents are allowed to override the freedom of expression of individuals'. The censorship or distortion of news to suit the political or commercial goals of proprietors is also a feature of the UK press.[4] It is necessary to remove these kinds of control, rather than add to them. Post-publication correction of inaccuracies, however, coupled with positive efforts to raise standards, would not constitute pre-publication censorship. Indeed, as the media law specialist Eric Barendt has argued, a newspaper's freedom to speak is not affected by its being subject to a requirement to publish a reply; its freedom 'is not infringed merely because [the editor] is required by law to publish a proposition he does not agree with. It is only invaded if he is compelled to say or write something in circumstances in which it would appear to a reasonable bystander that he believes in its truth.'[5]

The idea that the state should create a law to enable this to happen has generated the argument that the state should not interfere with the freedom of the press. As this book has shown, the state has always 'interfered' in the press, sometimes for the good, such as in granting immunities from libel for the press or anonymity for the victims of certain crimes, sometimes for the bad as in the case of secrecy laws; sometimes with the support of proprietors and journalist, sometimes not. A law therefore can be good, bad or indifferent depending on how and why it was framed and how it is implemented.

Another concern is that even a good law might be 'turned' or abused by the state or by powerful private interests to produce an outcome contrary to the original intentions of the legislators. Thus a right of reply law might be used by the government to harass left wing, polemical journals, regardless of whether those journals were printing inaccuracies, so as to drain their resources. A privacy law might, no matter how well framed, become, like the libel laws, a licence for harassing the press through the use of pre-publication injunctions, or might simply provide a shield behind which corrupt politicians, civil servants, military personnel, police and business people could hide.

Whilst these are real risks, much would depend on how such measures were framed and how well they were implemented and monitored. In addition, this concern could apply to many laws; contempt of court laws that shield the legal process from abuse can, and have been, used to restrain fair and accurate reporting; laws designed to raise educational standards by introducing a national curriculum can be used to enhance government control over the content of what is taught in schools. These problems are in the very nature of law making, and so it would be wrong to rule out press laws designed to promote higher standards and give rights to citizens because they might be abused in the future.

A further objection to a statutory measure was advanced by the 1974–77 Royal Commission. This was the principle that 'the press should not be subjected to a special regime of law, and that it should neither have special privileges nor labour under special disadvantages compared with the ordinary citizen. That argues against a special measure for ensuring a right of reply.' Geoffrey Robertson dealt persuasively with this argument in 1983. He attacked the Commission's argument as 'riddled with mistakes':

The press should not be subjected to a special regime of law. The press is already subjected to special legal regimes. The laws which deal with copyright, contempt, defamation, court reporting, rehabilitation of offenders, official secrecy, elections, local council meetings, matrimonial proceedings, race relations – to name but a few – have special provisions applying only the media.

The press should not have special privileges. The press already has some special privileges, and it needs more. Journalists have, for example, the privilege of remaining in certain courts and meetings when members of the public have been excluded ...

There should be no special legal measure for securing corrections. A special and legal measure for securing corrections already exists, namely, the law of defamation ...

The Royal Commission has formulated a nonsensical proposition ... to define the relationship between the people and the press.[6]

If you hold the view that the state in the UK is incapable of any form of positive response to pressure for reform then, quite rightly, you will not support any form of legislative reform. If you hold the view that the state should not be involved in regulating the media, or should only in so far as it provides a level playing field for economic competition and some minimum standards for content then you can justifiably be accused of agreeing to hand power in the media to the partisan, sectional interests of large-scale commercially driven communications conglomerates.

If we assume that some reforms are possible then the problem becomes one of devising a workable legal framework for promoting press freedom and improving standards; this is precisely what many of the campaigners from the 1940s to the 1990s have tried to do, in the face of vigorous opposition from proprietors. The kind of law that could be devised to raise standards is debatable, but there seems no good argument from principle why such a law should not be devised and implemented.

Overseas experience

There are many examples of European states that have established a legal right of reply or some form of binding sanctions on the press. This has usually been part of a constitutional or legal framework that also grants rights and freedoms to the press. In West Germany, before unification, press laws were established. Most of these laws, as well as guaranteeing freedoms to the press 'contained an obligation of accuracy and thoroughness, requiring the newspapers and magazines to check the content, origin and accuracy of all news prior to publication'. In addition these laws included a right of reply which obliged newspapers 'to publish an accredited reply by any individual or organisation who had been misrepresented over a matter of fact'. Whilst right of reply provisions have 'very often been ignored' and the voluntary German Press Council judged 'generally successful in deflecting state measures against the press, but rather less effective as a means of self-regulation', the existence of a statutory framework for the press incorporating a right of reply did not result in state control of the press.[7]

In France a press law granting freedoms and imposing responsibilities on the press, including a right of reply, has existed since 1881. The French system has 'provided some notable positive rights and freedoms: the principle of right of access to official information, a right of reply, strict privacy laws protecting individuals against unwarranted press intrusion, and ... protection afforded to journalists and their sources'.[8] There is no evidence that this framework has resulted in state control of the press.

Indeed by the 1990s a number of other European countries had both privacy and right of reply laws, including Austria, Denmark, the Netherlands, Norway and Spain. In Sweden a voluntary Press Council operated, but with teeth; having the power to fine newspapers and magazines that breached the Council's code and working within a framework in which publications were bound by contract to respond to its criticisms. It has been argued that the Swedish system has 'provided for an effective and publicly accountable system of self-regulation'.[9] We are not aware of any sustained attempt in the UK to argue that the existence of such laws and measures in other European countries has proven impractical or that they have constituted a threat to press freedom.

The 1974–77 Commission rejected a statutory right of reply on principle, but in the same breath accepted that such a law could work:

> There would clearly be practical difficulties in establishing a legal right of reply, and detailed regulations would be required. But since the system worked for a number of years in West Germany we see no practical reason why it could not do so here. The right provides a prompt remedy, acts as a sanction, and promotes accuracy of reporting.[10]

The existence of right of reply laws in states other than Germany also indicates that they are a practical option and that the UK has the opportunity to look to European good practice in this area and adapt it for domestic use.

A context for reform

A number of things shape the context in which any reform might take shape. They include the incorporation of the European Convention on Human Rights, the Data Protection Act and the libel laws.

European Convention on Human Rights (ECHR)

The incorporation into British law of the ECHR, as the Human Rights Act 1998, has been seen by many as the answer to the problem of privacy and freedom of expression. The relevant articles are:

Article 8. Right to Respect for Private and Family Life
1. Everyone has the right to respect for his private and family life, his home and his correspondence.
2. There shall be no interference by a public authority with the exercise of this right except such as is in accordance with the law and is necessary in a democratic society in the interests of national security, public safety or the economic well-being of the country, for the prevention of disorder or crime, for the protection of health or morals, or for the protection of the rights and freedoms of others ...

Article 10. Freedom of Expression
1. Everyone has the right to freedom of expression. This right shall include freedom to hold opinions and to receive and impart information and ideas without interference by public authority and regardless of frontiers. This Article shall not prevent States from requiring the licensing of broadcasting, television or cinema enterprises.
...
3. The exercise of these freedoms, since it carries with it duties and responsibilities, may be subject to such formalities, conditions, restrictions or penalties as are prescribed by law and are necessary in a democratic society, in the interests of national security, territorial integrity or public safety, for the prevention of disorder or crime, for the protection of health or morals, for the protection of the reputation or rights of others, for preventing the disclosure of information received in confidence, or for maintaining the authority and impartiality of the judiciary.[11]

The act therefore provides opportunities for the UK courts to develop the law on privacy and freedom of expression in the light of the requirements of Articles 8 and 10. This process may impact on the interests of newspapers. It will require several test cases for the effect of this process to emerge. The courts may also be required to develop a view on the question of the accuracy of newspapers in relation to the requirement in Article 10, paragraph 2 that protects the reputation of individuals. It might be that in the development of law the UK courts give too much prominence to Article 8 to the detriment of investigative journalism. The Human Rights Act could therefore provide an important context for the development of law that will affect the press, and therefore it may impact on the issues discussed in this book. Nonetheless, everything depends on interpretation by the courts. This, at the time of writing, is unknown territory for Britain.

Data Protection Act

The first Data Protection Act appeared in 1984. It was revised to give effect to EU Directive 95/46EC (The Data Protection Directive) as the Data Protection Act 1998.

This act has important consequences for the press. It requires all organisations that hold information about individuals either manually (as defined under Section 1 (1)(c) of the act) or on an electronic database to register with the Data Protection Commissioner, formerly known as the Data Protection Registrar.[12] The intention is to protect the individual from the improper use of personal information and to give them the power to correct inaccuracies.[13] It is this last element that brings the press into the picture. Under the act the press has a general duty (with some exemptions) to disclose the information it holds on individuals; the individual has the power to challenge inaccuracies and insist on their correction, not just at the point of publication, but on the database, to prevent a recurrence. The act, however, is not as clear in relation to the press as it perhaps should be; there remains plenty of room for different interpretations of how the act relates to questions of accuracy in the press.

Libel

At present, the libel laws constitute a powerful sanction on the press, but we would argue they act in a negative way. Legal aid is not available for libel, so essentially it remains a resort for the rich who fear press intrusion. Even in 'no win, no fee' cases the person who brings the action can be liable for the other side's costs, though this can be mitigated by insurance policies offered by solicitors to protect clients. Leaving aside the problem of financing an action, the press face serious restrictions on their ability to expose wrongdoing because the threat of a libel action can stop an investigation at an early stage. The fact that in the past juries have awarded damages of hundreds of thousands of pounds makes even the richer newspaper owners think twice before facing the prospect of a long and expensive legal action. For a small paper the costs can be potentially lethal.

So, libel fails to protect the less well off while posing a real threat to smaller newspapers and magazines. One of the reasons that a method of getting a factual correction displayed with appropriate prominence is desirable is because it could be an inexpensive and affordable alternative to libel. A greater willingness by the press to own up to errors would certainly lend weight to the argument that the libel laws should be made less onerous.

All of the measures outlined in this section have a bearing on the press, but they do not, individually, or cumulatively, provide a mechanism for promoting press freedom, enhancing standards and providing an inexpensive form of redress for the citizen.

Press freedom and ownership

The link between the economics of the industry and standards has always been strong. The private ownership of a newspaper confers on the owner the need to make profits, and to this end standards have often been sacrificed on the altar of circulation. The power of private ownership when concentrated in a few hands is open to abuse. In the late twentieth century newspaper proprietors have used their influence to attack mercilessly their political opponents, promote their commercial interests and to mobilise support for xenophobic sentiment.[14] It would be naive to think that measures such as a right to reply to inaccuracies would not have an influence on the ability of proprietors to use their publications to promote their own views at the expense of accuracy and truth. In fact in this book we have argued that the reason why proprietors and editors have objected to statutory regulation is because it would, through the devices of exposure and penalties, restrain their freedom to say what they like regardless of accuracy.

A number of measures could, and should, be taken to create a better climate for improving press standards. Foremost amongst these would be measures to prevent further concentration of ownership in the hands of a few media companies and to promote media diversity. This would involve setting strict limits on how many media outlets any one company could own.

Similarly there should be an organisation, possibly called a Media Diversity Board, funded by a levy on media advertising revenue. The funds raised by a levy could be used to promote diversity and, where necessary, to aid important but financially ailing publications. State support for the press has existed in Europe for many years, for example in Austria, France, Norway and Sweden. The experience of these countries could be analysed and developed to fit UK conditions. The press in the UK in the 1990s received a massive subsidy from the state in the form of exemption from value added taxation (VAT), so the industry has, in fact, conceded the principle that it can, under certain conditions, receive state-directed finances.[15]

Promoting media diversity is therefore a precondition, in the long term, for creating a system of press regulation that balances the right to freedom of expression with the need for media accountability to the public. Only a diverse media can adequately reflect the range of views and opinions that exist in society; a media concentrated in a few hands leaves far too much room for abuse of power.

An equally important development would be the implementation of a genuinely effective Freedom of Information Act that puts the onus on government to prove that the withholding of information was against the public interest, and which seriously confronted the long-established preference for secrecy amongst top politicians and civil servants.[16] A reform of secrecy legislation, of the law of contempt and the 'D' Notice system, plus some form of legal protection for editors and journalists from the fear of dismissal because they refuse to distort the news in line with proprietorial wishes, would also be major steps forward. If these measures were enacted, then part of the package might be a carefully framed privacy law, but only within a context that protected the right of journalists to publish material which was genuinely in the public interest as well as providing legitimate, affordable, protections for the citizen.

Ideally these changes would occur alongside the general reform of mass communications policy. By 2000, 23 years had passed since the report of the 1974–77 Royal Commission on the Press and of the Annan Commission on Broadcasting which reported in 1977. In that period the spread of computer-based communications technologies and changes in broadcasting policy had contributed to the proliferation of channels of communication. Policy-making proceeded in this period without any major attempt at public scrutiny such as that which had in the past been offered by the mechanism of a Royal Commission. There needs to be a clear commitment from governments to subject communications policy, including the question of the regulation of press standards, to periodic high-profile open public review, as a way of injecting a much needed degree of public accountability into the policy-making process in this important area.

Standards and freedom

The reform of the system of self-regulation should, ideally, proceed as part of the wider reforms we outline above. It would however be possible to take steps, based on the 1992–93 Press Freedom and Responsibility Bill, that would constitute real progress. We print the bill, as it was amended by Committee, in the Appendix. The bill provides a basis for thinking through some of the things that could be done.

The mechanisms within the bill were designed to promote high standards and press freedom. An Independent Press Authority (IPA) would be appointed by a procedure designed to maximise the independence and the representative nature of the people on it. The IPA would, through its Press Complaints Advisor, seek to help the public gain their right of correction, ideally by conciliation, although, if necessary, it would adjudicate on the complaint. In the case of non-compliance with an order to print a correction, the IPA could seek enforcement via an application to the courts. This last measure would provide the IPA with the sanctions that self-regulation has always lacked.

The other function of the IPA would be to promote high standards of journalism, to investigate and monitor issues relating to freedom of the press, to monitor the industry's structure and ownership, and to produce codes of standards and to conduct research. In a sense, under this model, the IPA would be doing the kind of thing the 1947–49 Commission envisaged a voluntary Press Council would do.

Defining 'inaccuracy' would, at times, present problems. But this has not prevented the PCC from adjudicating in this area and the bulk of the complaints it adjudicated on in the 1990s related to accuracy. It might be that the two functions, of enforcing the right to a correction, and promoting press standards, could be separated into two separate bodies. This would have the advantage of clearly distinguishing the role of promoter of press freedom and high standards from that of adjudicating on press conduct. In that case the press freedom aspects of the IPA could be part of a new Press Freedom law which had at its centre a clear legal defence of press freedom, establishing a right to print and publish and reasserting the right of freedom of expression subject to the normal constraints of the law.

To balance the rights of the press with those of the citizen a Press Freedom Act might also include a provision which makes the PCC Code enforceable in law or one which requires the courts to have regard to the code when adjudicating on any case against the press. On the face of it this is an attractive option because the code has been drawn up by the press and it is difficult for them to argue that it can't or shouldn't be enforced. It would also be a relatively simple piece of legislation, probably involving a few clauses added to an existing or proposed bill. If this were the situation then some cases we have discussed would perhaps have not occurred because the papers would have been unable to defend them in court under any article of the code. In addition such provisions might encourage swift, out-of-court settlements of disputes. Faced with statutory power, however, there would be nothing to stop the press simply withdrawing from the PCC or radically changing the existing code. To avoid this, legislation might give the courts the power to take into account any future changes to the code – so it would always remain relevant to the court's deliberations.

One difficulty with this approach is the problem of sanctions. What would the sanctions be for breaches of the code? We should always avoid sanctions which put at risk the future publication of a paper (which is one of the reasons why libel poses such a threat to press freedom) or that makes it likely that an editor or journalist faces imprisonment. By far the best form of sanctions and quite probably the most effective would be the requirement for the newspaper to print a correction, an apology or simply allow a right of reply. These are not onerous sanctions. Most newspapers would want to avoid having to publish such corrections regularly and would therefore have an incentive to seek higher standards. Serious consequences would only arise if an editor chose to defy the court. This risk already applies in all countries. Being an editor, however, does not mean being above the law.

There are, however other difficulties with this approach. Enshrining the PCC Code in law places too much power in the hands of the courts. Court proceedings are costly and therefore of limited value to most people. The idea also does not overcome the problem of allowing the PCC as presently constituted to have a major say in the framing the code and promoting press standards. The code as it stands is an employers' code, and the PCC does not represent the main trade union in the industry nor its code. Putting it into law also does not allow for the need to create a body that is independent of the press and the courts and acts for the complainant when other methods fail.

Conclusion

A new Press Freedom Law plus a version of the Freedom and Responsibility of the Press Bill might go some way towards removing the power of employers over the complaints process and involve more fully and effectively both journalists and the public in the task of framing and upholding press standards. They would also help to challenge the ability of employers and editors to claim that their interests are to be equated with press freedom by providing mechanisms that would allow others to have a say in defining press freedoms and responsibilities.

A 'fast track' system to correct complaints, backed by sanctions, would give authority to the complaints procedures. By its very existence the system would support the day-to-day work of those journalists who want to see the highest standards applied in their work. In addition, the production of a code of conduct that reflected the views of all sections of the industry, something that the employers have never yet agreed to, would provide a set of criteria by which the public could judge the activities of the press.

We do not believe that the mere correction of inaccuracy would solve wider problems of distortion and misrepresentation. We do, however, think that statutory measures of the sort we describe here would be a major step forward, benefiting both journalists and the public. These measures would help break the postwar cycle of self-regulation of reluctant reform, followed by more scandals, followed by public pressure, followed by minor, reluctant reform. They would help lay to rest the sterile general debate about whether the interests of press freedom are, or are not, promoted by statutory intervention, and focus minds on making laws and structures that were fair and worked. The proprietors have had their chance to make self-regulation work; as we have shown, they have repeatedly failed to do so. We need to build on the insights of the postwar reformers described in this book to create an effective statutory framework that balances the right of journalists to investigate and publish, with the reasonable expectation of citizens that the press should act fairly and responsibly. This would be a way of genuinely improving the quality of communications in our society and contributing, in a way that arguably self-regulation never did, to developing a media that enhances the democratic process.

Appendix[1]

A

BILL

[AS AMENDED IN STANDING COMMITTEE 'F']

TO

Require newspapers to present news with due accuracy; to secure the free dissemination of news and information in the public interest; to prescribe certain professional and ethical standards; to make provision with respect to enforcement, complaints and adjudication; and for connected purposes.

BE IT ENACTED by the Queen's most Excellent majesty, by and with the advice and consent of the Lords Spiritual and Temporal, and Commons, in this present Parliament assembled, and by the authority of the same: as follows: -

1. There shall be a body, to be called the Independent Press Authority (the Authority), which shall –
    (a) seek the presentation of news by newspapers and periodicals with due accuracy;
    (b) secure the free dissemination of news and information in the public interest and the promotion of professional and ethical standards;
    (c) have the duties and powers set Out in section 2 below; and
    (d) be constituted as set out in the Schedule to this Act.

2. (1) The Authority shall have the following duties –
    (a) to promote the highest standards of journalism in newspapers;
    (b) to investigate and monitor issues relating to freedom of the press and to report to Parliament on any measure it may consider appropriate;

(c) to investigate and monitor ethical standards of the press, distribution of newspapers, ownership and control of the media, access to information and restrictions on reporting and any related matter it may consider appropriate;
(d) to produce and promote codes of professional and ethical standards for the press;
(e) in support of the duties above, to conduct research into and make recommendations on the training and education of journalists;
(f) to issue advice and guidance to the press on matters within its responsibilities;
(g) to report annually to Parliament; and
(h) to consider any matter referred to it by either House of Parliament.

(2) The Authority shall have the following powers –
(a) to determine the question of factual inaccuracy where an application is made to the Authority under section 4 below; and
(b) where it is satisfied that a complainant is entitled to a correction under section 3 below, to order the editor or the publisher of the newspaper, or both of them, to publish a correction in the manner specified in that section; and
(c) in the case of non-compliance by an editor or publisher the High Court or, in Scotland, the Court of Session or, in Northern Ireland, the Supreme Court, may, on application by the Authority, enforce an order made under paragraph (b) above.

3. (1) There shall be a right to a published correction of a factual inaccuracy in editorial material published in a newspaper.

(2) A person, group of persons, or body (the complainant) may exercise the right contained in subsection (1), whether or not that complainant is directly affected by the inaccuracy.

(3) A correction shall be printed free of charge in the next possible edition of the same newspaper.

(4) The correction shall be given a prominence equivalent to that of the material complained of and shall be of the length necessary to correct the material, having regard to its original context.

4. (1) Where an editor or publisher fails or refuses to publish a correction, a complainant may apply to the Authority for the enforcement of the right to a correction.

(2) An application under subsection (1) above shall be referred by the Authority to the Press Complaints Advisor.

(3) A complainant applying under subsection (1) above for the enforcement of the right to a correction shall do so in writing within three months of the date of publication of the relevant editorial material.

(4) The Authority may consider an application made more than three months from the date of publication of the relevant material if it considers that it was not reasonably practicable to make that application within the time limit specified above.

(5) The Authority may dismiss any application which it reasonably considers to be vexatious or trivial.

5. (1) In determining the question of factual inaccuracy, the Authority shall take account of any evidence put forward by the complainant and the editor or publisher of the newspaper concerned or any other person who appears to have been responsible for the editorial material complained of, and those people shall be given the opportunity to put forward such evidence, and may give evidence to the authority at an oral hearing of the application.

(2) The Authority shall give its decision within 28 days of receiving an application unless it is not reasonably practicable to do so within that time limit.

(3) If an editor or publisher does not respond in time to allow the Authority to give a decision within 28 days of receiving a complaint, the Authority may nevertheless order the publication of a correction.

(4) A decision of the Authority shall be binding upon the parties to the decision.

6. (1) There shall be a Press Complaints Advisor (the Advisor), appointed as set out in the Schedule to this Act, to provide advice and Advisor assistance to complainants who are applying for the enforcement of their right to a correction under this Act.

(2) The Advisor may take up a case on behalf of a complainant.

(3) Where requested by the complainant, the Advisor may seek conciliation between the complainant and the newspaper to obtain redress other than a correction under section 3 above.

(4) The Advisor shall make an annual report to the Authority on his work and may make recommendations to the Authority on any aspect of its work.

7. There shall be paid out of money provided by Parliament –

(a) any expenses of any Minister or of the Authority under this Act;

(b) the salaries and expenses of the Secretary, the Advisor and other officers and staff of the Authority; and

(c) subject to a limit specified by the Secretary of State by order made by statutory instrument, the expenses necessarily incurred by the members of the Authority in connection with their duties.

8. In this Act –

'editor' means any person with overall responsibility for editorial content of a newspaper;

'editorial material' means any written, photographic or graphic material which is not an advertisement or cartoon; and 'material' shall be construed accordingly; and

'newspaper' includes 'periodical'.

9. (1) This Act may be cited as the Freedom and Responsibility of the Press Act 1993.

(2) This Act shall come into force on 1st January 1994.

(3) This Act shall extend to Northern Ireland.

Schedules
The Independent Press Authority

The Independent Press Appointments Committee

1. The Authority shall be constituted in accordance with the following provisions.

2. The Secretary of State shall appoint seven persons who shall constitute the Appointments Committee (hereinafter referred to as 'the Committee') who shall be responsible for the appointment of the members to the Council of the Authority. The Secretary of State shall thereafter appoint such persons necessary to replace those members who cease for whatever reason to serve on the Committee so that the Committee shall at all times be convened with seven members.

3. Before appointing a person to be a member of the Committee the Secretary of State shall satisfy himself that that person will have no such financial or other interest as is likely to affect prejudicially the discharge by him or her of his or her functions as a member of the Committee; and the Secretary of State shall satisfy himself from time to time with respect to every member of the Committee that he or she has no such interest.

4. Each member of the Committee may serve for a maximum of five years as a member of the Committee. No member shall serve on the Committee beyond the fifth anniversary of his or her appointment to the Committee.

5. The members of the authority shall receive no remuneration for serving on the Committee.

6. The Committee members shall appoint one of their number to be the Chairman of the Committee for a term of two years. A person so appointed may serve up to two terms as Chairman provided that no person's service as Chairman shall extend beyond the fifth anniversary of that person's appointment to the Committee.

Appointment of the authority

7. The sole responsibility of the Committee shall be from time to time to appoint persons as members to the Council of the Authority.

8. No person shall be considered for appointment who is: -
   (1) A member of the House of Commons.
   (2) A member of the House of Lords who holds a ministerial position.
   (3) An employer, partner, co-director or employee of any member of the Committee.
   (4) An ancestor, sibling or descendant of any member of the Committee.
   (5) Presently serving or subject to a term of imprisonment or a suspended sentence of imprisonment or is unrehabilitated within the terms of the Rehabilitated Offenders Act 1974.

9. The Committee shall within three months of its inaugural meeting select and appoint to serve on the Council of the Authority 21 persons.

10. The Committee shall from time to time thereafter select and appoint within 30 days of the vacancy occurring on the Council of the Authority such person or persons to the Council of the Authority as shall be required to maintain at 21 the number of members of the Council of the Authority.

11. The Committee shall invite nominations for membership of the Council of the Authority from all bodies and concerns involved or interested in the promotion of free speech and all the rights of individuals in a democratic society.

12. A person shall be appointed to serve on the Council of the Authority if, when nominated, he or she receives the vote of not less than five members of the Committee.

13. Save as otherwise expressly provided under this Section no person may serve on the Council beyond the eighth anniversary of his or her appointment to the Council of the Authority.

14. Eleven of the initial appointees of the Council of the Authority shall be entitled to serve an initial term of eight years as a member of the Council. The remaining initial appointees shall be entitled only to serve an initial term of four years on the Council. The initial length of term of an appointee shall be determined by lot.

15. A member of the Council may be appointed immediately following the expiry of his or her term but may not serve on the Council for a period in aggregate of more than 16 years.

16. Any person who is or whom the Committee proposes to appoint as a member of the Council of the Authority shall whenever requested by the Secretary of State to do so furnish the Secretary of State with such information as the Secretary of State considers necessary for the performance by that member of his or her duties.

17. Except as otherwise provided in this Act, the Authority may determine its own procedure.

18. The Authority shall elect annually a member as chair of the Authority by a simple majority of those present.

19. The Authority shall meet as often as it deems necessary and at least twice every year.

20. Members of the Authority shall be entitled to a reasonable amount of time off from their employment in order to carry out their functions as members of the Authority.

Officers of the Authority

21. The Authority shall appoint a Secretary who shall be responsible for the administration of the work of the Authority and shall carry out such duties as the Authority may direct.

22. The person appointed as Secretary may be relieved of office at his own request or may be removed from office by a resolution of the Authority supported by majority of the members.
23. The Authority may also appoint such officers and staff as are necessary to assist the Secretary in carrying out the duties in paragraph 8 above.

Press Complaints Advisor

24. The Authority shall appoint a Press Complaints Advisor and such officers and staff as are necessary to assist the Advisor in carrying out the duties specified in section 6 of this Act.
25. The Advisor shall be appointed for a term not exceeding five years, but may be reappointed.

Hearings

26. Decisions of the Authority on the enforcement of the right to a correction under this Act shall be made by a panel consisting of at least five members appointed for that purpose.

Notes

Notes to Chapter 1

1. H.C. Strick, 'British newspaper journalism 1900–1956: a study in industrial relations' (PhD thesis: University of London, 1957), p. 2.
2. R. Williams, *The Long Revolution* (London: Pelican, 1973), pp. 195–236.
3. R. Williams, 'The Press we don't deserve', in J. Curran (ed.), *The British Press: A Manifesto* (London: Macmillan, 1978), p. 18.
4. G. Boyce, 'The Fourth Estate; the reappraisal of a concept', in G. Boyce, J. Curran and P. Wingate (eds), *Newspaper History: from the seventeenth century to the present day* (London: Constable, 1978), pp. 20–21.
5. J. Curran, 'The Press as an agency of social control: an historical perspective', ibid., pp. 51–75.
6. B. Harrison, 'Press and pressure group in modern Britain', in J. Shattock and M. Wolff (eds), *The Victorian Periodical Press: Samplings and Soundings* (Leicester: Leicester University Press, 1982), p. 261. For another critique which stresses the importance of considering press reform within the context of campaigns for a wider franchise and free trade, see S. Koss, *The Rise and Fall of the Political Press in Britain* (London: Fontana, 1990), pp. 53–55, 65–67.
7. P.T. O'Malley, 'The politics of defamation: the state, Press interests and the evolution of the English libel laws' (PhD thesis: London School of Economics, University of London, 1975), p. 2.
8. A. Jones, *Powers of the Press. Newspapers, Power and the Public in Nineteenth-century England* (Aldershot: Scolar Press, 1996), p. 202.
9. J. Frank, *The Beginnings of the English Newspaper, 1620–1660* (Cambridge: Harvard University Press, 1961), pp. 1–3. In Chapters 1–3 we use the terms 'newspaper', 'news serial' and 'newsbook' interchangeably.
10. B. Harris, *Politics and the Rise of the Press. Britain and France, 1620–1800* (London: Routledge, 1996), pp. 26–27.
11. Frank, *Beginnings*, pp. 13, 57.
12. T. O'Malley, 'Religion and the newspaper Press, 1660–1685: a study of the "London Gazette"', in M. Harris and A. Lee (eds), *The Press in English Society from the Seventeenth to Nineteenth Centuries* (London and Toronto: Associated University Press, 1986), p. 31.
13. Harris, *Politics*, pp. 13–14.
14. O'Malley, 'Religion', pp. 28–29. For an account of news in the early seventeenth century, see R. Cust, 'News and politics in early seventeenth-century England', *Past & Present*, 112 (1986), pp. 60–90.
15. J. Black, *The English Press in the Eighteenth Century* (London: Croom Helm, 1987), p. 141.

16. The evidence of total circulations from 1712 until the mid-nineteenth century are based on the returns for the stamp tax, which was levied on all newspapers from that date. The difficulties with this evidence are discussed in A.P. Wadsworth, *Newspaper Circulations 1800–1954* (Manchester: Manchester Statistical Society, 1955), Appendix.

17. Harris, *Politics*, pp. 10–12.

18. For the reasons behind this growth, see Williams, *Long Revolution*, pp. 195–236; A. Lee, 'The structure, ownership and control of the press, 1855–1914', in Boyce *et al.*, *Newspaper History*, pp. 117–29; J. Moore, 'Communications', in C. Chant (ed.), *Science, Technology and Everyday Life 1870–1950* (London: Open University Press/Routledge, 1989), pp. 200–49.

19. Wadsworth, *Newspaper Circulations*, pp. 2–3.

20. Ibid., pp. 11–12. See also V. Berridge, 'Popular Sunday papers in mid-Victorian society', in Boyce *et al.*, *Newspaper History*, pp. 247–64.

21. S. Bennett, 'Revolutions in thought: serial publication and the mass market for reading', in Shattock and Wolff, *Victorian Periodical Press*, p. 226.

22. Bennett, 'Revolutions'; Harrison, 'Press and pressure group', p. 277; Lee, 'Structure, ownership and control'; W. Houghton, 'Periodical literature and the articulate classes', in Shattock and Wolff, *Victorian Periodical Press*, p. 3.

23. Williams, *Long Revolution*, pp. 198–99, 213.

24. O'Malley, 'Religion'.

25. Harris, *Politics*, pp. 16, 93; M. Harris, 'Sport in the newspapers before 1750: representations of cricket, class and commerce in the London press', *Media History* vol. 4, no. 1 (1998), pp. 19–28.

26. Koss, *Rise and Fall*, p. 56; Williams, *Long Revolution*, p. 198. See also Berridge, 'Popular Sunday papers'.

27. A. Lee, *The Origins of the Popular Press* (London: Croom Helm, 1976), pp. 117–25; Koss, *Rise and Fall*, pp. 344–47.

28. D.F. Mitch, *The Rise of Popular Literacy in Victorian England. The Influence of Private Choice and Public Policy* (Philadelphia: University of Pennsylvania Press, 1992), pp. xvi–xvii, 2; Harris, *Politics*, pp. 15, 17, 108.

29. Mitch, *Rise of Popular Literacy*, p. 2; figures refer to the signing of marriage registers.

30. Lee, *Origins*, p. 33; Mitch, *Rise of Popular Literacy*, p. xvi.

31. Mitch, *Rise of Popular Literacy*, pp. 41–61, 77; T. Mason, 'Sporting news, 1860–1914', in Harris and Lee, *Press in English Society*, pp. 168–86.

32. Lee, *Origins*, pp. 35–37; a list of papers held in one nineteenth-century reading room is in Wadsworth, *Newspaper Circulations*. For material on reading in coffee houses, see C.J. Sommerville, *The News Revolution in England. Cultural Dynamics of Daily Information* (Oxford: Oxford University Press, 1996).

33. F.S. Siebert, *Freedom of the Press in England 1476–1776* (Urbana: University of Illinois Press, 1965), p. 21.

34. Ibid., pp. 14–16; T. O'Malley, 'Defying the powers and tempering the spirit: a review of Quaker control over their publications, 1672–1689', *Journal of Ecclesiastical History*, 33 (1982), pp. 72–88; Harris, *Politics*, p. 8.

35. O'Malley, 'Politics of Defamation', pp. 112 on the lapse of the Licensing Act; Harris, *Politics*, pp. 29–30.

36. Harris, *Politics*, pp. 15, 36, 43–45; Boyce *et al.*, *Newspaper History*, p. 407; S. Targett, '"The Premier Scribbler himself": Sir Robert Walpole and the

management of political opinion', in M. Harris and T. O'Malley (eds), *Studies in Newspaper and Periodical History. 1994 Annual* (Connecticut: Greenwood Press, 1996), pp. 19–33.

37. O'Malley, 'Politics of Defamation', p. 146. On the working-class agitation in this period, see E.P. Thompson, *The Making of the English Working Class* (London: Penguin, 1991).

38. See Notes 5 and 6 above. See also Jones, *Powers*, Chapter 1.

39. Lee, *Origins*, pp. 42–49; Boyce *et al.*, *Newspaper History*, pp. 407–408.

40. J. Curran and J. Seaton, *Power Without Responsibility*, 5th edn (London: Routledge, 1997), Chapters 1–7; Koss, *Rise and Fall*. The question of commercial censorship in the press would repay greater historical study.

41. Moore, 'Communications', p. 231; D. Hooper, *Official Secrets. The Use and Abuse of the Act* (London: Coronet, 1988), pp. 29–42; C. Lovelace, 'British Press censorship during the First World War', in Boyce *et al.*, *Newspaper History*, pp. 307–19.

42. K. Williams, *Get Me A Murder A Day! A History of Mass Communication in Britain* (London: Arnold, 1998), Chapters 5 and 7; N. Pronay, 'Rearmament and the British public: policy and propaganda', in J. Curran, A. Smith and P. Wingate (eds), *Impacts and Influences* (London: Methuen, 1987), pp. 53–96; T. Aldgate, 'Comedy, class and containment: the British domestic cinema of the 1930s', in J. Curran and V. Porter (eds), *British Cinema History* (London: Weidenfeld and Nicolson, 1983), pp. 257–71; J. Richards, *The Age of the Dream Palace. Cinema and Society in Britain 1930–1939* (London: Routledge, 1984), pp. 89–152.

43. Curran and Seaton, *Power Without Responsibility*, pp. 111–50; P. Scannell, 'Broadcasting and the politics of unemployment 1930–1935', in R. Collins, J. Curran, N. Garnham, P. Scannell, P. Schlesinger and C. Sparks (eds), *Media, Culture and Society. A Critical Reader* (London: Sage, 1986), pp. 214–27.

44. For a more detailed account of the circumstances surrounding the establishment of the first Royal Commission, see T. O'Malley, 'Labour and the 1947–49 Royal Commission on the Press', in M. Bromley and T. O'Malley, *A Journalism Reader* (London: Routledge, 1997), pp. 126–58.

Notes to Chapter 2

1. T. O'Malley, 'Labour and the 1947–49 Royal Commission on the Press', in M. Bromley and T. O'Malley, *A Journalism Reader* (London: Routledge, 1997), pp. 126–58; T. O'Malley, 'Demanding accountability: the Press, the Royal Commissions and the pressure for reform, 1945–77', in H. Stephenson and M. Bromley (eds), *Sex, Lies and Democracy. The Press and the Public* (London: Longman, 1998), pp. 84–96.

2. A. Jones, *Powers of the Press. Newspapers, Power and the Public in Nineteenth-century England* (Aldershot: Scolar Press, 1996), p. 202.

3. Ibid., p. 180.

4. *Report of the Committee on Financing the BBC*, Cmnd. 9824 (London: HMSO, 1986), para. 23.

5. For some criticisms of the ideas associated with this version of history, see J. Keane, *The Media and Democracy* (Oxford: Polity, 1991), pp. 37–50; R. Wacks, *Privacy and Press Freedom* (London: Blackstone, 1995), pp. 27–28;

G. Boyce, 'The Fourth Estate; the reappraisal of a concept', in G. Boyce, J. Curran and P. Wingate (eds), *Newspaper History: from the seventeenth century to the present day* (London: Constable, 1978), p. 29; M. Harris, *London Newspapers in the Age of Walpole* (London and Toronto: Associated University Press, 1987), p. 8. This chapter does not attempt to analyse the different political currents that underpinned criticisms of the press, nor to identify which opinions carried greatest weight at different times. The purpose here is simply to establish that there have always been different assessments of the value of the press and of its proper relationship to state and society.

6.   Keane, *Media and Democracy*, pp. 11–13.
7.   H. Fielding, *Jonathan Wild* (New York: Signet, 1962), Book III, Chapter 5, p. 127.
8.   W. Blackstone, *Commentaries* (1765), Book IV, pp. 151–52, cited in G. Robertson, *Freedom, the Individual and the Law* (London: Penguin, 1991), p. 255.
9.   Anon., *The Letters of Junius. Complete in One Volume* (London, 1791), p. xv.
10.   J. Mill, 'Review', in *Edinburgh Review* (May 1811), cited in M. Bromley and T. O'Malley, *A Journalism Reader* (London: Routledge, 1997), pp. 16–17.
11.   J.S. Mill, 'Essay on Liberty' (1859), in ibid., p. 22. Brackets inserted.
12.   Jones, *Powers*, p. 52.
13.   T. Hobbes, *Leviathan* (London: Penguin, 1981), p. 379. See also F.S. Siebert, *Freedom of the Press in England 1476–1776* (Urbana: University of Illinois Press, 1965), pp. 249–56.
14.   C.J. Sommerville, *The News Revolution in England. Cultural Dynamics of Daily Information* (Oxford: Oxford University Press, 1996), pp. 29, 35, 65–66, 89.
15.   Ibid., p. 14; B. Harris, *Politics and the Rise of the Press. Britain and France, 1620–1800* (London: Routledge, 1996), pp. 42–45.
16.   Koss, *Rise and Fall*, p. 35; F. Williams, *Dangerous Estate. The Anatomy of Newspapers* (London: Arrow, 1959), p. 15.
17.   One way they became transmitted was by journalists reproducing them. For example, the 1852 quote from *The Times* was reproduced by Francis Williams, who was a leading journalist from the 1930s to the 1960s, in *Dangerous Estate*, p. 15; the same quote was used in 1962 by the *Daily Mirror*'s Hugh Cudlipp, in his *At Your Peril* (London: Weidenfeld and Nicolson, 1962), p. 12. Similarly the quote from C.P. Scott cited in Note 18 is endlessly reproduced by journalists; for example, see the NUJ's first official history, F.J. Mansfield, *'Gentlemen! The Press'* (London: W.H. Allen, 1943), p. 520.
18.   C.P. Scott, 'The *Manchester Guardian*'s first hundred years', *Manchester Guardian*, 5 May 1921, in Bromley and O'Malley, *Journalism Reader*, p. 108.
19.   H. Wickham Steed, *The Press* (London: Penguin, 1938), p. 14.
20.   Wilson Harris, *The Daily Press* (Cambridge: Cambridge University Press, 1943), pp. 9–10, 12–13. For biographical details on Wilson Harris and other people in the industry, see D. Griffiths (ed.), *The Encyclopaedia of the British Press 1422–1992* (London: Macmillan, 1992).
21.   *Royal Commission on the Press 1947–1949. Report*, Cmnd. 7700 (London: HMSO, reprinted 1962), paras. 366, 369. Hereafter, *RCP 1947–49*.
22.   Ibid., paras. 362, 383–84.
23.   This section draws on the ideas developed for the nineteenth century by Aled Jones, in *Powers*. For a much more detailed sense of the flux of opinion

about the press in nineteenth-century England, Scotland and Wales readers should consult his book.

24. J. Raymond, 'The Great Assises Holden on Parnassus. The reputation and reality of seventeenth-century newsbooks', in M. Harris and T. O'Malley (eds), Studies in Newspaper and Periodical History. 1994 Annual (Connecticut: Greenwood Press, 1996), p. 4.

25. Koss, Rise and Fall, p. 31.

26. R. Williams, The Long Revolution (London: Pelican, 1973), p. 218.

27. Koss, Rise and Fall, pp. 39, 41.

28. Ibid., p. 51; W. Cobbett, Cobbett's Political Register (London, 11 April 1807), p. 3, in Keane, Media and Democracy, p. 32.

29. Koss, Rise and Fall, p. 431; A. Jones, Press, Politics and Society: A History of Journalism in Wales (Cardiff: University of Wales Press, 1993), p. 154; S. Bennett, 'Revolutions in thought: serial publication and the mass market for reading', in J. Shattock and M. Wolff (eds), The Victorian Periodical Press: Samplings and Soundings (Leicester: Leicester University Press, 1982), pp. 252–53; Griffiths, Encyclopaedia, entry for J. William Croker.

30. Koss, Rise and Fall, p. 47.

31. Jones, Press, Politics and Society, p. 164.

32. Jones, Powers, pp. 135; B. Harrison, 'Press and pressure group in modern Britain', in Shattock and Wolff, Victorian Periodical Press, p. 268.

33. Jones, Powers, pp. 99, 189, 194, 196.

34. A. Jones, 'Workmen's advocates: ideology and class in a mid-Victorian labour newspaper system', in Shattock and Wolff, Victorian Periodical Press, pp. 297, 309, 312; Jones, Press, Politics and Society, p. 138.

35. Harrison, 'Press and pressure group', p. 270.

36. B. Maidment, 'John Ruskin and the periodical press', in Shattock and Wolff, Victorian Periodical Press, p. 37.

37. J. Carey, The Intellectuals and the Masses (London: Faber, 1992), p. 275.

38. Harrison, 'Press and pressure group', p. 275.

39. Jones, Powers, pp. 198–99.

40. Harrison, 'Press and pressure group', p. 280; Jones, Powers, pp. 63–65.

41. W.T. Stead, 'The future of journalism', Contemporary Review (1886), in Bromley and O'Malley, Journalism Reader, pp. 50–51.

42. C. Bainbridge, 'One hundred years of journalism', in C. Bainbridge (ed.), One Hundred Years of Journalism. Social Aspects of the Press (London: Macmillan, 1984), pp. 36–37.

43. Koss, Rise and Fall, p. 343; D. Porter, 'City editors and the modern investing public: establishing the integrity of the new financial journalism in late nineteenth-century London', Media History, vol. 4, no. 1 (1998), p. 55.

44. Jones, Powers, p. 200; T. Mason, 'Sporting news, 1860–1914', in M. Harris and A. Lee (eds), The Press in English Society from the Seventeenth to Nineteenth Centuries (London and Toronto: Associated University Press, 1986), p. 168.

45. J.O. Baylen, 'A contemporary estimate of the London daily press in the early twentieth century', in Bromley and O'Malley, Journalism Reader, pp. 99–101.

46. T. Nevett, 'Advertising and editorial integrity in the nineteenth century', in Harris and Lee, Press in English Society, p. 159.

47. Mansfield, Gentlemen!, pp. 517, 524; Koss, Rise and Fall, p. 434.

48. H. Richards, The Bloody Circus. The Daily Herald and the Left (London: Pluto Press, 1997), pp. 4–5, 12.

49. Labour Research Department, *The Press* (London: Labour Publishing Company, nd, but 1922), pp. 6, 13–14, 43–45. Brackets inserted.
50. Mansfield, *Gentlemen!*, p. 518.
51. Jones, *Press, Politics and Society*, p. 215; B. Kingsley Martin, 'The Press', in H.B. Lees-Smith (ed.), *The Encyclopaedia of the Labour Movement*, Volume III (London: Caxton Publishing, nd, but 1928), p. 59; O'Malley, 'Labour and the 1947–49 Royal Commission'.
52. J. Carey, *Intellectuals*, pp. 7, 15.
53. P.T. O'Malley, 'The politics of defamation: the state, Press interests and the evolution of the English libel laws' (PhD thesis: London School of Economics, University of London, 1975), pp. 245–50.
54. D. Thomson, *England in the Twentieth Century* (London: Penguin, 1966), p. 133.
55. M. Engel, *Tickle the Public. One Hundred Years of the Popular Press* (London: Victor Gollancz, 1996), pp. 124–25; Mansfield, *Gentlemen!*, pp. 525–26; Wickham Steed, *The Press*, p. 61. See also Koss, *Rise and Fall*, p. 1022, Note 2, and R. Cockett, *Twilight of Truth. Chamberlain, Appeasement and the Manipulation of the Press* (London: Weidenfeld and Nicolson, 1989), pp. 59–60, 126–27.
56. Koss, *Rise and Fall*, pp. 1006–1007; Wickham Steed, *The Press*, pp. 100–101, 104, 150–51.
57. Mansfield, *Gentlemen!*, p. 529.
58. I. Thomas, *The Newspaper* (Oxford: Oxford University Press, 1943), p. 22.
59. W. Harris, *The Daily Press* (Cambridge: Cambridge University Press, 1943), pp. 70–71, 90–91, 126–27.
60. Koss, *Rise and Fall*, pp. 1052–1053; W. Jaehnig, 'Kith and sin: Press accountability in the USA', in Stephenson and Bromley, *Sex, Lies and Democracy*, pp. 100–101.
61. J. Curran, 'Advertising as a patronage system', in H. Christian (ed.), *The Sociology of Journalism and the Press* (Keele: University of Keele, 1980), p. 87; G. Orwell, 'The prevention of literature', *Polemic* (1946), in Bromley and O'Malley, *Journalism Reader*, p. 161; O'Malley, 'Labour and the 1947–49 Royal Commission on the Press'.
62. *Royal Commission on the Press 1947–1949. Report*, Cmnd. 7700 (London: HMSO, reprinted 1962), p. iii.
63. Ibid. para. 489.
64. O'Malley, 'Labour and the 1947–49 Royal Commission on the Press', pp. 130–31.
65. Thus the assertions made in 1987 by Denis MacShane that until the 1970s the Labour Party 'in opposition or government had shown little interest in the media' and that in there 'was no tradition of concern on which present-day policy-makers' could draw are wide of the mark; D. MacShane, 'Media policy and the Left', in J. Seaton and B. Pimlott (eds), *The Media in British Politics* (Aldershot: Avebury, 1987), p. 219.

Notes to Chapter 3

1. H.C. Strick, 'British newspaper journalism 1900–1956: a study in industrial relations' (PhD thesis: University of London, 1957), pp. 67–71.

2. Ibid., pp. 67–75, 83–87; A. Jones, *Press, Politics and Society: A History of Journalism in Wales* (Cardiff: University of Wales Press, 1993), pp. 86–87; F.J. Mansfield, *'Gentlemen! The Press'* (London: W.H. Allen, 1943), p. 201.

3. G. Page, 'The Guild of British Newspaper Editors', in D. Griffiths (ed.), *The Encyclopaedia of the British Press 1422–1992* (London, Macmillan, 1992), p. 643; *Royal Commission on the Press 1947–1949. Report*, Cmnd. 7700 (London: HMSO, reprinted 1962), para. 636. Hereafter, *RCP 1947–49*.

4. B. Franklin, *Newszak and News Media* (London: Arnold, 1997), p. 51; Jones, *Press, Politics and Society*, p. 7; L. Brown, *Victorian News and Newspapers* (Oxford: Oxford University Press, 1985), p. 85; see also M. Bromley, 'The end of journalism? Changes in workplace practices in the Press and broadcasting in the 1990s', in M. Bromley and T. O'Malley, *A Journalism Reader* (London: Routledge, 1997), pp. 330–50.

5. Jones, *Press, Politics and Society*, p. 142; T. Nevett, 'Advertising and editorial integrity in the nineteenth century', in M. Harris and A. Lee (eds), *The Press in English Society from the Seventeenth to Nineteenth Centuries* (London and Toronto: Associated University Press, 1986), p. 154; Mansfield, *Gentlemen!*, p. 17.

6. B. Harrison, 'Press and pressure group in modern Britain', in J. Shattock and M. Wolff (eds), *The Victorian Periodical Press: Samplings and Soundings* (Leicester: Leicester University Press, 1982), p. 271; Strick, 'British newspaper journalism', p. 472.

7. Jones, *Press, Politics and Society*, p. 228.

8. Brown, *Victorian News*, pp. 76, 80–81; A. Jones, *Powers of the Press. Newspapers, Power and the Public in Nineteenth-century England* (Aldershot: Scolar Press, 1996), p. 127.

9. Jones, *Press, Politics and Society*, p. 57; Jones, *Powers*, pp. 120–23.

10. W.D. Rubenstein, 'Wealth, elites and class structure of modern Britain', *Past and Present*, no. 76 (1977), p. 122, Note 54.

11. Strick, 'British newspaper journalism', pp. 103–107; Jones, *Powers*, pp. 124–25; C. Bainbridge, 'One hundred years of journalism', in C. Bainbridge (ed.), *One Hundred Years of Journalism. Social Aspects of the Press* (London: Macmillan, 1984), pp. 44, 151–55.

12. Bainbridge, *One Hundred Years*, pp. 4–56; Strick, 'British newspaper journalism', p. 105; Jones, *Press, Politics and Society*, p. 60; figures on membership of both organisations can be found in H. Christian, 'Journalists' occupational ideologies and Press commercialisation', in H. Christian (ed.), *The Sociology of Journalism and the Press* (Keele: University of Keele, 1980), p. 298.

13. Jones, *Powers*, p. 125; Christian, 'Journalists' occupational ideologies', pp. 278–79.

14. Bainbridge, *One Hundred Years*, pp. 88–89.

15. Mansfield, *Gentlemen!*, pp. 24, 31, 524.

16. Ibid., pp. 332, 524–25.

17. Ibid., pp. 526, 28; Christian, 'Journalists' occupational ideologies', p. 279.

18. Mansfield, *Gentlemen!*, pp. 528–29.

19. Ibid., p. 550; see also T. O'Malley, 'Labour and the 1947–49 Royal Commission on the Press', in M. Bromley and T. O'Malley, *A Journalism Reader* (London: Routledge, 1997).

20. Mansfield, *Gentlemen!*, p. 524; Christian, 'Journalists' occupational ideologies', p. 297; Strick, 'British newspaper journalism', pp. 409–12.

21. S. Koss, *The Rise and Fall of the Political Press in Britain* (London: Fontana, 1990), pp. 442–43.
22. See J. Curran and J. Seaton, *Power Without Responsibility*, 5th edn (London: Routledge, 1997), chapters on Press; C. Seymour-Ure, *The British Press and Broadcasting since 1945* (Oxford: Blackwell, 1991); M. Hollingsworth, *The Press and Political Dissent* (London: Pluto Press, 1986); T. O'Malley, *Closedown? The BBC and Government Broadcasting Policy 1979–92* (London: Pluto Press, 1994).
23. Koss, *Rise and Fall*, pp. 412–13; for Wales, see Jones, *Powers*, p. 148.
24. Brown, *Victorian News*, p. 55.
25. Koss, *Rise and Fall*, p. 93.
26. Jones, *Press, Politics and Society*, pp. 158–60; Jones, *Powers*, p. 154; Koss, *Rise and Fall*, p. 9; Harrison, 'Press and pressure group', p. 271. See also P. Brett, 'Early nineteenth–century reform newspapers in the provinces: the *Newcastle Chronicle* and the *Bristol Mercury*', in M. Harris and T. O'Malley (eds), *Studies in Newspaper and Periodical History, 1995 Annual* (Connecticut: Greenwood, 1997), pp. 49–67.
27. Koss, *Rise and Fall*, pp. 10, 216; P.T. O'Malley, 'The politics of defamation: the state, Press interests and the evolution of the English libel laws' (PhD thesis: London School of Economics, University of London, 1975), pp. 216–17, 232, Note 41.
28. Mansfield, *Gentlemen!*, p. 459–61; Koss, *Rise and Fall*, pp. 1074–1075; Strick, 'British newspaper journalism', p. 408.
29. H. Street, *Freedom, the Individual and the Law* (London: Pelican, 1975), p. 119; Mill in Bromley and O'Malley, *Journalism Reader*, p. 17; O'Malley, 'Politics of defamation', p. 154.
30. O'Malley, 'Politics of defamation', pp. 159–69; Jones, *Press, Politics and Society*, p. 22.
31. Jones, *Press, Politics and Society*, p. 22; Jones, *Powers*, p. 152; D.J. Gray, 'Early Victorian scandalous journalism', in Shattock and Wolf, *Victorian Periodical Press*, p. 343; Street, *Freedom*, p. 139.
32. O'Malley, 'Politics of defamation', pp. 191–97, 200–205; Jones, *Powers*, p. 189.
33. O'Malley, 'Politics of defamation', pp. 203–204, 208–10; Jones, *Press, Politics and Society*, p. 22.
34. O'Malley, 'Politics of defamation', pp. 216–17; G. Robertson, *People Against the Press. An Enquiry into the Press Council* (London: Quartet, 1983).
35. Street, *Freedom*, p. 141–42; G. Robertson, *Freedom, the Individual and the Law* (London: Penguin, 1991), p. 131; D. Hooper, *Official Secrets. The Use and Abuse of the Act* (London: Coronet, 1988), pp. 28–31.
36. Mansfield, *Gentlemen!*, pp. 108–109.
37. Hooper, *Official Secrets*, pp. 38–41; C. Lovelace, 'British Press censorship during the First World War', in G. Boyce, J. Curran and P. Wingate (eds), *Newspaper History: from the seventeenth century to the present day* (London: Constable, 1978), p. 319.
38. Street, *Freedom*, p. 99; Mansfield, *Gentlemen!*, p. 534. See also M. Engel, *Tickle the Public. One Hundred Years of the Popular Press* (London: Victor Gollancz, 1996), p. 223–24.
39. Street, *Freedom*, p. 120; I. Thomas, *The Newspaper* (Oxford: Oxford University Press, 1943), p. 31; O'Malley, 'Politics of defamation', p. 251–55.
40. Robertson, *Freedom*, p. 254.

Notes to Chapter 4

1. T. O'Malley, 'Demanding accountability: the Press, the Royal Commissions and the pressure for reform, 1945–77', in H. Stephenson and M. Bromley (eds), *Sex, Lies and Democracy. The Press and the Public* (London: Longman, 1998), pp. 84–96.

2. For a more detailed account of the political background to the 1947–49 Royal Commission on the Press, see T. O'Malley, 'Labour and the 1947–49 Royal Commission on the Press', in M. Bromley and T. O'Malley (eds), *A Journalism Reader* (London: Routledge, 1997), pp. 126–58.

3. *Political and Economic Planning, Report on the British Press* (London: PEP, 1938), pp. 36–37, 284–85.

4. K. Morgan, *The People's Peace: British History 1945–1990* (Oxford: Oxford University Press, 1992), p. 16; S. Koss, *The Rise and Fall of the Political Press in Britain* (London: Fontana, 1990, p. 1052; F.J. Mansfield, *'Gentlemen! The Press'* (London: W.H. Allen, 1943), p. 558.

5. C. Seymour-Ure, *The Political Impact of the Mass Media* (London: Constable, 1974), pp. 166–67; Koss, *Rise and Fall*, p. 1076.

6. C.J. Bundock, *The National Union of Journalists. A Jubilee History 1907–1957* (Oxford: Oxford University Press, 1957), pp. 185–86; O'Malley, 'Labour and the 1947–49 Royal Commission'; *Royal Commission on the Press 1947–1949. Report*, Cmnd. 7700 (London: HMSO, reprinted 1962), p. iii [hereafter, *RCP 1947–49*]; see also O'Malley, 'Demanding accountability'.

7. Public Record Office (PRO): 'Policy Committee. Note by the Secretary', 7 October 1947, HO 251/213; 'Notes of discussion between Sir David Ross, Sir Geoffrey Vickers and Mr Hull on 17th March 1948', HO 251/216; *RCP 1947–49*, pp. 179–80.

8. *RCP 1947–49*, paras. 642–45; *Report of the Committee on the Law of Defamation 1948*, Cmnd. 7536, paras. 24–26, cited in *Committee on Privacy 1972*, Cmnd. 5012 (London: HMSO, 1972), para. 136.

9. *RCP 1947–49*, para. 684.

10. House of Commons Debates: H.C.Debs, 5s, vol. 467, cols. 2683, 2696, 2699, 2715, 28 July 1949. An explanation of the abbreviations is given in the Bibliography (see 'Parliamentary Debates').

11. V. Juusela, 'The Finnish Council for Mass Media and the Press Complaints Commission. A comparative study of two Press watchdogs' (MPhil thesis: University of Wales, Cardiff, 1992), pp. 34–35; Press Council, *The Press and the People. The Tenth Annual Report of the Press Council* (London: Press Council, 1963), p. 1. Hereafter Press Council Annual Reports (AR) will be cited in abbreviated form indicating the year covered by the report, rather than the year of publication, e.g. *P&P 10th AR 1953–54*.

12. H.C.Debs, 5s, vol. 480, col. 1885, 16 November 1950; ibid., vol. 483, written answers, cols. 152–53, 2 February 1951; PRO, Cabinet Minutes, Cab.128.19, CM.4(51)1, 18 January 1951. See Bibliography for an explanation of abbreviations ('Public Record Office', 'Cabinet Papers').

13. H.C.Debs, 5s, vol. 508, col. 967, 28 November 1952; ibid., vol. 494, cols. 1510–1511, 28 November 1951; ibid., vol. 504, cols. 1670–1671, 31 July 1952; H. Levy, *The Press Council. History, Procedure and Cases* (London: Macmillan, 1967), p. 9.

14. PRO, Cab.128.25, cc 99(52)2, 20 November 1952.

15. H.C.Debs, 5s, vol. 508, cols. 962–1062, 28 November 1952.

16. PRO, Cab.128.26 Part I, cc 30(53)2, 5 May 1953; H.C.Debs, 5s, vol. 515, cols. 748–806.

17. *P&P 1st AR 1953–54*, pp. 32–36, 'Constitution' clauses, 2, 3, 4, 14, Schedule; *RCP 1947–49*, para. 684.

18. *P&P 1st AR 1953–54*, p. 17; H.C.Debs. 5s, vol. 543, col. 1739, 12 July 1955.

19. F. Williams, *Dangerous Estate. The Anatomy of Newspapers* (London: Arrow, 1959), p. 237; Strick, 'British newspaper journalism', p. 3; *P&P 3rd AR 1955–56*, p. 36.

20. H.C.Debs, 5s, vol. 570, cols. 725–819, 17 May 1957.

21. R. Hoggart, *The Uses of Literacy* (London: Penguin, 1973), p. 335, first published 1957; Williams, *Dangerous Estate*, p. 229; *P&P 4th AR 1956–57*, p. 2.

22. J. Tunstall, *The Media in Britain* (London: Constable, 1983), pp. 80–83; H.C.Debs, 5s, vol. 630, cols. 545–47, 17 November 1960; ibid., vol. 631, cols. 719–822, 2 December 1960.

23. H.C.Debs, 5s, vol. 631, col. 867, 5 December 1960; ibid., cols. 1443–1447, 8 December 1960; ibid., vol. 632, cols. 186–87, 13 December 1960; ibid., vol. 633, written answers, cols. 11–12, 24 January 1961; ibid., vol. 634, cols. 1742–1743, 16 February 1961.

24. PRO, Cab.128.35, cc 5(61)4, 7 February 1961; H.C.Debs, 5s, vol. 634, cols. 625–33, 9 Feb 1961; *Royal Commission on the Press 1961–1962. Report*, Cmnd. 1811 (London: HMSO, 1962), p. 3 [hereafter, *RCP 1961–62*].

25. *P&P 8th AR 1960–61*, pp. 19–20; letter, L. Scott to A. Hetherington, 17 March 1961, cited in G. Taylor, *Changing Faces. A History of The Guardian 1956–88* (London: Fourth Estate, 1993), pp. 56–57; H. Cudlipp, *At Your Peril* (London: Weidenfeld and Nicolson, 1962), pp. 365–66.

26. *RCP 1961–62*, para. 325, p. 117.

27. Anon., 'Physician heal thyself' and Anon., 'Press Council plan welcomed by the NUJ', *The Times*, 20 September 1962; 'Minute to Prime Minister', 8 October 1962, PRO, FO 1109/437; *P&P 9th AR 1961–62*, pp. 3, 9.

28. *P&P 10th AR 1963–64*, pp. 65–69.

29. H.C.Debs, 5s, vol. 679, cols. 947–49, 23 June 1963.

30. M. Engel, *Tickle the Public. One Hundred Years of the Popular Press* (London: Victor Gollancz, 1996, p. 237; S. Somerfield, *Banner Headlines* (Shoreham by Sea: Scan Books, 1979), p. 145; *Lord Denning's Report*, Cmnd. 2152 (London: HMSO 1963), paras. 341–43; G. Martin, 'The Press', in D. Thompson (ed.), *Discrimination and Popular Culture* (London: Penguin, 1964), p. 95.

31. J. Northcott, *Why Labour?* (London: Penguin, 1964), p. 92; T. Benn, *Out of the Wilderness. Diaries 1963–67* (London: Hutchinson, 1987), 29 September and 7 October 1964, 3 February 1965; A. Quicke, *Tomorrow's Television* (Berkhamsted: Lion Publishing, 1976), p. 208; R. Williams, *Communications* (London: Penguin, revised edition 1966, reprinted 1970), pp. 140–41.

32. A. Hetherington, *Guardian Years* (London: Chatto & Windus, 1981), p. 138; J. Tunstall, *Media*, pp. 83, 267; Levy, *Press Council*.

33. H.C.Debs, 5s, vol. 687, cols. 684–85, 20 Jan 1964; ibid., vol. 694, cols. 1255–1256, 6 May 1964.

34. *P&P 12th AR 1964–65*, pp. 25–26; H.C.Debs, 5s, vol. 728, cols. 400–403, 22 February 1966; Levy, *Press Council*, pp. 438–47; Somerfield, *Banner*, pp. 116–17.
35. H.C.Debs, 5s, vol. 740, cols. 1732, 8 February 1967; *P&P 14th AR 1966–67*, pp. 24–29; *P&P 15th AR 1967–68*, pp. 115–18.
36. Taylor, *Changing Faces*, pp. 242–43; W. Shawcross, *Murdoch* (London: Pan, 1993), pp. 144–45.
37. H.C.Debs, 5s, vol. 790, cols. 825–26, 4 November 1969; *P&P 18th AR 1970–71*, pp. 64–66, 72.
38. *P&P 18th AR 1970–71*, pp. 67–68; H. Evans, *Good Times, Bad Times* (London: Coronet, 1984), p. 211.
39. *Committee on Privacy 1972*, paras. 116, 123, 125, 128, 129, 189–93.
40. *P&P 19th AR 1971–72*, pp. 1–4, 80; *P&P 20th AR 1972–73*, p. 109.
41. *Committee on Privacy 1972*, para. 191.

Notes to Chapter 5

1. T. O'Malley, 'Demanding accountability: the Press, the Royal Commissions and the pressure for reform, 1945–77', in H. Stephenson and M. Bromley (eds), *Sex, Lies and Democracy. The Press and the Public* (London: Longman, 1998), pp. 84–96.
2. H.C.Debs, 5s, vol. 870, cols. 1320–1322, 21 March 1974; ibid., vol. 871, cols. 392–93, 26 March 1974; ibid., vol. 872, cols. 631–34, 709–19, 11 April 1974; ibid., vol. 872, cols. 1327–1332, 2 May 1974.
3. H.C.Debs, 5s, vol. 873, cols. 1118–1240, 14 May 1974.
4. Labour Party, *The People and the Media* (London: Labour Party, 1974), pp. 4, 7, 12–13, 31.
5. H.C.Debs, 5s, vol. 874, written answers, col. 536, 11 June 1974; ibid., vol. 891, written answers, col. 151, 30 April 1975; ibid., vol. 901, written answers, col. 235, 27 November 1975; ibid., vol. 905, written answers, cols. 621–22, 17 February 1976.
6. For example, H.C.Debs, 5s, vol. 881, cols. 1318–1325, 20 November and written answers, cols. 494–95, 21 November 1974; M. Jones, *Michael Foot* (London: Gollancz, 1975), pp. 370–75, 391–93. The sheer acrimony of Wilson's relationship with the press in this period can be gleaned from S. Dorrill and R. Ramsay, *Smear! Wilson and the Secret State* (London: Grafton, 1992) and B. Pimlott, *Harold Wilson* (London: HarperCollins, 1993).
7. M. Hollingsworth, *The Press and Political Dissent* (London: Pluto Press, 1986), p. 44; H.C.Debs, 5s, vol. 906, cols. 615–17, 26 February 1976.
8. O'Malley, 'Demanding accountability'.
9. *Royal Commission on the Press. Final Report*, Cmnd. 6810 (London: HMSO, 1977), paras. 2.12, 19.15–19.18. Hereafter, *RCP 1974–77*.
10. Ibid., paras. 20.1, 20.12, 20.15, 20.19.
11. Ibid., para. 20.39.
12. Ibid., para. 20.83.
13. Ibid., pp. 235–36.
14. J. Curran (ed.), *The British Press: A Manifesto* (London: Macmillan, 1978), p. 9. This book contains a good deal of contemporary criticism of the Commission.
15. H.C.Debs, 5s, vol. 959, written answers, cols. 480–81, 4 December 1978.

16. *P&P 25th AR 1978*, pp. 1–3.
17. T. O'Malley, *Closedown? The BBC and Government Broadcasting Policy 1979–92* (London: Pluto Press, 1994); G. Williams, *Britain's Media – How They are Related*, 2nd edn (London: CPBF, 1996); P. Goodwin, *Television under the Tories. Broadcasting Policy 1979–1997* (London: BFI, 1998).
18. Campaign for Press Freedom, *Towards Press Freedom* (London: CPF, 1979), p. 14; A. Richardson and M. Power, 'Media freedom and the CPBF', in J. Curran, J. Ecclestone, G. Oakley and A. Richardson (eds), *Bending Reality. The State of the Media* (London: Pluto Press, 1986), p. 197.
19. H.C.Debs, 5s, vol. 979, written answers, cols. 132–33, 19 February 1980; ibid., vol. 985, written answers, col. 787, 5 June 1980; ibid., vol. 996, written answers, cols. 628–29, 16 January 1981; ibid., 6s, vol. 4, written answers, col. 364, 15 May 1981; G. Robertson, *People Against the Press. An Enquiry into the Press Council* (London: Quartet, 1983), pp. 3–4.
20. H.C.Debs, 6s, vol. 5, cols. 792–94, 2 June 1981; F. Allaun, 'Make the right of reply legal', *Free Press*, no. 8, July/August 1981; Anon., 'Journalists take space on page one', *Free Press*, no. 9, September/October 1981.
21. Curran, *Bending Reality*; Hollingsworth, *The Press and Political Dissent*.
22. H.C.Debs, 6s, vol. 16, col. 404, 28 Jan 1982; Richardson and Power, 'Media freedom', p. 199; Hollingsworth, *Press and Political Dissent*, p. 292. Frank Allaun's backers in December 1982 were Sir Derek Walker Smith, Arthur Davidson, Sir Nigel Fisher, Phillip Whitehead, Patrick Cormack, Michael Meacher, Sydney Chapman, John Tiley, Alan Hazelhurst, Norman Atkinson, and W. Benyon: H.C.Debs, 6s, vol. 33, cols. 269–70, 1 December 1992; Right of Reply in the Media Bill (London: House of Commons, 1982).
23. *Guardian* cited in Robertson, *People Against the Press*, p. 155; Anon., 'Self discipline not state discipline', *The Times*, 18 February 1983; NUJ, 'Press statement from Mr Jonathan Hammond, President NUJ' (London: NUJ, 17 February 1983).
24. H.C.Debs, 6s, vol. 37, cols. 571–637, 18 February 1983; C. Brown, 'Commons warns media to put house in order', *Guardian*, 19 February 1983. See also C. Wintour, 'A warning shot from the House of Commons', *Observer*, 20 February 1982, which also recognised the seriousness of the bill.
25. Robertson, *People Against the Press*, pp. 6–7, 150–51; CPBF, 'Secretary's report to the CPBF 1984 Annual General Meeting' (London: CPBF 1984, unpublished manuscript).
26. H.C.Debs, 6s, vol. 46, written answers, col. 94, 19 July 1983; J. Jennings, 'TUC call for communications council', *Free Press*, no. 20, September/October 1983; D. Barker, 'GLC funds Right of Reply group', *Guardian*, 19 October 1983; Richardson and Power, 'Media freedom', p. 209.
27. J. Curran and J. Seaton, *Power Without Responsibility*, 5th edn (London: Routledge, 1997), pp. 71–108, 209–36; L. Melvern, *The End of the Street* (London: Methuen, 1986).
28. M. Power, 'Gotcha! Miners reply in the *Sun*', *Free Press*, no. 21, January/February 1984; Anon., 'On avoiding legislation', and S. Collings, 'Suggesting a statutory alternative', *Journalist*, February 1984.
29. H.C.Debs, 6s, vol. 61, cols. 169–71, 5 June 1984, and cols. 779–81, 12 June 1984.

30. Anon., 'Solidarity in print', *Free Press*, no. 24, July/August 1984; A. Richardson, 'Make it legal', *Free Press*, no. 25, September/October 1984.

31. P. Foot, 'Paul Foot on right of reply', *Free Press*, no. 26, November/December 1984; M. Power, 'What are we to do about Paul Foot?', *Free Press*, no. 27, January/February 1985; Hollingsworth, *Press and Political Dissent*, p. 294.

32. Curran and Seaton, *Power Without Responsibility*; Melvern, *End of the Street*; G. Gall, 'Looking in the *Mirror*. A case study of industrial relations in a national newspaper', in M. Bromley and T. O'Malley, *A Journalism Reader* (London: Routledge, 1997), pp. 233–46; K. Morgan, *The People's Peace: British History 1945–1990* (Oxford: Oxford University Press, 1992), p. 479.

33. *P&P 34th AR 1987*, p. 269; H.C.Debs, 6s, vol. 119, cols. 17–74, 6 July 1987; ibid., vol. 121, col. 307, 28 October 1987; Ann Clywd's supporters were Merlyn Rees, Michael Foot, Norman Buchan, Roland Boyes, Dafydd Ellis Thomas, Paddy Ashdown, Geraint Howells, Charles Kennedy, Robin Squire, Peter Temple-Morris and Roger Gale, a mix of Labour, Liberal, Conservative and Plaid Cymru MPs; Unfair Reporting and Right of Reply Bill (London: House of Commons, 1987).

34. H.C.Debs, 6s, vol. 121, col. 815, 3 November 1987; ibid., vol. 123, cols. 509–64, 27 November 1987.

35. H.C.Debs, 6s, vol. 144, col. 455, 21 December 1988; D. Trelford, 'Publish and be jailed', in TUC, *The Role of the Media in a Democracy* (London: TUC, 1989), p. 19 – this was a keynote speech to a TUC conference held on 16 March 1989; M. Doornaert and S.E. Omdal, *IFJ Special Report. Press Freedom under Attack in Britain* (Brussels: International Federation of Journalists, 1989), p. 21.

36. H.C.Debs, 6s, vol. 146, cols. 548, 550, 592–94, 611, 3 February 1989.

37. H. Stephenson, 'Tickle the public: consumerism rules', in Stephenson and Bromley, *Sex, Lies and Democracy*, pp. 13–14; H.C.Debs, 6s, vol. 151, cols. 561–626, 21 April 1989.

38. *Report of the Committee on Privacy and Related Matters*, Cmnd. 1102 (London: HMSO, 1990), p. 1.

39. Labour Party, *Looking to the Future* (London: Labour Party, 1990), p. 41; *P&P 36th AR 1989*, pp. 341–42; W. Shawcross, *Murdoch* (London: Pan, 1993), p. 494; R. Snoddy, *The Good, the Bad and the Unacceptable* (London: Faber, 1992), pp. 92–114.

40. *Committee on Privacy and Related Matters*, pp. xi–xii; paras. 14.28–14.38, 16.9–16.24, 17.12.

41. H.C.Debs, 6s, vol. 174, cols. 1125–1127, 21 June 1990; B. Jones, *The Road to Calcutt and Beyond* (Cambridge: Wolfson College, 1991), p. 19.

42. Press Complaints Commission, *First Annual Report 1991* (London: PCC, nd), p. 2; ibid., *Submission to the Review of Press Self-Regulation* (London: PCC, 1992), pp. 11–12.

43. Snoddy, *The Good, the Bad*, pp. 10–11; B. McNair, *News and Journalism in the UK* (London: Routledge, 1994), pp. 153–57; H.C.Debs, 6s, vol. 198, written answers, col. 438, 12 November 1991; J. Morgan, 'Blom-Cooper calls for Press ethics committee', *UK Press Gazette*, 2 March 1992; Home Office Circular, 'Review of Press self-regulation' (London: Home Office, July 1992); National Heritage Committee, 'Press Notice' (London: House of Commons, 22 October 1992).

44. McNair, *News and Journalism*, p. 158; *Freedom and Responsibility of the Press Bill* (London: House of Commons, 1992). Soley's sponsors were Mark Fisher, Nick Raynsford, Angela Eagle, Chris Smith, Harriet Harman, Bruce Grocott, Glenda Jackson, Charles Kennedy, Jeff Rooker, Andrew F. Bennett and Clare Short. A copy of the bill (as revised in Committee for Third Reading) is printed in the Appendix.

45. Anon., 'Backbenchers may use Soley's bill for revenge', *British Editor*, vol. 4, no. 5, Autumn 1992; M. Brown, 'McGregor defends regulation of press', *Independent*, 16 October 1992; J. Slattery, 'Soley to grant access to complaints letters', *UK Press Gazette*, 2 November 1992.

46. M. Jempson (ed.), *Report of Special Parliamentary Hearings on Freedom and Responsibility of the Press* (Bristol: Crantock Communications, 1993); A. Travis, 'Claims of higher press standards leave MPs cold', *Guardian*, 4 December 1992; B. Franklin, *Newszak and News Media* (London: Arnold, 1997), p. 224.

47. Jempson, *Report*, pp. 65–71; Anon., 'Put up or shut UP, Mr Soley', *Sun*, 12 December 1992; Anon., 'Press excesses and the law', *Daily Telegraph*, 1 December 1992; Anon., 'Without apology', *The Times*, 15 December 1992; M. Brown, 'Calcutt "wants statutory controls on Press"', *Independent*, 4 January 1993.

48. Letters Page, *Tribune*, 29 January 1993; P. Foot and L. Howson, 'Stop Press', *Socialist Review*, no. 161, February 1993.

49. National Heritage Committee, *Fourth Report. Privacy and Media Intrusion*, Volume I (London: HMSO, 1993), paras. 25–28; H.C.Debs, 6s, vol. 217, col. 1296–1368, 29 January 1993; House of Commons, *Standing Committee 'F': Freedom and Responsibility of the Press Bill* (London: House of Commons, 3 March 1993) – record of proceedings; K.J. McKeown, 'The right to reply to the Press in the United Kingdom' (MA thesis: Leeds University, 1993), p. 118. One important consequence of the work on the Soley bill was the establishment of an organisation, Press Wise, that was set up to work with people inside and outside the media to promote high standards and empower victims of unfair press or media intrusion and inaccurate or irresponsible reporting.

50. National Heritage Committee, *Fourth Report*, para. 110.

51. See Campaign for Press and Broadcasting Freedom, *Putting People First. The Campaign for Press and Broadcasting Freedom's Response to Regulating Communications: Approaching Convergence in the Information Age [CM 4022, HMSO, July 1998]* (London: CPBF, 1998).

52. Franklin, *Newszak*, pp. 218–19; A. Culf, 'Privacy adjudicator to watch over the Press', *Guardian*, 10 January 1994.

53. S. Harris, '... and even on its platforms!', *Journalist*, August/September 1994; on the shift in Labour policy, see also Goodwin, *Television*, pp. 145–47, and T. O'Malley, 'Losing a sense of ownership', *Free Press*, no. 96, January/February 1997.

54. C. Mullin, 'Regulation to save the nation', *Journalist*, February/March 1995; K. Brown, 'Blair seeks to persuade Murdoch', *Financial Times*, 17 July 1995; M. White and A. Culf, 'Blair's New Left warning to Murdoch', *Guardian*, 17 July 1995; A. Culf, 'Government retreat on Press privacy' and 'How the editors avoided the Last Chance Saloon', *Guardian*, 18 July 1995.

55. NUJ, *Your Union at Work. Report and Accounts for 1995* (London: NUJ, 1996), p. 26; ibid., *Your Union at Work. Annual Report 1996* (London: NUJ,

1997), p. 19; A. Culf, 'Wakeham to make self-regulation more open',
Guardian, 24 October 1995; J. Dugdale, 'Love, lies and loopholes', *Guardian*,
29 April 1996.
56. A. Culf, 'Wakeham acts over intrusion', *Guardian*, 11 October 1996; ibid.,
'Tabloids condemned over Euro 96 own goals', *Guardian*, 30 October 1996;
ibid., 'MPs attack witness Press deals', *Guardian*, 23 January 1997.
57. Labour Party, *New Labour. Because Wales Deserves Better* (London: Labour
Party, 1997), p. 31; Anon., 'The Sun backs Blair', *Sun*, 18 March 1997;
NUJ, *Your Union at Work. Annual Report 1999* (London: NUJ, 1999), p. 26.

Notes to Chapter 6

1. *P&P 10th AR 1962–63*, p. 1.
2. *P&P 27th and 28th ARs, 1980 and 1981*, p. 298.
3. *P&P 8th AR 1960–61*, p. 6.
4. Source for Tables 6.3: Press Council Annual Reports.
5. Tulloch, 'Managing the Press in a medium-sized European power', in H.
Stephenson and M. Bromley (eds), *Sex, Lies and Democracy. The Press and the
Public* (London: Longman, 1998), p. 73.
6. Tulloch, 'Managing', pp. 75–77.
7. *P&P 1st AR 1953–54*, p. 4; *P&P 5th AR 1957–58*, p. 1.
8. *P&P 7th AR 1959–60*, p. 4; *P&P 8th AR 1960–61*, p. 7.
9. *P&P 13th AR 1965–66*, pp. 2–3; *P&P 15th AR 1967–68*, p. 115; *P&P 24th
AR 1976–77*, p. 1; *P&P 35th AR 1988*, p. 9.
10. *P&P 1st AR 1953–54*, p. 3; *P&P 3rd AR 1955–56*, pp. 1, 6, 7.
11. *P&P 6th AR 1958–59*, p. 1; *P&P 7th AR 1959–60*, pp. 1, 6.
12. *P&P 10th AR 1962–63*, p. 69; *P&P 13th AR 1965–66*, p. 112; H. Levy,
The Press Council. History, Procedure and Cases (London: Macmillan, 1967),
p. 465.
13. *P&P 17th AR 1969–70*, p. 1; *P&P 20th AR 1972–73*, p. 1; *P&P 22nd AR
1974–75*, p. 2; *P&P 26th AR 1979*, p. 1.
14. *P&P 29th and 30th ARs, 1982 and 1983*, pp. 278–85; *P&P 31st AR 1984*,
p. 10; *P&P 32nd AR 1985*, p. 262; *P&P 34th AR 1987*, pp. 10–11.
15. *P&P 1st AR 1953–54*, p. 1; *P&P 2nd AR 1954–55*, p. 51; *P&P 5th AR
1957–58*, p. 7.
16. *P&P 4th AR 1956–57*, p. 1; *P&P 5th AR 1957–58*, p. 8; *P&P 6th AR
1958–59*, p. 5.
17. *P&P 5th AR 1957–58*, p. 19; *P&P 7th AR 1959–60*, p. 2.
18. *P&P 7th AR 1959–60*, p. 1; *P&P 8th AR 1960–61*, pp. 49, 57.
19. *P&P 11th AR 1963–64*, pp. 1–3, 16, 87.
20. *P&P 13th AR 1965–66*, p. 143.
21. *P&P 14th AR 1966–67*, p. 184.
22. *P&P 15th AR 1967–68*, p. 114.
23. Levy, *Press Council*, p. 27; *Royal Commission on the Press. Final Report*, Cmnd.
6810 (London: HMSO, 1977), paras. 20.43–20.49 [hereafter, *RCP
1974–77*]; G. Robertson, *People Against the Press. An Enquiry into the Press
Council* (London: Quartet, 1983), p. 30.
24. *P&P 20th AR 1972–73*, p. 75; *P&P 21st AR 1973–74*, p. 78.
25. *P&P 22nd AR 1974–75*, p. 6. By the 1970s the Council's administrative
machinery had slowed down considerably, and it entered a long period

when its annual reports were published between one and two years after the events covered: see *P&P 23rd AR 1975–76*, p. 1; *P&P 31st AR 1984*, p. 7.

26. *P&P 25th AR 1977–78*, p. 120; M. Hollingsworth, *The Press and Political Dissent* (London: Pluto Press, 1986), pp. 181–85; the waiver demand is first referred to in the 'Procedure for Making Complaints' section in *P&P 29th and 30th ARs, 1982 and 1983*, p. 28, which was printed late and refers to the 1984 'fast track' procedure; *P&P 31st AR 1984*, p. 244.

27. PCC, *First Annual Report 1991*, p. 13; B. Franklin, *Newszak and News Media* (London: Arnold, 1997), p. 227; Lord Wakeham, 'Can self-regulation achieve more than the law?' (London: PCC, http://www.pcc.org.uk/adjud/press/pr150598.htm 19 May 1999 – Text of the Wynne Baxter Godfree Lecture ... at the University of Sussex on Friday 15 May 1998).

28. *P&P 1st AR 1953–54*, pp. 5, 9; *P&P 3rd AR 1955–56*, p. 9. For two brief surveys of some of the shifts in the 1950s and 1960s, see J. Seed, 'Hegemony postponed: the unravelling of the culture of consensus in Britain in the 1960s', in B. Moore-Gilbert and J. Seed (eds), *Cultural Revolution? The Challenge of the Arts in the 1960s* (London: Routledge, 1992), pp. 15–44 and D. Porter, 'Downhill all the way: thirteen Tory years 1951–64', in R. Coopey, S. Fielding and N. Tiratsoo (eds), *The Wilson Governments 1964–70* (London: Pinter, 1993), pp. 10–28.

29. *P&P 2nd AR 1954–55*, pp. 1–2; *P&P 3rd AR 1955–56*, pp. 1–3.

30. *P&P 5th AR 1957–58*, p. 11; *P&P 6th AR 1958–59*, pp. 7–8.

31. *P&P 10th AR 1962–63*, p. 2

32. Levy, *Press Council*, p. 467; *P&P 16th AR 1968–69*, p. 1.

33. Franklin, *Newszak*, p. 228.

34. *P&P 2nd AR 1954–55*, pp. 6, 10.

35. *P&P 3rd AR 1955–56*, p. 4; *P&P 4th AR 1956–57*, pp. 1–2.

36. *P&P 5th AR 1957–58*, pp. 1–2.

37. *P&P 7th AR 1959–60*, pp. 3–5; *P&P 8th AR 1960–61*, p. 8.

38. *P&P 11th AR 1963–64*, pp. 2–3; *P&P 22nd AR 1974–75*, pp. 113–14; PCC, *First Annual Report 1991*, p. 13.

Notes to Chapter 7

1. *P&P 1st AR 1953–54*, pp. 10–11; *P&P 2nd AR 1954–55*, pp. 12–13; *P&P 3rd AR, 1955–56*, pp. 14–15, 24–25; *P&P 4th AR 1956–57*, pp. 17–19; *P&P 5th AR 1957–58*, pp. 16, 24; *P&P 8th AR 1960–61*, p. 2; *P&P 9th AR 1961–62*, pp. 8–11, 61–65.

2. For example, *P&P 10th AR 1962–63*, pp. 21–24; *P&P 11th AR 1963–64*, pp. 21–27.

3. *P&P 12th AR 1964–65*, p. 1; *P&P 13th AR 1965–66*, pp. 8–9; *P&P 14th AR 1966–67*, pp. 12–13, 28–29; H. Levy, *The Press Council. History, Procedure and Cases* (London: Macmillan, 1967), p. 419.

4. *P&P 16th AR 1968–69*, p. 85; *P&P 18th AR 1970–71*, p. 70; *P&P 19th AR 1971–72*, p. 93.

5. *P&P 21st AR 1973–74*, p. 80; *P&P 23rd AR 1975–76*, p. 11ff.

6. *P&P 22nd AR 1974–75*, pp. 106, 122; *P&P 24th AR 1976–77*, p. 116. On the media coverage of the conflict in Ireland, see L. Curtis, *Ireland: The Propaganda War* (London: Pluto Press, 1984), and D. Miller, *Don't Mention*

the War: Northern Ireland, Propaganda and the Media (London: Pluto Press, 1994).

7. For example, *P&P 36th AR 1989*, pp. 223–25, 240–41.
8. *P&P 34th AR 1987*, p. 9.
9. *Royal Commission on the Press 1947–1949. Report*, Cmnd. 7700 (London: HMSO, reprinted 1962), para. 684 [hereafter, *RCP 1947–49*]; *P&P 2nd AR 1954–55*, p. 5; *P&P 3rd AR 1955–56*, pp. 12–13; *P&P 5th AR 1957–58*, p. 9.
10. *P&P 6th AR 1958–59*, pp. 2, 7; *P&P 12th AR 1964–65*, p. 2; Levy, *Press Council*.
11. *P&P 14th AR 1966–67*, pp. 8–9; *P&P 23rd AR 1975–76*, pp. 150–53; *P&P 31st AR 1984*, pp. 232–35.
12. Anon., 'Problems of the Press', *Financial Times*, 8 July 1977; R. Mead, *The Press Council* (Cheshire: Brennan Publications, 1978), p. 7; N.S. Paul, *Principles for the Press. A Digest of Press Council Decisions 1953–84* (London: Press Council, 1985), p. 1.
13. *P&P 26th AR 1989*, pp. 8–9, 245–47; PCC, *First Annual Report 1991*, p. 16.
14. *P&P 1st AR 1953–54*, p. 6; *P&P 2nd AR 1954–55*, p. 8; *P&P 3rd AR 1955–56*, p. 11; *P&P 12th AR 1965–66*, p. 3; *P&P 27th and 28th ARs, 1980 and 1981*, p. 211; B. McNair, *News and Journalism in the UK* (London: Routledge, 1994), pp. 155–59.
15. *P&P 5th AR 1957–58*, pp. 4, 11.
16. *P&P 17th AR 1969–70*, p. 85; *P&P 18th 1970–71*, pp. 65–66. See also Press Council, *Privacy, Press and Public* (London: Press Council, 1971).
17. *P&P 27th and 28th ARs, 1980 and 1981*, pp. 8, 9, 211; *P&P 37th AR 1990*, pp. 7, 28.
18. *P&P 2nd AR 1954–55*, pp. 4, 24.
19. *P&P 23rd AR 1975–76*, p. 148.
20. *P&P 18th AR 1970–71*, pp. 2–3; *P&P 24th AR 1976–77*, pp. 105–107; T. Benn, *Conflicts of Interest. Diaries 1977–80* (London: Hutchinson, 1990), p. 181.
21. *P&P 29th and 30th ARs, 1982 and 1983*, pp. 286–7, 306, 310. On the Council's response to the industrial action in support of the miners, see *P&P 31st AR 1984*, p. 248.
22. *P&P 32nd AR 1985*, pp. 260–61.
23. *P&P 34th AR 1987*, p. 266; *P&P 35th AR 1988*, pp. 8–9; *P&P 36th AR 1989*, pp. 332, 340–41.
24. PCC, *First Annual Report 1991*, p. 16.
25. Robertson, *People Against the Press. An Enquiry into the Press Council* (London: Quartet, 1983).
26. PCC, *Annual Report 1991*, p. 13.

Notes to Chapter 8

1. For example, see D. Miller, J. Kitzinger, K. Williams and P. Beherrall, *The Circuit of Mass Communication. Media Strategies, Representation and Audience Reception in the AIDS Crisis* (London: Sage, 1998); for a review of some of the issues, see G. Cumberbatch, 'Media effects: the continuing controversy',

in A. Briggs and P. Cobley (eds), *The Media: An Introduction* (London: Longman, 1998), pp. 262–74.

2. Sale of Goods Act 1979, Section 13 (1)–(4).
3. Broadcasting Act 1990, Section 6 (1) (b).
4. See Chapters 2 and 3 on the background to the NUJ's code.
5. Advertising Standards Association, *British Code of Advertising Practices 1988* (London: ASA, 1988), Part B, 5.1.
6. NUJ, 'Code of conduct', in M. Jempson (ed.), *Report of Special Parliamentary Hearings on Freedom and Responsibility of the Press* (Bristol: Crantock Communications, 1993), p. 169.
7. Press Complaints Commission, *Code of Practice* (http://www.pcc.org.uk/ complain/code.htm/ 5 November 1997). The PCC, technically, administers a code drawn up by the editors in the industry. For the purpose of brevity we refer to it as the PCC Code. Between 1991 and 1998 the PCC had three codes. Its first code was superseded by a revised one in October 1993 and that by a third one in late November 1997. We give the date of the particular version we are using at any one time.
8. The most obvious example was the coverage of the Labour-controlled Greater London Council in the 1980s, for which see M. Hollingsworth, *The Press and Political Dissent* (London: Pluto Press, 1986) and J. Curran, 'Culturist perspectives of news organizations: a reappraisal and a case study', in M. Ferguson (ed.), *Public Communication. The New Imperatives* (London: Sage, 1990), pp. 114–34.
9. B. Akass, 'Now it's Baa Baa Black Sheep', *Daily Star*, 15 February 1986.
10. Media Research Group, *Media Coverage of London Councils, Interim Report* (London: University of London, Goldsmith's College, 1987), pp. 1, 6.
11. Ibid.
12. 'Statement of evidence: Baroness Hollis of Heigham', in Jempson, *Report*, p. 38.
13. 'Bob Borzello: statement of evidence' in ibid., p. 115.
14. Soley Correspondence: letter from Robert Fleming to Tony Fowler, 26 June 1991.
15. 'Evidence of Mr Bob Borzello, Tuesday 1 December 1992', in Jempson, *Report*, p. 24.
16. Soley Correspondence: letter from Tony Fowler to Bob Borzello, 8 August 1991.
17. Soley Correspondence: letter from Max Davidson to Bob Borzello, 3 September 1991.
18. 'Evidence of Mr Bob Borzello', in Jempson, *Report*, p. 24.
19. See C. Searle, *Your Daily Dose: Racism and The Sun* (London: Campaign for Press and Broadcasting Freedom, 1989) and T.A. Van Dijk, *Racism and the Press* (London: Routledge, 1991).
20. 'Statement of evidence: Brendan and Teresa McKeever', in Jempson, *Report*, pp. 14–17.
21. Letter from Professor Walsh to Mr McKeever, 20 September 1991, in Jempson, *Report*, p. 16, where copies of more accurate accounts from *The Times*, the *Independent* and the *Telegraph* of 29 August 1991 are reproduced.
22. C. Davis, 'Human tide Labour would let in', *Sun*, 4 April 1992.
23. Searle, *Daily Dose*.

24. Conservative Central Office, 'Baker warns 'Proportional Representation has helped Fascists march again' (London: Conservative Central Office, Press Statement, April 6 1992).

25. P. Hooley, 'Baker's migrant flood warning', *Daily Express*, 7 April 1992.

26. PCC, *Code of Practice* (5 November 1997).

27. Anon., 'Boy, 12, held for Jamie murder', *Sun*, 17 February 1993.The reporting of the Bulger case was riddled with inaccuracies, some of which fed into a campaign that led to the government changing the law relating to the classification of videos for home use. See Cumberbatch, 'Media effects' for a discussion of the way in which inaccurate reporting got fed into the policy-making process in this case.

28. Soley Correspondence: letter from Leo Adamson to PCC, 22 February 1993.

29. Race was covered by Article 15 of the PCC Code (5 November 1997).

30. 'Statement of evidence: Brendan and Teresa McKeever', in Jempson, *Report*, p. 14.

Notes to Chapter 9

1. PCC, *Code of Practice* (5 November 1997).

2. J.B. Sykes (ed.), *The Concise Oxford Dictionary of Correct English*, 6th edn (Oxford: Clarendon Press, 1980).

3. Social Security Act 1988, Sec. 4; Joseph Rowntree Foundation, *Inquiry into British Housing, Second Report* (York: Joseph Rowntree Foundation, 1991).

4. S. Grey, 'Beggar who pulls in £18,000 a year', *Daily Express*, 9 May 1994.

5. N. Briggs, 'Bank account beggar sets the law on Express', *Daily Express*, 10 May 1994; J. Cooper, 'Tell them to beggar off for the good of everyone', *Daily Express*, 11 May 1994.

6. J. Pyatt, '"Beggar" makes £1000 per week selling *Big Issue*', *Sun*, 28 October 1996.

7. *Big Issue*, no. 206, 4–10 November 1996, cover page.

8. O. Bowcott, 'Buyers turn backs on *Big Issue* after *Sun*'s £1000 a week claims', *Guardian*, 28 October 1996.

9. 'Editorial', PCC, *Report* (London: PCC, 1997, no. 38).

10. B. Pittaway, 'It's madness', *Sunday Mirror*, 17 August 1997.

11. Public Order Act 1986, Part III, Sections (17)–(26).

12. PCC, *Code* (5 November 1997).

13. See C. Searle, *Your Daily Dose: Racism and The Sun* (London: Campaign for Press and Broadcasting Freedom, 1989) and T.A. Van Dijk, *Racism and the Press* (London: Routledge, 1991).

14. Anon., 'This is the real discrimination', *Daily Mail*, 12 April 1990.

15. Searle, *Your Daily Dose* and Van Dijk, *Racism and the Press*.

16. PCC, *Code* (5 November 1997).

17. T. Brooks, 'Vindaloot: Indian dad winner of £18 million takeaway', *Daily Star*, 14 December 1994.

18. J. Troup and A. Taylor, 'The Chosen One', *Sun*, 14 December 1994.

19. G. Patrick, 'What a rich chap-ati', *Sun*, 14 December 1994.

20. F. Corless and P. Mulchrone, '£18m win's a sin', *Daily Mirror*, 14 December 1994.

21. PCC, *Code* (5 November 1997).

218   REGULATING THE PRESS

22. Soley Correspondence, letter from T. Coleman to N. Lloyd, 11 November 1993; Letters Page, *Daily Express*, 19 November 1993.
23. Soley Correspondence, letter from Bernard Shrimsley to Tony Colman, 17 November 1993.
24. Anon., 'Left wing councillors ... want to ban the story of the Ugly Duckling', *Sun*, 16 November 1993; Soley Correspondence, letter from Michael Toner to Tony Colman, 16 November 1993.
25. Prince of Wales, 'A vision for the millennium', *Perspectives*, February/March 1996.
26. D. Williams and J. Burt, 'Charles: Let Lottery money go to mosques', *Daily Mail*, 25 January 1996; I. Trueman, 'You mosque be joking', *Daily Star*, 25 January 1996.
27. Searle, *Your Daily Dose*.
28. PCC, *Report* (London: PCC, no. 34, 1996); PCC, *Code* (5 November 1997).

Notes to Chapter 10

1. PCC, *Code* (5 November 1997).
2. See Chapter 2.
3. PCC, *Annual Report 1995*.
4. R. Snoddy, *The Good, the Bad and the Unacceptable* (London: Faber, 1992); R. Wacks, *Privacy and Press Freedom* (London: Blackstone, 1995); I. Cram, 'Beyond Calcutt: the legal and extra legal protection of privacy interests in England and Wales', in M. Kiernan (ed.), *Media Ethics* (London: Routledge, 1998), pp. 97–110.
5. Cram, 'Beyond Calcutt'; Wacks, *Privacy*.
6. *Committee on Privacy 1972*, Cmnd. 5012 (London: HMSO, 1972), para. 3.20.
7. Lord Chancellor's Department and Scottish Office, *Infringement of Privacy: Consultation Paper* (London: Lord Chancellor's Department, July 1993).
8. Department of National Heritage, *Privacy and Media Intrusion: The Government's Response*, Cmnd. 2918 (London: HMSO, 1995).
9. Cram, 'Beyond Calcutt', p. 105.
10. For a discussion of this, see M. Frankel, 'Freedom of Information setback', *Free Press*, no. 106, September/October 1998; D. Hencke, 'Straw slows Freedom of Information legislation', *Guardian*, 30 September 1998.
11. Official Secrets Act 1911 and Official Secrets Act 1989.
12. G. Robertson, 'Law for the Press', in J. Curran (ed.), *The British Press: A Manifesto* (London: Macmillan, 1978), pp. 203–28.
13. See Chapter 2.
14. Anon., 'David Mellor and the actress', and R. Levine, 'I am exhausted. I'm so knackered', *Sunday People*, 19 July 1992.
15. PCC, *First Annual Report 1991* (London: PCC, nd), p. 16.
16. R. Dore, 'Mellor story "Was in public interest"', Press Association Story, 22 July 1992.
17. Anon., 'David Mellor and the actress'; Levine, 'I am exhausted. I'm so knackered'.
18. Ibid.
19. A. Boshoff and R. Sylvester, 'Every editor that has paid for intrusive photographs has blood on their hands', *Daily Telegraph*, 1 September 1997.

The whole issue would merit a fuller study as it touches on many of the most important issues about the relationship between the media and social stability, the media and the state, and, the question of the power of the media to mobilise public opinion around very narrow social and political agendas.

20. M. Brown, 'Press watchdog urges restraint in Royal coverage', *Independent*, 9 June 1992.
21. J. Carvel and D. Campbell, 'DPP quits over kerb crawling: Establishment stunned as Alan Green tells of "regret"', *Guardian*, 4 October 1991.
22. G. Hay, 'Woman at the centre of law wife tragedy', *Daily Mirror*, 1 February 1993.
23. R. Pendlebury, 'Adoption disaster: inquiry backs man who banned "naïve" couple from giving black child a home', *Daily Mail*, 13 September 1993.
24. R. Pendlebury, 'My years with the gay social worker', *Daily Mail*, 13 September 1993.
25. PCC, *First Annual Report 1991*, p. 16.
26. T. Woodward, 'Why I sent my daughter to prison', *Daily Mail*, 7 May 1998.
27. PCC, *Report no. 44* (London: PCC, 1996), p. 23.
28. Soley Correspondence: letter, L. Sear, Managing Editor *Daily Mail*, to C. Soley, 13 May 1998.
29. Soley Correspondence: letter, Lord Wakeham to C. Soley, 13 May 1998.
30. The changes that came into force at the end of November 1997.
31. PCC, 'Lord Wakeham underlines PPC's commitment to protection of children' (London: PCC, 8 May 1998 – Press Statement); Soley Correspondence, Lord Wakeham to C. Soley, 1 June 1998.
32. Anon., 'Naming children banned even if order not made', *The Times*, 9 December 1998; Soley Correspondence, C. Soley to Lord Wakeham, and C. Soley to L. Sear, both on 16 December 1998.

Notes to Chapter 11

1. J. Curran and J. Seaton, *Power Without Responsibility*, 5th edn (London: Routledge, 1997).
2. T. O'Malley, 'A degree of uncertainty: aspects of the debate over the regulation of the press in the UK since 1945', in D. Berry (ed.), *Ethics and Media Culture. Practice and Representations* (Oxford: Focal Press, 2000), pp. 297–310.
3. See discussion of Paul Foot's views in Chapter 5 and 'Evidence of Mr Paul Lashmar, Mr John Ware and The Cross Media Group', in M. Jempson (ed.), *Report of Special Parliamentary Hearings on Freedom and Responsibility of the Press* (Bristol: Crantock Communications, 1993), pp. 65–71.
4. R. Collins and C. Murroni, *New Media, New Policies* (Cambridge: Polity, 1996), pp. 94–95; M. Hollingsworth, *The Press and Political Dissent* (London: Pluto Press, 1986); T. O'Malley, *Closedown? The BBC and Government Broadcasting Policy 1979–92* (London: Pluto Press, 1994).
5. E. Barendt, *Freedom of Speech* (Oxford: Oxford University Press, 1987), pp. 65–66.
6. *Royal Commission on the Press. Final Report*, Cmnd. 6810 (London: HMSO, 1977), para. 20.39 [hereafter, *RCP 1974–77*]; G. Robertson, *People Against*

the Press. An Enquiry into the Press Council (London: Quartet, 1983), pp. 157–58.

7. P.J. Humphreys, Media and Media Policy in Germany. The Press and Broadcasting since 1945, 2nd edn (Oxford: Berg, 1994), pp. 55–58; ibid., Mass Media and Media Policy in Western Europe (Manchester: Manchester University Press, 1996), p. 64.

8. Humphreys, Mass Media, pp. 63–64.

9. Ibid., pp. 57–62; for a brief overview of the range of laws in different countries, see also Euromedia Research Group, The Media in Western Europe. The Euromedia Handbook (London: Sage, 1992).

10. RCP 1974–77, para. 20.39

11. Human Rights Act 1998, Schedule 1, Part 1, Articles 8 and 10.

12. Data Protection Act 1998, Part I, Section 6 (1).

13. Ibid., Part II, Sections 7–15.

14. Hollingsworth, Press and Political Dissent; O'Malley, Closedown?; G. Philo (ed.), Glasgow Media Group Reader. Volume 2: Industry, Economy, War and Politics (London: Routledge, 1995); R. Keeble, 'The myth of Saddam Hussein: new militarism and the propaganda function of the human interest story', M. Kiernan (ed.), Media Ethics (London: Routledge, 1998), pp. 66–81; J. Pilger, 'Acts of murder', Guardian, 18 May 1999.

15. See P. Murschetz, 'State support for the daily press in Europe: a critical appraisal. Austria, France, Norway and Sweden compared', European Journal of Communication, vol. 13, no. 3, 1998, pp. 291–313; Humphreys, Mass Media, 91–93, 105–106, 298.

16. During 1999 the Labour Government announced Freedom of Information legislation, which was criticised by those who had been campaigning for such a measure as a reversal, in fact, of the principle enunciated in the title. See Anon., 'Labour retreats on Information Bill', Free Press, no. 110, May/June 1999; L. Ward, W. Woodward and D. Hencke, 'Pressure mounts over public right to know', Guardian, 21 June 1999.

Note to Appendix

1. Freedom and Responsibility of the Press Bill, as amended in Standing Committee 'F' (London: HMSO, 10 March 1993). Parliamentary copyright material from the Freedom and Responsibility of the Press Bill is reproduced with the permission of the Controller of Her Majesty's Stationery Office on behalf of Parliament.

Bibliography

Public Record Office, London

Documents relating to the 1947–49 Royal Commission

HO 251/213   'Policy Committee. Note by the Secretary', 7 October 1947.
HO 251/216   'Notes of discussion between Sir David Ross, Sir Geoffrey Vickers and Mr Hull on 17th March 1948'.

Cabinet papers

Cab.128.19
Cab.128.25

For Cabinet Minutes, references are to Class Mark (i.e. Cab.128), file number (e.g. '19'), Cabinet Meeting Number (e.g. 'CM4'), the year of the meeting (e.g. '(51)'), and the minute number (e.g. '1'), plus a date where appropriate: for example, 'Cab.128.19, CM.4(51)1, 18 January 1951'. Sometimes 'cc' is used instead of 'CM'. This is an abbreviation for 'cabinet conclusion'; it is then followed by details of the meeting number, year of meeting, minute number and date: for example, 'Cab.128.25, cc 99(52)2, 20 November 1952'.

Other documents

FO 1109/437   'Minute to Prime Minister', 8 October 1962.

Parliamentary debates

House of Commons Debates. References are given to the series, i.e. 'H.C.Debs, 5s'; to the volume number, e.g. 'vol. 467'; and to the columns, e.g. 'cols. 2696–2699'.

Government reports and official publications

Royal Commission on the Press 1947–1949. Report, Cmnd. 7700 (London: HMSO, reprinted 1962).
Royal Commission on the Press 1961–1962. Report, Cmnd. 1811 (London: HMSO, 1962).
Lord Denning's Report, Cmnd. 2152 (London: HMSO, 1963).

Committee on Privacy 1972, Cmnd. 5012 (London: HMSO, 1972).
Royal Commission on the Press. Final Report, Cmnd. 6810 (London: HMSO, 1977).
Report of the Committee on Financing the BBC, Cmnd. 9824 (London: HMSO, 1986).
Report of the Committee on Privacy and Related Matters, Cmnd. 1102 (London: HMSO, 1990).
National Heritage Committee, *Fourth Report. Privacy and Media Intrusion, Volume I* (London: HMSO, 1993).
House of Commons, *Standing Committee 'F': Freedom and Responsibility of the Press Bill* (London: House of Commons, 3 March 1993) – record of proceedings.
Lord Chancellor's Department and Scottish Office, *Infringement of Privacy: Consultation Paper* (London: Lord Chancellor's Department, July 1993).
Department of National Heritage, *Privacy and Media Intrusion: The Government's Response*, Cmnd. 2918 (London: HMSO, 1995).

Statutes and Private Member's Bills

Official Secrets Act 1911
Sale of Goods Act 1979
Right of Reply in the Media Bill (London: House of Commons, 1982)
Public Order Act 1986
Unfair Reporting and Right of Reply Bill (London: House of Commons, 1987)
Social Security Act 1988
Local Government Act 1989
Official Secrets Act 1989
Broadcasting Act 1990
Freedom and Responsibility of the Press Bill (London: House of Commons, 1992)
Freedom and Responsibility of the Press Bill, as amended in Standing Committee 'F' (London: HMSO, 10 March 1993)
Data Protection Act 1998
Human Rights Act 1998

The Press Council's annual reports

Press Council, *The Press and the People* (London: Press Council, various dates, 1954–90). The Council published 37 annual reports, from the first covering 1953–54 to the last for the year 1990, all of which have been used in this study.

Press statements

Home Office Circular, 'Review of Press self-regulation' (London: Home Office, July 1992).
National Heritage Committee, Press Notice (London: House of Commons, 22 October 1992).
NUJ, 'Press statement from Mr Jonathan Hammond, President NUJ' (London: NUJ, 17 February 1983).
PCC, 'Lord Wakeham underlines PCC's commitment to protection of children' (London: PCC, 8 May 1998).

Wakeham, Lord, 'Can self-regulation achieve more than the law?' (London: PCC, http://www.pcc.org.uk/adjud/press/pr150598.htm 19 May 1999 – Text of the Wynne Baxter Godfree Lecture ... at the University of Sussex on Friday 15 May 1998).

Articles and books

Advertising Standards Association, *British Code of Advertising Practices 1988* (London: ASA, 1988).
Akass, B., 'Now it's Baa Baa, Black Sheep', *Daily Star*, 15 February 1986.
Aldgate, T., 'Comedy, class and containment: the British domestic cinema of the 1930s', in Curran, J. and Porter, V. (eds), *British Cinema History* (London: Weidenfeld and Nicolson, 1983).
Allaun, F., 'Make the Right of Reply legal', *Free Press*, no. 8, July/August 1981.
Anon., *The Letters of Junius. Complete in One Volume* (London, 1791).
——, 'Physician heal thyself', *The Times*, 20 September 1962.
——, 'Press Council plan welcomed by the NUJ', *The Times*, 20 September 1962.
——, 'Problems of the Press', *Financial Times*, 8 July 1977.
——, 'Journalists take space on page one', *Free Press*, no. 9, September/October 1981.
——, 'Self discipline not state discipline', *The Times*, 18 February 1983.
——, 'On avoiding legislation', *Journalist*, February 1984.
——, 'Solidarity in print', *Free Press*, no. 24, July/August 1984.
——, 'This is the real discrimination', *Daily Mail*, 12 April 1990.
——, 'David Mellor and the actress', *People*, 19 July 1992.
——, 'Backbenchers may use Soley's bill for revenge', *British Editor*, vol. 4, no. 5, Autumn 1992.
——, 'Press excesses and the law', *Daily Telegraph*, 1 December 1992.
——, 'Put up or shut UP, Mr Soley', *Sun*, 12 December 1992.
——, 'Without apology', *The Times*, 15 December 1992.
——, 'Boy, 12, held for Jamie murder', *Sun*, 17 February 1993.
——, 'Left wing councillors ... want to ban the story of the Ugly Duckling', *Sun*, 16 November 1993.
——, 'The Sun backs Blair', *Sun*, 18 March 1997.
——, 'Naming children banned even if order not made', *The Times*, 9 December 1998.
——, 'Labour retreats on Information Bill', *Free Press*, no. 110, May/June 1999.
Bainbridge, C. (ed.), *One Hundred Years of Journalism. Social Aspects of the Press* (London: Macmillan, 1984).
Barendt, E., *Freedom of Speech* (Oxford: Oxford University Press, 1987).
Barker, D., 'GLC funds Right of Reply group', *Guardian*, 19 October 1983.
Baylen, J.O., 'A contemporary estimate of the London daily press in the early twentieth century', in Bromley, M. and O'Malley, T. (eds), *A Journalism Reader* (London: Routledge, 1997).
Benn, T., *Out of the Wilderness. Diaries 1963–67* (London: Hutchinson, 1987).
——, *Conflicts of Interest. Diaries 1977–80* (London: Hutchinson, 1990).
Bennett, S., 'Revolutions in thought: serial publication and the mass market for reading', in Shattock, J. and Wolff, M. (eds), *The Victorian Periodical Press: Samplings and Soundings* (Leicester: Leicester University Press, 1982).

Berridge, V., 'Popular Sunday papers in mid-Victorian society', in Boyce, G., Curran, J. and Wingate, P. (eds), *Newspaper History: from the seventeenth century to the present day* (London: Constable, 1978).

Berry, D. (ed.), *Ethics and Media Culture. Practice and Representations* (Oxford: Focal Press, 2000).

Big Issue, no. 206, 4–10 November, 1996.

Black, J., *The English Press in the Eighteenth Century* (London: Croom Helm, 1987).

Boshoff, A. and Sylvester, R., 'Every editor that has paid for intrusive photographs has blood on their hands', *Daily Telegraph*, 1 September 1997.

Bowcott, O., 'Buyers turn backs on *Big Issue* after *Sun*'s £1000 a week claims', *Guardian*, 28 October 1996.

Boyce, G., 'The Fourth Estate; the reappraisal of a concept', in Boyce, G., Curran. J. and Wingate, P. (eds), *Newspaper History: from the seventeenth century to the present day* (London: Constable, 1978).

Brett, P., 'Early nineteenth-century reform newspapers in the provinces: the *Newcastle Chronicle* and the *Bristol Mercury*', in Harris, M. and O'Malley, T. (eds), *Studies in Newspaper and Periodical History, 1995 Annual* (Connecticut: Greenwood, 1997).

Briggs, A. and Cobley, P. (eds), *The Media: An Introduction* (London: Longman, 1998).

Briggs, N., 'Bank account beggar sets the law on Express', *Daily Express*, 10 May 1994.

Bromley, M. and O'Malley, T. (eds), *A Journalism Reader* (London: Routledge, 1997).

——, 'The end of journalism? Changes in workplace practices in the Press and broadcasting in the 1990s', in Bromley, M. and O'Malley, T. (eds), *A Journalism Reader* (London: Routledge, 1997).

Brooks, T., 'Vindaloot: Indian dad winner of £18 million takeaway', *Daily Star*, 14 December 1994.

Brown, C., 'Commons warns media to put house in order', *Guardian*, 19 February 1983.

——, 'Press watchdog urges restraint in Royal coverage', *Independent*, 9 June 1992.

Brown, K., 'Blair seeks to persuade Murdoch', *Financial Times*, 17 July 1995.

Brown, L., *Victorian News and Newspapers* (Oxford: Oxford University Press, 1985).

Brown, M., 'McGregor defends regulation of Press', *Independent*, 16 October 1992.

——, 'Calcutt "wants statutory controls on press"', *Independent*, 4 January 1993.

Bundock, C.J., *The National Union of Journalists. A Jubilee History 1907–1957* (Oxford: Oxford University Press, 1957).

Campaign for Press Freedom, *Towards Press Freedom* (London: CPF, 1979).

Campaign for Press and Broadcasting Freedom, *Putting People First: The Campaign for Press and Broadcasting Freedom's Response to Regulating Communications: Approaching Convergence in the Information Age [CM 4022, HMSO, July 1998]* (London: CPBF, 1998).

Carey, J., *The Intellectuals and the Masses* (London: Faber, 1992).

Carvel, J. and Campbell, D., 'DPP quits over kerb crawling: Establishment stunned as Alan Green tells of "regret"', *Guardian*, 4 October 1991.

Chant, C. (ed.), *Science, Technology and Everyday Life 1870–1950* (London: Open University Press/Routledge, 1989).

Christian, H. (ed.), *The Sociology of Journalism and the Press* (Keele: University of Keele, 1980).

——, 'Journalists' Occupational Ideologies and Press Commercialisation', in Christian, H. (ed.), *The Sociology of Journalism and the Press* (Keele: University of Keele, 1980).

Cockett, R., *Twilight of Truth. Chamberlain, Appeasement and the Manipulation of the Press* (London: Weidenfeld and Nicolson, 1989).

Collings, S., 'Suggesting a statutory alternative', *Journalist*, February 1984.

Collins, R., Curran, J., Garnham, N., Scannell, P., Schlesinger, P. and Sparks, C. (eds), *Media, Culture and Society. A Critical Reader* (London: Sage, 1986).

Collins, R. and Murroni, C., *New Media, New Policies* (Cambridge: Polity, 1996).

Cooper, J., 'Tell them to beggar off for the good of everyone', *Daily Express*, 11 May 1994.

Coopey, R., Fielding, S. and Tiratsoo, N. (eds), *The Wilson Governments 1964–1970* (London: Pinter, 1993).

Corless, F. and Mulchrone, P., '£18m win's a sin', *Daily Mirror*, 14 December 1994.

Cram, I., 'Beyond Calcutt: the legal and extra legal protection of privacy interests in England and Wales', in Kiernan, M. (ed.), *Media Ethics* (London: Routledge, 1998).

Cudlipp, H., *At Your Peril* (London: Weidenfeld and Nicolson, 1962).

Culf, A., 'Privacy adjudicator to watch over the Press', *Guardian*, 10 January 1994.

——, 'Government retreat on press privacy', *Guardian*, 18 July 1995.

——, 'How the editors avoided the Last Chance Saloon', *Guardian*, 18 July 1995.

——, 'Wakeham to make self-regulation more open', *Guardian*, 24 October 1995.

——, 'Wakeham acts over intrusion', *Guardian*, 11 October 1996.

——, 'Tabloids condemned over Euro 96 own goals', *Guardian*, 30 October 1996.

——, 'MPs attack witness press deals', *Guardian*, 23 January 1997.

Cumberbatch, G., 'Media effects: the continuing controversy', in Briggs, A. and Cobley, P. (eds), *The Media: An Introduction* (London: Longmans, 1998).

Curran, J., 'The Press as an agency of social control: an historical perspective', in Boyce, G., Curran, J. and Wingate, P. (eds), *Newspaper History: from the seventeenth century to the present day* (London: Constable, 1978).

——, 'Advertising as a patronage system', in Christian, H. (ed.), *The Sociology of Journalism and the Press* (Keele: University of Keele, 1980).

——, 'Culturist perspectives of news organizations: a reappraisal and a case study', in Ferguson, M. (ed.), *Public Communication. The New Imperatives* (London: Sage, 1990).

Curran, J. (ed.), *The British Press: A Manifesto* (London: Macmillan, 1978).

Curran, J., Ecclestone, J., Oakley, G. and Richardson, A. (eds), *Bending Reality. The State of the Media* (London: Pluto Press, 1986).

Curran, J. and Porter, V. (eds), *British Cinema History* (London: Weidenfeld and Nicolson, 1983).

Curran, J. and Seaton, J., *Power Without Responsibility*, 5th edn (London: Routledge, 1997).

Curran, J., Smith, A. and Wingate, P. (eds), *Impacts and Influences* (London: Methuen, 1987).

Curtis, L., *Ireland: The Propaganda War* (London: Pluto Press, 1984).

Cust, R., 'News and politics in early seventeenth-century England', *Past & Present*, 112 (1986).

Daily Express, 19 November 1993, Letters Page.

Davis, C., 'Human tide Labour would let in', *Sun*, 4 April 1992.

Doornaert, M. and Omdal, S.E., *IFJ Special Report. Press Freedom under Attack in Britain* (Brussels: International Federation of Journalists, 1989).

Dore, R., 'Mellor story "Was in Public Interest"', Press Association Story, 22 July 1992.

Dorrill, S. and Ramsay, R., *Smear! Wilson and the Secret State* (London: Grafton, 1992).

Dugdale, J., 'Love, lies and loopholes', *Guardian*, 29 April 1996.

Engel, M., *Tickle the Public. One Hundred Years of the Popular Press* (London: Victor Gollancz, 1996).

Euromedia Research Group, *The Media in Western Europe. The Euromedia Handbook* (London: Sage, 1992).

Evans, H., *Good Times, Bad Times* (London: Coronet, 1984).

Ferguson, M. (ed.), *Public Communication. The New Imperatives* (London: Sage, 1990).

Fielding, H., *Jonathan Wild* (New York: Signet, 1962).

Foot, P., 'Paul Foot on Right of Reply', *Free Press*, no. 26, November/December 1984.

Foot, P. and Howson, L., 'Stop Press', *Socialist Review*, no. 161, February 1993.

Frank, J., *The Beginnings of the English Newspaper, 1620–1660* (Cambridge: Harvard University Press, 1961).

Frankel, M., 'Freedom of Information setback', *Free Press*, no. 106, September/October 1998.

Franklin, B., *Newszak and News Media* (London: Arnold, 1997).

Gall, G., 'Looking in the *Mirror*. A case study of industrial relations in a national newspaper', in Bromley, M. and O'Malley, T. (eds), *A Journalism Reader* (London: Routledge, 1997).

Goodwin, P., *Television under the Tories. Broadcasting Policy 1979–1997* (London: BFI, 1998).

Gray, D.J., 'Early Victorian scandalous journalism', in Shattock, J. and Wolff, M. (eds), *The Victorian Periodical Press: Samplings and Soundings* (Leicester: Leicester University Press, 1982).

Grey, S., 'Beggar who pulls in £18,000 a year', *Daily Express*, 9 May 1994.

Griffiths, D. (ed.), *The Encyclopaedia of the British Press 1422–1992* (London: Macmillan, 1992).

Harris, B., *Politics and the Rise of the Press. Britain and France, 1620–1800* (London: Routledge, 1996).

Harris, M., 'Sport in the newspapers before 1750: representations of cricket, class and commerce in the London press', *Media History*, vol. 4, no. 1 (1998).

Harris, M. and Lee, A. (eds), *The Press in English Society from the Seventeenth to Nineteenth Centuries* (London and Toronto: Associated University Press, 1986).

——, *London Newspapers in the Age of Walpole* (London and Toronto: Associated University Press, 1987).

Harris, M. and O'Malley, T. (eds), *Studies in Newspaper and Periodical History, 1994 Annual* (Connecticut: Greenwood Press, 1996).

——, *Studies in Newspaper and Periodical History, 1995 Annual* (Connecticut: Greenwood Press, 1997).

Harris, S., ' ... and even on its platforms!', *Journalist*, August/September 1994.

Harris, W., *The Daily Press* (Cambridge: Cambridge University Press, 1943).

Harrison, B., 'Press and pressure group in modern Britain', in Shattock, J. and Wolff, M. (eds), *The Victorian Periodical Press: Samplings and Soundings* (Leicester: Leicester University Press, 1982).

Hay, G., 'Woman at the centre of law wife tragedy', *Daily Mirror*, 1 February 1993.

Hencke, D., 'Straw slows Freedom of Information legislation', *Guardian*, 30 September 1998.

Hetherington, A., *Guardian Years* (London: Chatto & Windus, 1981).

Hobbes, T., *Leviathan* (London: Penguin, 1981).

Hoggart, R., *The Uses of Literacy* (London: Penguin, 1973).

Hollingsworth, M., *The Press and Political Dissent* (London: Pluto Press, 1986).

Hooley, P., 'Baker's migrant flood warning', *Daily Express*, 7 April 1992.

Hooper, D., *Official Secrets. The Use and Abuse of the Act* (London: Coronet, 1988).

Houghton, W., 'Periodical literature and the articulate classes', in Shattock, J. and Wolff, M. (eds), *The Victorian Periodical Press: Samplings and Soundings* (Leicester: Leicester University Press, 1982).

Humphreys, P.J., *Media and Media Policy in Germany. The Press and Broadcasting since 1945*, 2nd edn (Oxford: Berg, 1994).

——, *Mass Media and Media Policy in Western Europe* (Manchester: Manchester University Press, 1996).

Jaehnig, W., 'Kith and sin: Press accountability in the USA', in Stephenson, H. and Bromley, M. (eds), *Sex, Lies and Democracy. The Press and the Public* (London: Longman, 1998).

Jempson, M. (ed.), *Report of Special Parliamentary Hearings on Freedom and Responsibility of the Press* (Bristol: Crantock Communications, 1993).

Jennings, J., 'TUC call for Communications Council', *Free Press*, no. 20, September/October 1983.

Jones, A., 'Workmen's advocates: ideology and class in a mid-Victorian labour newspaper system', in Shattock, J. and Wolff, M. (eds), *The Victorian Periodical Press: Samplings and Soundings* (Leicester: Leicester University Press, 1982).

——, *Press, Politics and Society: A History of Journalism in Wales* (Cardiff: University of Wales Press, 1993).

——, *Powers of the Press. Newspapers, Power and the Public in Nineteenth-century England* (Aldershot: Scolar Press, 1996).

Jones, B., *The Road to Calcutt and Beyond* (Cambridge: Wolfson College, 1991).

Jones, M., *Michael Foot* (London: Gollancz, 1975).

Joseph Rowntree Foundation, *Inquiry into British Housing, Second Report* (York: Joseph Rowntree Foundation, 1991).

Keane, J., *The Media and Democracy* (Oxford: Polity, 1991).

Keeble, R., 'The myth of Saddam Hussein: new militarism and the propaganda function of the human interest story', in Kiernan, M. (ed.), *Media Ethics* (London: Routledge, 1998).

Kiernan, M. (ed.), *Media Ethics* (London: Routledge, 1998).

Koss, S., *The Rise and Fall of the Political Press in Britain* (London: Fontana, 1990).

Labour Party, *The People and the Media* (London: Labour Party, 1974).

——, *Looking to the Future* (London: Labour Party, 1990).

——, *New Labour. Because Wales Deserves Better* (London: Labour Party, 1997).

Labour Research Department, *The Press* (London: Labour Publishing Company, nd, but 1922).

Lee, A., *The Origins of the Popular Press* (London: Croom Helm, 1976).

——, 'The structure, ownership and control of the press, 1855–1914', in Boyce, G., Curran, J. and Wingate, P. (eds), *Newspaper History: from the seventeenth century to the present day* (London: Constable, 1978).

Lees-Smith, H.B. (ed.), *The Encyclopaedia of the Labour Movement*, Volume III (London: Caxton Publishing, nd, but 1928).

Levine, R., 'I am exhausted. I'm so knackered', *People*, 19 July 1992.

Levy, H., *The Press Council. History, Procedure and Cases* (London: Macmillan, 1967).

Lovelace, C., 'British Press censorship during the First World War', in Boyce, G., Curran, J. and Wingate, P. (eds), *Newspaper History: from the seventeenth century to the present day* (London: Constable, 1978).

McNair, B., *News and Journalism in the UK* (London: Routledge, 1994).

MacShane, D., 'Media policy and the Left', in Seaton, J. and Pimlott, B. (eds), *The Media in British Politics* (Aldershot: Avebury, 1987).

Maidment, B., 'John Ruskin and the periodical Press', in Shattock, J. and Wolff, M. (eds), *The Victorian Periodical Press: Samplings and Soundings* (Leicester: Leicester University Press, 1982).

Mansfield, F.J., *'Gentlemen! The Press'* (London: W.H. Allen, 1943).

Martin, B.K., 'The Press', in Lees-Smith, H.B. (ed.), *The Encyclopaedia of the Labour Movement, Volume III* (London: Caxton Publishing, nd, but 1928).

Martin, G., 'The Press', in Thompson, D. (ed.), *Discrimination and Popular Culture* (London: Penguin, 1964).

Mason, T., 'Sporting news, 1860–1914', in Harris, M. and Lee, A. (eds), *The Press in English Society from the Seventeenth to Nineteenth Centuries* (London and Toronto: Associated University Press, 1986).

Mead, R., *The Press Council* (Cheshire: Brennan Publications, 1978).

Media Research Group, *Media Coverage of London Councils, Interim Report* (London: University of London, Goldsmith's College, 1987).

Melvern, L., *The End of the Street* (London: Methuen, 1986).

Miller, D., *Don't Mention the War: Northern Ireland, Propaganda and the Media* (London: Pluto Press, 1994).

Miller, D., Kitzinger, J., Williams, K. and Beherrall, P., *The Circuit of Mass Communication. Media Strategies, Representation and Audience Reception in the AIDS Crisis* (London: Sage, 1998).

Mitch, D.F., *The Rise of Popular Literacy in Victorian England. The Influence of Private Choice and Public Policy* (Philadelphia: University of Pennsylvania Press, 1992).

Morgan, J., 'Blom-Cooper calls for Press ethics committee', *UK Press Gazette*, 2 March 1992.

Morgan, K., *The People's Peace: British History 1945–1990* (Oxford: Oxford University Press, 1992).

Moore, J., 'Communications', in C. Chant (ed.), *Science, Technology and Everyday Life 1870–1950* (London: Open University Press/Routledge, 1989).

Moore-Gilbert, B. and Seed, J. (eds), *Cultural Revolution? The Challenge of the Arts in the 1960s* (London: Routledge, 1992).

Mullin, C., 'Regulation to save the nation', *Journalist*, February/March 1995.

Murschetz, P., 'State support for the daily Press in Europe: a critical appraisal. Austria, France, Norway and Sweden compared', *European Journal of Communication*, vol. 13, no. 3, 1998.

National Union of Journalists, *Your Union at Work. Report and Accounts for 1995* (London: NUJ, 1996).

——, *Your Union at Work. Annual Report 1996* (London: NUJ, 1997).

——, *Your Union at Work. Annual Report 1999* (London: NUJ, 1999).

Nevett, T., 'Advertising and editorial integrity in the nineteenth century', in Harris, M. and Lee, A. (eds), *The Press in English Society from the Seventeenth to Nineteenth Centuries* (London and Toronto: Associated University Press, 1986).

Northcott, J., *Why Labour?* (London: Penguin, 1964).

O'Malley, T., 'Defying the powers and tempering the spirit: a review of Quaker control over their publications, 1672–1689', *Journal of Ecclesiastical History*, 33 (1982).

——, 'Religion and the newspaper Press, 1660–1685: a study of the "London Gazette"', in M. Harris and A. Lee (eds), *The Press in English Society from the Seventeenth to Nineteenth Centuries* (London and Toronto: Associated University Press, 1986).

——, *Closedown? The BBC and Government Broadcasting Policy 1979–92* (London: Pluto Press, 1994).

——, 'Labour and the 1947–49 Royal Commission on the Press', in Bromley, M. and O'Malley, T. (eds), *A Journalism Reader* (London: Routledge, 1997).

——, 'Losing a sense of ownership', *Free Press*, no. 96, January/February 1997.

——, 'Demanding accountability: the Press, the Royal Commissions and the pressure for reform, 1945–77', in Stephenson, H. and Bromley, M. (eds), *Sex, Lies and Democracy. The Press and the Public* (London: Longman, 1998).

——, 'A degree of uncertainty: aspects of the debate over the regulation of the press in the UK since 1945', in Berry, D. (ed.), *Ethics and Media Culture. Practice and Representations* (Oxford: Focal Press, 2000).

Page, G., 'The Guild of British Newspaper Editors', in Griffiths, D. (ed.), *The Encyclopaedia of the British Press 1422–1992* (London: Macmillan, 1992).

Patrick, G., 'What a rich chap-ati', *Sun*, 14 December 1994.

Paul, N.S., *Principles for the Press. A Digest of Press Council Decisions 1953–1984* (London: Press Council, 1985).

Pendlebury, R., 'Adoption disaster: inquiry backs man who banned "naïve" couple from giving black child a home', *Daily Mail*, 13 September 1993.

——, 'My years with the gay social worker', *Daily Mail*, 13 September 1993.

Philo, G. (ed.), *Glasgow Media Group Reader. Volume 2: Industry, Economy, War and Politics* (London: Routledge, 1995).

Pilger, J., 'Acts of murder', *Guardian*, 18 May 1999.

Pimlott, B., *Harold Wilson* (London: HarperCollins, 1993).

Pittaway, B., 'It's madness', *Sunday Mirror*, 17 August 1997.

Political and Economic Planning, *Report on the British Press* (London: PEP, 1938).

Porter, D., 'Downhill all the way: thirteen Tory years 1951–64', in Coopey, R., Fielding, S. and Tiratsoo, N. (eds), *The Wilson Governments 1964–1970* (London: Pinter, 1993).

——, 'City editors and the modern investing public: establishing the integrity of the new financial journalism in late nineteenth-century London', *Media History*, vol. 4, no. 1 (1998).

Power, M., 'Gotcha! Miners reply in the *Sun*', *Free Press*, no. 21, January/February 1984.

——, 'What are we to do about Paul Foot?', *Free Press*, no. 27, January/February 1985.

Press Complaints Commission, *First Annual Report 1991* (London: PCC, nd).

——, *Submission to the Review of Press Self-Regulation* (London: PCC, 1992).

——, *Press Complaints Commission Review* (London: PCC, 1994).

——, *Annual Report 1995* (London: PCC, nd).

——, *Report* (London: PCC, 1996, no. 34).

——, http://www.pcc.org.uk/annual/96/review.htm

——, *Code of Practice* (http://www.pcc.org.uk/complain/code.htm – 5 November 1997).

——, http://www.pcc.org.uk/annual/97.htm

——, *Report* (London: PCC, 1997, no. 38).

——, *Reports* (London: PCC, 1998, nos. 41–44).

Press Council, *Privacy, Press and Public* (London: Press Council, 1971).

Prince of Wales, 'A vision for the millennium', *Perspectives*, February/March 1996.

Pronay, N., 'Rearmament and the British public: policy and propaganda', in Curran, J., Smith, A. and Wingate, P. (eds), *Impacts and Influences* (London: Methuen, 1987).

Pyatt, J., '"Beggar" makes £1000 per week selling *Big Issue*', *Sun*, 28 October 1996.

Quicke, A., *Tomorrow's Television* (Berkhamsted: Lion Publishing, 1976).

Raymond, R., '*The Great Assises Holden on Parnassus*. The reputation and reality of seventeenth-century newsbooks', Harris, M. and O'Malley, T. (eds), *Studies in Newspaper and Periodical History. 1994 Annual* (Connecticut: Greenwood Press, 1996).

Richards, H., *The Bloody Circus. The Daily Herald and the Left* (London: Pluto Press, 1997).

Richards, J., *The Age of the Dream Palace. Cinema and Society in Britain 1930–1939* (London: Routledge, 1984).

Richardson, A., 'Make it legal', *Free Press*, no. 25, September/October 1984.

Richardson, A. and Power, M., 'Media freedom and the CPBF', in Curran, J., Ecclestone, J., Oakley, G. and Richardson, A. (eds), *Bending Reality. The State of the Media* (London: Pluto Press, 1986).

Robertson, G., 'Law for the Press', in Curran, J. (ed.), *The British Press: A Manifesto* (London: Macmillan, 1978).

——, *People Against the Press. An Enquiry into the Press Council* (London: Quartet, 1983).

——, *Freedom, the Individual and the Law* (London: Penguin, 1991).

Rubenstein, W.D., 'Wealth, elites and class structure of modern Britain', *Past and Present*, no. 76 (1977).

Scannell, P., 'Broadcasting and the politics of unemployment 1930–1935', in Collins, R., Curran, J., Garnham, N., Scannell, P., Schlesinger, P. and Sparks, C. (eds), *Media, Culture and Society. A Critical Reader* (London: Sage, 1986).

Searle, C., *Your Daily Dose: Racism and The Sun* (London: Campaign for Press and Broadcasting Freedom, 1989).

Seaton, J. and Pimlott, B. (eds), *The Media in British Politics* (Aldershot: Avebury, 1987).

Seed, J., 'Hegemony postponed: the unravelling of the culture of consensus in Britain in the 1960s', in Moore-Gilbert, B. and Seed, J. (eds), *Cultural Revolution? The Challenge of the Arts in the 1960s* (London: Routledge, 1992).

Seymour-Ure, C., *The Political Impact of the Mass Media* (London: Constable, 1974).

——, *The British Press and Broadcasting since 1945* (Oxford: Blackwell, 1991).

Shattock, J. and Wolff, M. (eds), *The Victorian Periodical Press: Samplings and Soundings* (Leicester: Leicester University Press, 1982).

Shawcross, W., *Murdoch* (London: Pan, 1993).

Siebert, F.S., *Freedom of the Press in England 1476–1776* (Urbana: University of Illinois Press, 1965).

Slattery, J., 'Soley to grant access to complaints letters', *UK Press Gazette*, 2 November 1992.

Snoddy, R., *The Good, the Bad and the Unacceptable* (London: Faber, 1992).

Somerfield, S., *Banner Headlines* (Shoreham by Sea: Scan Books, 1979).

Sommerville, C.J., *The News Revolution in England. Cultural Dynamics of Daily Information* (Oxford: Oxford University Press, 1996).

Stephenson, H. and Bromley, M. (eds), *Sex, Lies and Democracy. The Press and the Public* (London: Longman, 1998).

Street, H., *Freedom, the Individual and the Law* (London: Pelican, 1975).

Sykes, J.B. (ed.), *The Concise Oxford Dictionary of Correct English*, 6th edn (Oxford: Clarendon Press, 1980).

Targett, S., '"The Premier Scribbler himself": Sir Robert Walpole and the management of political opinion', in Harris, M. and O'Malley, T. (eds), *Studies in Newspaper and Periodical History. 1994 Annual* (Connecticut: Greenwood Press, 1996).

Taylor, G., *Changing Faces. A History of The Guardian 1956–88* (London: Fourth Estate, 1993).

Thomas, I., *The Newspaper* (Oxford: Oxford University Press, 1943).

Thompson, D. (ed.), *Discrimination and Popular Culture* (London: Penguin, 1964).

Thompson, E.P., *The Making of the English Working Class* (London: Penguin, 1991).

Thomson, D., *England in the Twentieth Century* (London: Penguin, 1966).

Trades Union Congress, *The Role of the Media in a Democracy* (London: TUC, 1989 – document issued for a TUC conference held on 16 March 1989).

Travis, A., 'Claims of higher Press standards leave MPs cold', *Guardian*, 4 December 1992.

Trelford, D., 'Publish and be jailed', in Trades Union Congress, *The Role of the Media in a Democracy* (London: TUC, 1989 – document issued for a TUC conference held on 16 March 1989).

Tribune, 29 January 1993, Letters Page.

Troup, J. and Taylor, A., 'The Chosen One', *Sun*, 14 December 1994.

Trueman, I., 'You mosque be joking', *Daily Star*, 25 January 1996.

Tulloch, J., 'Managing the Press in a medium-sized European power', in Stephenson, H. and Bromley, M. (eds), *Sex, Lies and Democracy. The Press and the Public* (London: Longman, 1998).

Tunstall, J., *The Media in Britain* (London: Constable, 1983).

Van Dijk, T.A., *Racism and the Press* (London: Routledge, 1991).

Wacks, R., *Privacy and Press Freedom* (London: Blackstone, 1995).

Wadsworth, A.P., *Newspaper Circulations 1800–1954* (Manchester: Manchester Statistical Society, 1955).

Ward, L., Woodward, W. and Hencke, D., 'Pressure mounts over public right to know', *Guardian*, 21 June 1999.

White, M. and Culf, A., 'Blair's New Left warning to Murdoch', *Guardian*, 17 July 1995.

Wickham Steed, H., *The Press* (London: Penguin, 1938).

Williams, D. and Burt, J., 'Charles: Let Lottery money go to mosques', *Daily Mail*, 25 January 1996.

Williams, F., *Dangerous Estate. The Anatomy of Newspapers* (London: Arrow, 1959).

Williams, G., *Britain's Media – How They Are Related*, 2nd edn (London: CPBF, 1996).

Williams, K., *Get Me A Murder A Day! A History of Mass Communication in Britain* (London: Arnold, 1998).

Williams, R., *Communications* (London: Penguin, revised edition 1966, reprinted 1970).

——, *The Long Revolution* (London: Pelican, 1973).

——, 'The Press we don't deserve', in Curran, J. (ed.), *The British Press: A Manifesto* (London: Macmillan, 1978).

Wintour, C., 'A warning shot from the House of Commons', *Observer*, 20 February 1982.

Woodward, T., 'Why I sent my daughter to prison', *Daily Mail*, 7 May 1998.

Unpublished theses

Juusela, V., 'The Finnish Council for Mass Media and the Press Complaints Commission. A comparative study of two Press watchdogs' (MPhil thesis: University of Wales, Cardiff, 1992).

McKeown, K.J., 'The right to reply to the Press in the United Kingdom' (MA thesis: Leeds University, 1993).

O'Malley, P.T., 'The politics of defamation: the state, Press interests and the evolution of the English libel laws' (PhD thesis: London School of Economics, University of London, 1975).

Strick, H.C., 'British newspaper journalism 1900–1956: a study in industrial relations' (PhD thesis: University of London, 1957).

Other unpublished manuscripts

Campaign for Press and Broadcasting Freedom, 'Secretary's report to the CPBF 1984. Annual General Meeting' (London: CPBF, 1984, unpublished manuscript).

Soley Correspondence. Letters relating to press standards held by Clive Soley at the House of Commons, London.

Index

Compiled by Sue Carlton

Abbot, Barrie 101
Aberfan disaster, press coverage of 67
accountability 71, 73, 83, 178
    and press freedom 186–7, 188
accuracy 22–5, 35, 53, 145–53, 185
adjudications 68, 88, 89, 113,
        131–41
    analysis of 136–8
    delays in 81, 82
    publishing 69–70, 76, 78, 79,
        105–6, 129
    see also complaints; corrections
advertising
    and accuracy 145–6
    advertising free broadcasting 32
    dependence on 17
    duty on 15, 16, 20, 36
    effect on standards 28, 29, 30
    government list 44–5
    influence on Press 32, 53
Advertising Standards Association
        (ASA) 145–6
Aims of Industry 71
Allaun, Frank 60, 66, 112, 130, 179
    and right of reply 79–80, 81, 82,
        130
almanacs 13
Andrews, Sir Linton 98, 105, 108,
        115, 116–17, 124
apologies and retractions 93
    see also corrections
appeasement policy 32
Arnold, Matthew 28
ASLEF 130
Association of British Editors 91
Astor, J.J. 98, 105
Attlee, Clement 19, 53

'Baa Baa, Black Sheep' 146–7
Baker, Kenneth 150
Baldwin, Stanley 31

ballads 10, 12, 13
Ballet Rambert 160, 163, 164
Barendt, Eric 180–1
Bax, Ernest Belfort 27
BBC 18, 20
    see also broadcasting
Beaverbrook newspapers 72
Benn, Tony 66, 73–4, 129–30
Benson, Preston 53
Bentham, Jeremy 23
Benyon, W. 81
Bevan, Aneurin 31
Bevin, Ernest 30
bias 34, 71, 76, 80
    against Labour Party 52, 146, 150
Big Issue sellers 157–8
Birmingham Ladies Debating Society
        27
Blackstone, William 21, 22
Blair, Tony 93, 94, 95
Blanc, Louis 27, 46–7
Blom-Cooper, Louis 86, 87, 98, 124
    ideas for reform 90, 104, 126, 131
Bonham-Carter, Violet 57
Borzello, Bob 147, 148, 160
Bourne, Henry Richard Fox 28
Boyce, George 8
Bradley, H.J. 56
bribery 43, 47
Bristol *Evening Post* 68
British Editor 91
British Medical Association 126–7
broadcasting
    and accuracy 145
    advertising free 32
    censorship 18, 20
    complaints bodies 66, 84
    proliferation of channels 187
    see also media
Brooke, Peter 93
Brooks, Edwin 67

Brown, Hugh 72
Brown, Lucy 38, 39, 44–5
Browne, John 86
Bulger, Jamie, murder of 151–2, 153
Butler, Peter 156
Butler, R.A. 61

Calcutt Inquiry (1989) 87–90, 123, 126, 128, 166
Calcutt Inquiry (1992-93) 91, 92, 93, 94, 167
Callaghan, Jim 71
cameras, long-range 67, 165
Campaign for Press and Broadcasting Freedom (CPBF) 79, 82, 86
Campaign for Press Freedom (CPF) 78–9, 80
    inquiry into Press Council 79, 82
capitalist press 28
    criticism by Labour movement 31, 33
    and profit-making 30
    restrictive forms of 8
Carnarven Advertiser 38
Cash, William 85–6, 131
censorship
    broadcasting 18, 20
    film industry 18
    post-publication penalties 21, 49, 180
    self-censorship 123
    see also pre-publication censorship
chapbooks 10, 13
Charles, Prince of Wales 162, 163, 169–70
Charles II 9, 15
Chartist publications 26
chequebook journalism 67, 82, 106, 121
    see also intrusion
Chesterton, G.K. 29
children
    and privacy 172–3
    witnesses 120
Churchill, Winston 57
circulation 9–12
    drive to increase 17
    rapid growth in 10–12, 29
civil servants, disclosing official information 48
class division 84

'closed shop' 71, 73
Clwyd, Ann 85–6, 131
Co-operative Press 24
Cobbett, William 26
Code of Professional Conduct 43
codes of conduct 69, 124–6
    editors 126, 131
    National Union of Journalists (NUJ) 73, 79, 95, 124, 145–6
    Press Council 88, 110–11, 124–6, 131
    see also ethical codes; Press Complaints Commission, code of practice; self-regulation
Collings, Simon 83
Collins, R. 180
Colman, Tony 161–2
communication, computer-based 187
compensation 89, 93
complaints
    categorisation of 132, 140
    difficulties of 161–4
    'fast track' procedure 112, 130, 189
    guidance 109–10, 111
    procedures 107–13
        failure of 163–4
    reaching adjudication 113, 132, 140
    records of 108, 132, 133–4
    redirected to editors 108–9, 110, 111–12
    subject of legal proceedings 111
    time limits for 111
    see also adjudications; corrections
Conservative government 71, 78, 121–2
    and proposals for Press Council 57
    and right of privacy 166
    and self-regulation 93, 180
contempt, law of 123, 187
Continuation, The 25
control see regulation; self-regulation
Cooper, Jonathan 157
'corantos' 9, 12
corrections 88, 91, 93, 131, 188, 189
    prominent publication of 76, 85, 129

Council (General Council of the
    Press), criticism of 59–61,
    63–4, 75, 81, 88, 105
Cowan, Sir Zelman 98, 106–7, 124
criminal libel 46
criminals
    employed as journalists 29
    payments to 62, 67, 83, 125
Croker, John William 26
Cudlipp, Hugh 62–3
Curl case 46
Curran, James 8, 17

'D' Notice system 187
Daily Courant 10, 23
Daily Express 24, 30, 83, 155–7,
    161–2
Daily Herald 17, 24, 33
Daily Mail 11, 13, 28, 30, 83, 106
    attitude to Press Council 164
    and Haringay council 146
    and intrusion 171, 172, 173
    misrepresentation 162, 163
    and racial discrimination 160,
        164
Daily Mirror 13, 33, 164
    and inaccuracy 149, 152
    intrusion 170
    and Labour party 33
    and racial discrimination 160–1
daily papers 10
    competition 68, 178
    content 13
    division into mass-market and
        quality 13
    increase in circulation 11–12, 14
Daily Star 83
    misrepresentation 146, 162, 163
    racism 147–8, 160, 161
Daily Telegraph 13, 92, 105
data protection 185
Davidson, Max 148
Deedes, W.F. 57, 66
defamation 49
    law of 123
    and legal aid 85
    see also libel laws
defendants, payment by media 79
democracy
    and freedom of the press 7, 20, 35,
        103

and truthfulness of press 25
Denning, Lord 65
Devlin, Lord 66, 67, 70, 98, 99
    and libel laws 121
    and number of adjudications 135
    and PC code of practice 110, 124
    and PC complacency 115–16
    welcoming criticism 118
Diana, Princess of Wales 94, 169
Disraeli, Benjamin 26
distortion 154–61, 180
    see also inaccuracy; misrepresenta-
        tion
Driberg, Tom 57
Dubbs, Alf 83
Dunning, Terry 171, 173

Eastern Morning News 28
Economist 33, 52
Edelman, Maurice 72
Edinburgh Advertiser 23
editor, use of term 38
editors
    code of conduct 126, 131
    and Press Council 107
    and statutory intervention 91, 92
Eliot, T.S. 31
Empire News 61
employers' organisations 36–7
English Civil War (1642-49) 9, 15,
    22
Ensor, Sir Robert 54
Erskine, Kenneth 159
ethical code
    impracticality of 125
    public demand for 126
    unwritten 110–11, 125–6
    see also codes of conduct
ethnic minorities
    misrepresentation 159–61, 163
    press bias against 80
Europe, support for press 186
European Convention on Human
    Rights (ECHR) 184–5
European Cup football tournament
    (1996) 95
Evans, Nicola 170
Evening Post 10
Evening Standard 68
Exclusion Crisis (1679-81) 9
Express 13

Fabricant, Michael 162
facts 23, 25
    and opinion 149–51
    selective presentation of 154–5
    see also accuracy; opinion; truth-
        fulness
'fast track' procedure 112, 130, 189
Faulks, Mr Justice 122, 123
Fielding, Henry 20
film industry, censorship 18
financial controls
    difficulties of 17
    lifting of 8
Financial Times 125
fines 93
Fleming, Robert 148
Foot, Michael 66
Foot, Paul 84
Foster, Reverend Christopher 22
Fowler, Tony 148
France, press laws 183
Frank, J. 9
Franks, Lord 122, 123
freedom of expression
    and European Convention on
        Human Rights 184
    importance of 21–2, 106
    and truth and error 22, 53
    within boundaries/necessary
        restraints 21, 180
    see also press freedom
freedom of information
    and Labour government 166
    and privacy 166–7
    and public interest 187
Freud, Clement 72
Fyfe, David Maxwell 57

Gardiner Committee on Terrorism in
    Northern Ireland 123
General Council of the Press *see* Press
    Council
General Strike 31
Gentle Lash 25
Germany, press laws 182–3
Gissing, George 27
Gordon Walker, Patrick 65
Gorst, John 72
Graham, William 45
Green, Lady Eva 170, 173
Green, Sir Alan 170

Greene, Graham 31
Greene, Sir Hugh 66
Grimond, Joe 57, 65
Grunwick dispute 129
Guardian 62, 68, 81, 83, 105
Guild of British Newspaper Editors
    67, 91, 98–9

Hackney Council 146
Hall, Radclyffe 49
Hamilton, Sir Dennis 101
Hardcastle, J.A. 45
Haringay Council 146–7
Harmsworth, Alfred 11
Harris, Wilson 24, 33
Harrison, Brian 8, 27, 38
Hattersley, Roy 81
Hayward, Ron 73
Heath, Edward 72
Herford, Reverend Brook 27
Hobbes, Thomas 22
Hoggart, Richard 61, 116, 117
Hollis, Baroness 147
homelessness 154–8, 163, 164
hospitals, press practice in 126–7
Humphreys, F.G 43
Hutchins Commission 33
hypocrisy 66

immigration 150, 152–3
impartiality 22–5, 35, 72
    see also accuracy; facts; opinion;
        truthfulness
inaccuracy 29, 34, 38, 41, 76, 86,
    146–7
    defining 188
    and distortion 130
    economic motives for 152, 180
    fact and opinion 149–51
    failure to deal with 152
    and justice 151–2
    political motives for 15, 180
Independent Press Authority (IPA)
    opposition to 93, 180
    proposals for 91, 92–3, 187–8
industrial action
    to influence content 80, 82,
        129–30
    see also strikes
industrialisation 16

information
    freedom of 166–7, 187
    means of obtaining 69
    official 48
    selling 47, 62, 67, 79, 83, 106,
        125
Institute of Journalists (IOJ) 33, 40–2,
    98–9
    attitude to trade unionism 43
    conference 28, 29
    Press Council membership 101
International Court of Honour 42
International Federation of
        Journalists 42
intrusion 34, 41, 52, 66, 87, 96
    defence of 168
    and economic competition 31, 42
    economic motives 166, 168, 173
    innocent subjects of 170–1, 172–3
    and lack of professional status 38
    and legislation 54, 67
    photographers at funerals 32
    political motives 168
    and press responsibility 169
    and self-regulation 43, 51
    see also privacy

Jenkins, Reverend, of Dowlais 26
jingoism 29
John Bull 24
Johnson, Paul 84
Johnson, Samuel 25
Jones, Aled 9, 19, 26, 38, 39
journalism
    courses 40
    effect on public morals 28–9
    entry examinations 40
    legal framework 42, 45–50, 82
    and professionalism 28
    social acceptability 39–40
    status of 25
Journalist 83
journalists
    commercial pressures on 38–9,
        42, 44
    education 38, 39
    elected to Parliament 45
    expressing public opinion 28
    increasing numbers of 38
    in law courts 39, 48

local government meetings 39, 48,
    120, 141
    and obscene publications
        legislation 48–9
    organisation 38
    and politicians 44–5
    professional status 37, 39–40
    protection for 187
    and responsibility 177
    rights of 141
    role of 38
    salaries and conditions 42
    separatism 39
    state registration 41, 42–3, 49, 51
    status in society 38, 39
    and trade unions 38
Justice 28

Keeler, Christine 65, 68, 88, 115
Kershaw, Anthony 60, 61
King, Cecil 66
Koss, Stephen 17, 44, 45

Labour councils, and press 146–7,
    161–2, 163
Labour government 65
    and freedom of information 166
    and press control 18, 93
    and Press Council 56
    and right of reply 84
Labour movement
    and media reform 73, 180
    newspapers 17, 27, 28, 30, 31
    press bias against 80
    and press freedom 78
Labour Party
    criticism of press 29–30, 31, 34,
        178
    media policy 94
    press bias against 52, 146, 150
    and right of reply 130
    and self-regulation 83, 94, 95–6,
        116
    and statutory intervention 87
    support by newspapers 33, 95
    21st Century Media Conference 94
Labour press 17, 27, 28, 30, 31
Lancashire Newspaper Society 37
Lawrence, D.H. 31
Leach, George 48
Leader-writer, use of term 38

Leavis, F.R. 31
'legal waiver' 111, 112
Letters of Junius 21, 22
Levy, Harold 124
libel laws
    and capitalist system 9
    and press freedom 21, 46, 185–6
    protection from 46–7
    reform 121
Licensing Act, lapse of (1694) 10, 15
lies 25
    see also inaccuracy; misrepresenta-
        tion; truthfulness
limited liability 46
Linotype Users' Association 37
Lipton, Lieutenant-Colonel 60
literacy, growth of 7, 13–14
Lloyds Weekly News 11
lobbying 120–4, 141
London Express Newspapers Ltd 24
London Gazette 9, 12, 17
London Press
    criticism of 29
    ownership of 30
'long argument' 19, 34, 177
Longford, Francis, Earl of 85
Lucas-Tooth, Hugh 57
Lyon, Alex 127

Macaulay, Thomas Babington 20
McGregor Commission 179
McGregor, Lord 89, 90, 91, 98, 168
McKeever family 149, 152, 153
Macmillan, Harold 62
Maerdy Institute 31
Major, John 78, 93, 166
malice 21
Manchester Guardian 13, 23
Manchester Literary Society 26–7
Mancroft, Lord 127
Mansfield, F.J. 43
Margaret, Princess 108, 110
Martin, Graham 65
Martin, Kingsley 31
Maude, Sir Angus 81
Mayhew, Christopher 61–2
media
    accuracy 145–6
    influence of 145
    policy 71, 72, 83, 94
    promoting diversity 186–7

reforms 72
    see also broadcasting
Mellor, David 81, 167–8
mental illness
    misrepresentation 158–9, 163,
        164
    PCC guidance 158
Merton Council 161–2, 163
Mill, James 21, 46
Mill, J.S. 21–2
Milton, John 20, 21, 22
misrepresentation 31, 33, 43,
    154–64, 189
    political motives 155, 156, 163
    and right of reply 83, 84
    see also accuracy; correction;
        inaccuracy; right of reply
Mitchell, Austin 83
Mitchell, Charles 38
monopoly *see* ownership, concentra-
    tion of
Moors Murderers trial 67
Morgan, Kenneth 84–5, 86
Morley, John 27
Morning Post 25
Morrison, Herbert 33–4, 43, 53, 56,
    57
Mowlam, Mo 94
murders and executions 12, 13
Murdoch, Rupert 68, 84, 85, 88, 92,
    94
Murray, George 97, 98, 99, 109, 115
Murroni, C. 180
muscular dystrophy, inaccurate
    information 149

National Association of Journalists
    (NAJ) 40
National Graphical Association
    (NGA) 80, 83
National Health Service workers 130
National Heritage Committee 91, 92,
    93, 94, 95
national security, and press freedom
    48
National Union of Journalists (NUJ)
    40, 42–4, 48–9
    attempts to raise standards 19, 29,
        33, 38, 42–3, 53
    code of conduct 73, 79, 95, 124,
        145–6

opposition to state intervention 48, 49
opposition to state register 41, 42–3
press attacks on 84
and Press Complaints Commission 95
and Press Council 64, 83, 98, 99, 101
and proposals for Press Council 56
salaries and conditions 42
and statutory right of reply 81
withdrawal from Press Council 79, 112, 178
see also trade unions
National Union of Mineworkers (NUM) 83
NATSOPA 71
Neil, Patrick 98, 106
'new journalism' 13, 28
News Chronicle 61
news periodicals, demand for 9–10
News of the World 11, 65, 67, 68
newsbooks 12
Newspaper Press Directory 38
Newspaper Proprietors' Association 33, 56, 57
Newspaper Publishers' Association 66, 89, 98–9, 101
Newspaper Society 33, 56, 89, 98–9, 101
    fragmentation 37
newspapers
    closures 61
    Conservative controlled 52
    content 12–13
    controls 14–18
    daily 10, 11–12, 13, 14, 68, 178
    and fascism 32
    financing 52–3
    government financial support 25–6
    political content 12–13
    and political parties 17, 44–5
    price of 11, 14, 15, 16
    readership 13–14
    shareholder system 46
    specialist 11
    subscription system 46
    taxes on 15–16, 27

trade 11
weekly 10–11
    see also ownership; press
newsreels 18
Norfolk Social Services 171
Normanbrook, Lord 66
Northcott, Jim 66
Northern Daily Express 27
Northern Ireland, news coverage 123

obscene libel 46
obscene publications 46, 47, 48–9
Observer 30, 59, 68, 129
Odhams Press Ltd 24
official secrets legislation 17–18, 47–8, 49, 123, 187
ombudsmen 82, 83, 93
    in-house 88, 131, 148
opinion 24–5, 146
    and facts 149–51
Orwell, George 33
owners see proprietors
ownership, concentration of 29, 33, 60–1, 64, 186–7
    and Labour government 93, 94
    and standards 44

pamphlets 12
paper, duty on 15, 16, 36
Parliament
    journalist MPs 45
    reporting on proceedings 39
peace movements, press bias against 80
Peacock enquiry 20
Pearce, Lord 69, 98, 106
People 60
People's Printing Society Ltd 24
Periodical Publishers Association 98–9
Perspectives 162
Phillimore, Lord Justice 122, 123
photography
    of children 171
    honest methods 43
    long-lens 67, 165
Pitman's phonetic shorthand 39
Political and Economic Planning (PEP) 32, 51–2
politicians, and journalists 44–5

popular press
  content of 12–13
  criticism of 31
  emergence of 7, 10
  influence of 26–7, 31
  see also tabloid newspapers
pornography 114
power, without responsibility 31
Power, Mike 84
pre-publication censorship 15, 49,
    122
  abolition of 9, 12, 20, 35, 46
  broadcasting 18
  and film industry 18
  and freedom of expression 180–1
  impracticality of 15, 17, 20
  see also censorship
preliminary hearings, magistrates'
    court 120
press
  commercialism of 26, 28
  as constitutional watchdog 8
  criticisms of 25–35
  debate on standards 85
  depoliticisation of 17
  as Fourth State of realm 8, 24, 34,
    47
  independence 19–20
  and law 45–50, 122–3, 181–2
  public confidence in 90, 115
  role in society 36, 74, 177
  self-censorship 123
  and social control 8
  and state 7, 14–18, 19, 36, 177,
    186
  subsidised 186
  voluntary regulation 51–2, 178
  wartime controls 18, 48
  see also newspapers; ownership;
    press freedom; press industry
Press Board of Finance (Presbof) 89
Press Complaints Commission (PCC)
    85, 88–90, 97
  and accessibility 113, 118
  and accuracy 145, 188
  adjudications 113, 132, 138–40
  aims 118, 141
  appointments commission 88,
    89–90
  chairmen 98
  and children 172–3

code of practice 90, 126, 132, 141
  accuracy 145–6, 151, 154
  discriminatory reporting 159,
    160, 161
  failure to enforce 164, 173–4
  privacy 165, 167, 170, 171,
    172
  and statutory power 188–9
  complaints procedures 112–13
  complaints upheld 135, 138–40
  criticism of 90, 93, 95
  defensiveness 118
  dominance of editors 95
  failure of 94, 164
  finance 89
  and independence from press
    89–90, 91, 93
  membership 102–3
  and misrepresentation 154
  and press freedom 95
  and privacy 94, 126, 169–70
  and race 147–8
  rejecting complaints 135
  and right of reply 131
  sanctions 89, 153, 188–9
  self-praise 116
  and third party complaints 147–9
  see also Wakeham, John
Press Council (General Council of the
    Press) 37, 49, 58–61, 97
  addressing middle-class 113, 114
  and adjudications 88, 131–41
  aims/objects of 55, 58–9, 86–7,
    103–5
  appointments commission 69,
    75–6, 77
  attitudes of 113–19
  and case law analysis 124–5
  chairmen 98
  code of conduct 88, 110–11,
    124–6, 131
  complaints procedures 107–12
  complaints upheld 133, 134–5
  Conciliator 76, 77, 112
  and conventional values 114
  disbanded 85, 88, 128
  and economics of industry 105,
    117
  and editors 107
  effectiveness of 65, 67–8, 70, 88,
    178

failure of 64, 65, 72, 74–5, 79, 81
'fast track' procedure 112, 130
finance 98–101
investigation of 62, 63, 72
and Labour government backing
    56
lay members 64–5, 74, 77, 97,
    178
    arguments for 54, 55, 60, 63,
        69, 75–6
    lack of 58, 59
    occupations of 101–3
    opposition to 54
and 'legal waiver' 111, 112
lobbying 120–4, 141
opposition to 56, 57
powers of 59, 105–7, 123–4
and press freedom 55, 58, 86–7,
    103, 104
and privacy 126–8
proposals for 51–8
and quality newspapers 62, 105
records of complaints 132, 133–4
redirecting complainants 108–9,
    110, 111–12
reform 64–5, 73, 79, 82, 88, 97,
    179
response to criticism 116–18
and right of reply 85–6, 128–31
Robertson Report on 82
Royal Commission (1947-49) rec-
    ommendations 54–6, 70
Royal Commission (1961-62) rec-
    ommendations 63–4, 70, 97
Royal Commission (1974-77) rec-
    ommendations 75–8, 97, 125
sanctions 72, 77, 105–6, 107
self-satisfaction 114–16
third party complaints 107, 108
voluntary basis 54, 58, 61
Younger Committee recommenda-
    tions 69–70, 73, 77, 97, 111
press freedom 7–8, 19–22, 53, 91,
    118
    effects of 26–7
    importance of 43
    and legal restraints 49, 53, 181
    and Press Complaints Commission
        95
    and Press Council 55, 58, 86–7,
        103, 104

and proprietors' control 130, 179,
    186–7
    protection of 141, 186
    and responsibility 186–9
    and standards 187–9
    and wartime controls 48
    see also freedom of expression
press industry
    competitiveness of 31, 34, 68,
        104, 178
    economic problems 61–2, 71
    expansion 9–10
    see also newspapers; press
Preston, Peter 91, 129
Preston Review and County Advertiser
    23
print workers, industrial action 130
printers
    laws to encourage 15
    publishing names of 46
privacy 68–9, 73, 74, 82, 88, 89,
    126–8
    defence of breaches 127
    and European Convention on
        Human Rights 184
    and freedom of information 166–7
    legislation 74, 85–6, 93, 94, 123,
        181, 183
    ordinary people 171–3
    pressure for change 127–8
    and public figures 168, 169–70
    and public interest 125, 128, 161,
        165–73
    and self-regulation 165–74
    see also intrusion
Privacy Commissioner, PCC 94, 113
professional status, journalists 37,
    39–40, 42
Profumo, John 65, 68, 115, 121
proprietors
    collective organisation 36–7
    elected to Parliament 45
    influence on government 94–5,
        178
    and legislative process 47
    objections to statutory regulation
        186
    and proposals for Press Council 56
    registration 47
    see also ownership
Provincial Newspaper Association 47

Provincial Newspaper Society 36
Public Advertiser 21
public figures, and right of privacy
    168, 169–70
public interest
    and freedom of information 187
    and privacy 125, 128, 161,
        165–73
    and third party complaints 147
public meetings, reporting on 46, 47
public servants, selling information
    47
puritanism 116

Quaker movement 15
qualified privilege 47

racial hatred, incitement 159
racism 95, 149–51, 159–61
radio, control 18
rape victims, anonymity 122
readers
    responsibility for standards 61,
        117
    and self-regulation 147
redress 27, 33, 47, 49
    see also adjudications; complaints;
        corrections; Press Complaints
        Commission; Press Council
registration
    of journalists 41, 42–3, 49, 51
    of presses 16
    of proprietors 47
regulation 14–18
    arguments for 21
    context for reform 183–7
    in Europe 182–3
    inconsistent approach of inquiries
        179
    methods of 14–15
    and political ambition 20–1
    statutory intervention 89, 90, 91,
        92, 93, 180, 182–3
    see also codes of conduct; Press
        Complaints Commission; Press
        Council; self-regulation
Reid, Sir Wemys 38
Renton, Timothy 87
reporter, use of term 38
Reynolds' Weekly News 11, 24, 33

right of reply 33, 47, 78–88, 128–31
    in Europe 75, 182, 183
    statutory 27, 96, 130–1, 181
Right of Reply Committee 79
Robertson, Geoffrey 79, 181–2
Robertson Report 82, 83, 111
Robinson, W.G. 19
Ross, Sir David 43, 57
Royal Commission on the Press
    (1947-49) 18, 19, 33–4, 37,
        43, 44, 178
    recommendations 54–6, 63, 70
    terms of reference 52, 53
    and truthfulness 24–5
Royal Commission on the Press
    (1961-62) 61–3, 105–6, 115,
        117, 120–1
    recommendations 63–4, 70, 97
Royal Commission on the Press
    (1974-77) 71–2, 74–8, 112,
        122, 181
    and 'legal waiver' 111
    recommendations 75–8, 97, 125
Royal Family, press coverage 26, 90,
        95, 124, 127, 169–70
Rubenstein, W.D. 39–40
Ruskin, John 27

sanctions 95
    Press Complaints Commission 89,
        153, 188–9
    Press Council 72, 77, 105–6, 107
Scargill, Arthur 83
Scott, C.P. 23
Scott, Laurence 62
Scottish Daily Newspaper Society
    98–9
Scottish Newspaper Proprietors
    Association 98–9, 101
secret service money, subsidies 16,
        17
Selborne, Earl of 60
self-regulation
    arguments for 33, 179
    criticism of 66, 178
    difficulties of 39, 68, 82
    dissatisfaction with 90–1, 92
    and employers' interests 178
    history of 51–96
    organisation of 97–119
    reform of 178–90

survival of 178–80
see also National Union of
    Journalists (NUJ), Institute of
    Journalists (IOJ); Press
    Complaints Commission; Press
    Council
sensationalism 29, 32–3, 38, 66, 85,
    167–70
    economic motives 152–3, 159,
        167, 168
    and registration of journalists 41
    in wartime 43
sex, exploitation of 114
sexuality, and privacy 171, 173
Sharpton, Al 147–8, 153
Shawcross, Commission 63–4, 65,
    134, 179
Shawcross, Lord 73–4, 75, 98, 104,
    106, 112, 118
Shrimsley, Bernard 162
Siebert, F.S. 14
Simmons, C.J. 57, 58
Simon, J.E.S. 61
slander 21
Smith, Chris 95
Smith, Phillip 171
Smith, Sir Geoffrey Johnson 81
Snowden, Philip 30, 45
Socialist Workers Party 84
socialists 27, 28
Soley, Clive
    and children's privacy 172–3
    criticism by *Sun* 92, 179
    and misrepresentation 163
    Private Member's Bill 90–1, 93,
        140, 180
    right of reply 85
Somerfield, Stafford 65, 67, 68
South Wales Daily News 31
Southend *Evening Echo* 68
Spectator 24
Spender, J.A. 28
sports coverage
    effect on public morals 29
    growth of 14
stamp duty 10, 15, 16, 20, 36
Stanley, Oliver 56
Star 61
state intervention 177
    caution about 8, 179
    history of 14–18

possible abuse of 181
and press freedom 19–22, 60,
    107, 122–3, 128, 180–1,
    182–3
privileges 45, 177
registration 16, 41, 42–3, 47, 49,
    51
see also regulation
Stationers Company 15, 18, 20
Stead, W.T. 28, 29
Steed, Henry Wickham 23, 32
Stratton-Mills, 66
Strick, H.C. 7, 36, 38, 45
strikes
    changes in law 85
    press coverage 30
    strike breaking 31
    see also industrial action
sub-editor, use of term 38
'suicide mania' 32
Sun 88, 129, 130
    abuse of critics 80, 92, 179
    inaccuracy 151–2
    misrepresentation 157–8, 162
    racism 150, 160, 161
    support for Labour 95
Sunday Dispatch 61
Sunday Express 24
Sunday Graphic 61
Sunday Mirror 158–9
Sunday People 167–8
Sunday press 10–11, 13
    encouraging atheism 26
Sunday Times 30, 105
Sutcliffe, Peter, news coverage 80,
    106, 159
Sweden, self-regulation 183

tabloid newspapers
    and inaccuracy 146
    and 'loony left' 147, 152–3
    and public opinion 91–2
    reform 88, 91
    see also popular press
taxes
    abolition of 16, 27
    on knowledge 16, 18, 26, 35
Taylor, Teddy 80
telegraph system, nationalised 17
terrorism, press coverage 123
Thatcher, Margaret 71, 78, 180

third parties, distress caused to
    148–9, 152
third party complaints 107, 108,
    147–9, 153, 157
Thomas, Ivor 33, 49
Thompson, Roy 66
Tias, Charles 10
Times, The 12, 13, 83, 130
    and advertising 29
    anti-fascist stance 32
    attacking popular press 60, 116
    correspondence 34
    government financial support 25–6
    removal to Wapping 84–5
    on Royal Commission 64
    on self-regulation 81, 92, 105
    and truthfulness 23
Today 13
Toner, Michael 162
Trade Union movement, criticism of
    press 29, 30
trade unions 37, 42
    'closed shop' 71, 73
    conflict with employers 84–5
    influence over content 83–4
    meetings 39
    and press freedom 78
    restrictive practices 62
    rights 71
    see also National Union of
        Journalists
Trades Union Congress 79, 80, 82,
    83, 84
Trelford, Donald 86
truthfulness 22–5, 33, 35
    half truths 31
    and opinion 24–5
    see also accuracy; facts; impartiality
Tucker Committee 120
Tulloch, John 102–3
21st Century Media Conference,
    Labour Party 94
Typographical Association 37

'Ugly Duckling' 161–2
United States, concerns about press
    33

Vassall, John 115
Vickers, Sir Geoffrey 54
Vincent, Henry 26

Waddington, David 89
Wakeham, Lord John 94–5, 98, 113,
    116, 173
Walden, Brian 68, 127
Walsh, Frank 149
Wapping 84–5
Ward, Stephen 115
Waters, Sir George 54
Waugh, Evelyn 31
weekly newspapers 10–11
Wells, H.G. 30
Western Mail 31
Williams, Francis 61
Williams, Raymond 7–8, 66
wills, publication of 120
Wilson, Harold 67, 68, 71, 72, 73,
    74
witnesses, payments to 62, 67, 83,
    106, 125
women's movements, press bias
    against 80
working-class press 11, 13, 27
    challenging political system 15
    restrictions on 16
    see also Labour movement
World War I (1914-18) 18, 29
World War II 32–3
Worthington, Tony 86, 87, 131, 180

xenophobia 95

York, James, Duke of 9
Younger Committee (1972) 68–70,
    97, 111, 122, 128
Younger, Kenneth 68, 122